Also by Jane and Michael Stern

Trucker: A Portrait of the Last American Cowboy
Roadfood • *Amazing America*
Auto Ads • *Friendly Relations*
Horror Holiday • *Goodfood*

SQUARE
MEALS

SQUARE MEALS

America's Favorite Comfort Food Cookbook

Jane and Michael Stern

LF LEBHAR-FRIEDMAN BOOKS
NEW YORK · CHICAGO · LOS ANGELES · LONDON · PARIS · TOKYO

Lebhar-Friedman Books
425 Park Avenue
New York, NY 10022

Published by Lebhar-Friedman Books
Lebhar-Friedman Books is a company of Lebhar-Friedman, Inc.

Printed in the United States of America

Library of Congress Cataloging-in-Publication Data on file at the Library of Congress

ISBN: 0-86730-820-6

COVER DESIGN BY KEVIN HANEK
COMPOSITION BY MILLER-WILLIAMS DESIGN ASSOCIATES

Visit our Web site at lfbooks.com

For Bob Gottlieb

Square Meals' special friend; ours too

Contents

Foreword

by M. F. K. Fisher

Dictionaries are always fun, but not always reassuring. This probably depends upon their lexicographers. Our omnibibulous H. L. Mencken, for instance, mentions *square meal* two or three times in his several volumes about the American language, but without really defining it as anything but an interesting proof of our "instinct for the terse, the vivid, and the picturesque," along with other scholarly examples like *cloudburst* and *firebug*.

Almost any American of more than a few months' citizenship knows what a square meal is, whether he teaches computer programming or picks crops. A few days ago a man said to me, "All I really need right now is somewhere to sleep, and three squares a day." And I knew what he meant: warmth, and then food, decent food, something to stick to his ribs and keep him upright and strong.

But he did not mean a bowl of beans, or meat between bread slices, no matter how sustaining either of these things may be. He meant a *square meal,* which perforce means tools and a place to use them, a knife and a spoon and perhaps even a plate, and a protected place for the enjoyment of all or almost all he could eat.

Most of us have eaten square meals in strange places. But no matter where we are or how the food looks, we feel without question that it must be eaten while we are sitting down, and it must be ample, to be truly square. It does not matter if we are sitting cross-legged on a flat rock above the Mexican desert, or crouched beside a trout stream in Idaho, or lolled in a dinner in Keokuk or Miami or even Beverly Hills. A square SQUARE S*Q*U*A*R*E meal means plenty of good hot or good cold familiar odorous decent FOOD.

Of course this is as true anywhere as it is here in our own country. Sometimes it is harder to find, in far lands. But any man will know, in his own language, what a square meal means, and will hope to eat one sooner or later.

It is human to need one, preferably of familiar foods from a person's past life and yearnings: a platter of noodles, a big plum tart, a slice of baked ham, plenty of everything and the time to eat and then eat more, without pretensions or social prejudices.

The title of this book that Jane and Michael Stem have written means, naturally, that it is American. We understand what SQUARE MEALS are in this country, where most of us have known them from early on and have believed that we could, at least occasionally, continue to enjoy them. The man who told me lately that all he wanted was a roof and three squares a day had just served time in a state prison, where he said he ate pretty well on the whole. But now that he was out again, he wanted his own version of a meal. And I think I know what it would be . . . and so do the Sterns.

On the off chance that my own views of what "three squares" might mean could sound slanted, I have asked a few other native Americans what the term means to them. A ninety-year-old ex-Rosicrucian Buddhist said with enviable repugnance that it must mean a huge hearty feast of meat-potatoes-gravy. Another friend, a plump small-town insurance salesman, said wistfully that it means the chow he got on holidays in Veetnamm: roast turkey, all the dressings, pumpkin pie, first come first served but orderly, in a camouflaged mess-tent in the jungle. Susan, a volunteer lunch-cook in the local grammar school who has been feeding kids since she was knee-high, thought hard and then said, "It has to be *big*, and it has to be *good* . . . and you have to *want* it."

In other words, the Sterns are right. They have written with love and respect about the square meals of our country, the kind our grandmothers and the ladies of the Church Society and the cookies out in the cattle-country have always managed to serve now and then, to keep us reassured as well as on our feet. Today, many of the things we eat are not exactly as Great-Aunt Jenny made them, but they are still much better than tol'able. Often they come from packages instead of cannisters and barrels down cellar or in the summer pantry, but in general the boughten stuff is instinctively rejected if it tastes *too* dishonest, and once accepted by the revered ladies in the kitchens (and by the Sterns!) it is treated with proper care.

Myself, I find this book about square meals, whether we have them three daily or only a few times a year, both funny and useful (as well as of real historical value). Most of us will recognize at least half of the recipes, if we have lived in this country more than a few months, and the nicest thing about this eminently *nice* discussion of how we have adapted our basic frontier-cooking to a gradual sophistication is that it is never mocking or supercilious, never guilty of the discreetly sneering haughtiness I have sometimes felt from people who are insecure about American eating habits.

Here, as in most countries, we eat very simply in rural or ethnic regions. A square meal once or twice a day is something we always hope to provide, and when we can make it for a church supper or a birthday we like to show off and be "fancy." Inevitably "convenience" cans and packages have come into our kitchens, and when they are properly used, they are almost as good as their originals. And of course human laziness is served: for instance, we can still buy unflavored natural gelatin, but many otherwise honest cooks use synthetic "instant" substitutes.

Once I went to a potluck supper for the 4-H club my children belonged to, and seventeen of the twenty women on the Food Committee brought quivering green and pink molded "salads" striped with marshmallows and store-bought mayonnaise. Their hardworking rancher husbands circled the three tuna-noodle casseroles like hungry coyotes until the desserts of packaged cake mixes heaped with aerosol Fudge Whippo were served forth. It was

dismal. (I got put on the Food Committee, at the risk of seeming both pushy and protective, and we ladies divided our jobs more evenly and produced some really good meals, hot and savory and *hearty* . . .)

Of course the dictionaries give several definitions of *square,* and a current one means anything from socially hidebound to plain stodgy, which makes the title of the Sterns' book sound a mite tongue in cheek. It is true that a square meal can be both stodgy and hidebound. Basically, though, it will consist of decent bread and butter, plenty of meat/fish/fowl and one or more seasonal vegetables, and then cake or pudding or fruit. This pattern should qualify for what Webster defines as a substantial satisfying meal, I think.

And the food that the Sterns list in their fond and fair and often funny pages is exactly that. It is what we Americans have agreed upon, no matter how grudgingly at times, as a decent facsimile of the plain pioneer food that boosted us through our beginnings. It is familiar, and when we cannot have it we dream of it. We feel OK and unaffected when we confess that we love most of it. It is what we really mean when we half-laugh about Mom-The-Flag-and-Apple-Pie. In other words, a square meal is . . . well . . . who doesn't *need* one, right now or soon?

Introduction

L ife is worrisome. Food shouldn't be. That is why we love square meals, and that is why we wrote this book.

There is no single sort of square meal, and the recipes we gathered to exemplify the best square meals range from hearty meat loaf and mashed potatoes inspired by truck-stop grub to featherweight cookies of the sort served in ladies tea rooms long ago. Nearly all square meals are easy to prepare and fun to serve, and they are always eater-friendly.

Every one of us has a favorite comfort food for those times when we need to feel mothered, when we yearn to feel close to home, when we want to share the kindest cooking with those we care about. It doesn't matter whether you are a great chef or someone who can barely boil water, the cooking and serving and eating of a good square meal provides sustenance that goes beyond nutrition into the realm of spiritual nurture.

So please, banish the anxiety generated by the need to be au courant in the kitchen or as clever as Martha Stewart; just say no to the fear tactics of the nutrition police who want us to feel guilt about everything we eat, and join us in recognizing the simple pleasure food can be. As our friend and mentor M.F.K. Fisher wrote about square meals in her Foreword to the first edition of this book in 1984, "Who doesn't *need* one, right now or soon?"

A square meal can be a joyful celebration of family togetherness or it can be as private and peaceful as a bowl of warm buttered noodles alone at midnight. It might be food that evokes nostalgia for times gone by—coddled eggs on toast points with a mug of cocoa some frosty morning; or it can be a meal that reminds us of our home and home town, like a church-supper casserole from the heartland. In a world fraught with worries, such honest and unaffected fare can be an oasis of serenity. Whether dining solo, with loved ones, or with good friends, there is something especially satisfying about a meal that is not pretentious, not trendy, not scary-exotic, but is just plain nice.

Having spent the last quarter century as food writers whose beat had us traveling from Bug Tussle, Georgia, to Gnaw Bone, Indiana, and from New York City to Los Angeles, we know first-hand that square meals are alive and well across America. Food trends come and go, but those dishes that make people feel good endure regardless of culinary fashion. Look through self-published cookbooks from PTAs and firehouses and you will see that the trends of food fashion have little effect on what Americans really like to eat.

When *Square Meals* was first published sixteen years ago, tortuously overwrought nouvelle cuisine was the leading-edge food trend of the moment, and *au courant* restaurants served huge plates with tiny portions of squid-ink pasta and reductions of kiwi and lemongrass. At the time, we joked with Bob Gottlieb, our editor and publisher at Knopf, that he needed to print only three copies of this cookbook—one for each of the three of us—because square meals were so totally against the grain of prevailing culinary style. With Bob's blessing and his frequent presence at our dinner table, we cooked our way through vintage cookbooks and food-product brochures from ages past. We concocted crazy Jell-O molds, Polynesian fantasies sweetened with grape juice, and casseroles that demanded no culinary talent beyond the skillful use of a can opener. Laughing all the way, we also found the secrets to many American classics: the best pot roasts, perfect bread pudding, quintessential tomato soup.

As it turned out, we were not alone in our affection for pot roast and Sunday supper, living-room luaus and wacky gelatin desserts. Cooks and eaters welcomed this book as a celebration of culinary innocence and a fun alternative to gastronomy that was more fashion statement than nourishment. In its own way, *Square Meals* pioneered the appreciation of comfort food, not as a "trend," but as a valuable legacy that transcends trends. Since 1984, square meals have once again become a fundamental part of the culinary landscape, at home as well as in restaurants plain and fancy. Many of America's trend-setting restaurant chefs offer pot pies and apple pan dowdies on their menus; and even the most ambitious epicures have come to appreciate the joy of a meal that dares to be square.

Acknowledgments

James Beard had the noblesse oblige to answer endless questions about tearoom dining, pink parties, and the proper way to construct a banana candle salad. Mr. Beard's wisdom has been a unique resource in helping us get a grasp on food as popular culture. We thank him for his unfailing good humor and generous open door policy.

Our editor, Martha Kaplan, appreciates the joys of a square meal better than anyone. When she groaned with delight at a three layer chocolate cake we set before her a few years ago, we knew this was a book we had to do together. Although Martha still can't stand tapioca pudding, she is a woman of taste.

We are indebted to Bob Gottlieb, our publisher, for leaving his lofty corner office to find us remarkable cookbook treasures in flea markets. *Square Meals* would not have happened without his encouragement, advice, and prune recipes. Mary Maguire, with her elegant telephone manner and enthusiasm for this book, has made working on it a pleasure.

Bob Cornfield, our agent, makes it easy for us to worry about nothing but writing and cooking. There is nobody with whom it is more fun to share a meal.

Special thanks to Harry and Florence Stern, who scoured antique stores throughout the Midwest to supply us with a steady stream of invaluable source material.

Dave Morris, Mary Ann Rumney, Rudi Besier, and Nancy Faber each contributed rare and wonderful cookbooks from their own collections.

Jan Longone of the Wine and Food Library in Ann Arbor, Michigan, allowed us to run wild through her fabulous stacks of vintage cookbooks, then stifled our ecstatic cries of discovery with delicious croissants and coffee.

Phyllis Richman of the *Washington Post* cheerfully parted with her mother's partyburger recipe. Carol Sama Sheehan, editor of posh *Houston Home & Garden,* was downhome enough to offer an irresistible recipe for five cup salad.

Carol Ann Story of Cleveland's *Morning Exchange* reassured us of the heartland's passion for Jell-O, and led us to Ohioans Joyce Ferring, Gloria Jean Minnick, Virginia Delp, and Sandra Lutz, whose recipes were a kaleidoscopic trove of invention.

Steve Poulos of the Sweet Shop in Winnetka, Illinois, parted with his father's hot fudge formula—an inspiration for the chapter on Lunch Counter Cooking. We could find no recipe anywhere for Iowa pea salad until Carroll Marshall of the White Way Cafe in Durant, Iowa, sent us his, and enriched the chapter on Sunday Dinner.

Closer to home, we thank our neighbors, John and Johanna Robohm, for the loan of their old cookbooks; and their parents, Dr. and Dr. Robohm and Mr. and Mrs. Jung, for their cookbooks, too. Benjamin and Suzanne Van Vechten served valiantly as culinary guinea pigs for meals that didn't work, as well as those that did. Jim and Judy Monteith took care of our dog Edwina when we left home, and also provided us with just the light touch to make the perfect tuna noodle casserole.

Square Meals was our first cookbook, published in 1984. It has been out of print for more than a dozen years—eternity in the world of publishing. What a joy it has been for us to work with Lebhar-Friedman to bring it back in a new edition with so much of the archival art that we have discovered since the 1980s. In particular, we thank Geoff Golson for his steady support, Frank Scatoni for making the process so easy, and Roger Friedman for his belief in us, and in the value of America's food heritage.

—JANE & MICHAEL STERN, WEST REDDING, CONNECTICUT.

SQUARE
MEALS

LADIES LUNCH

❦

Before the sexes insisted on barging into each other's business, there was a ritual called ladies' lunch, an interlude in Madame's busy day that allowed her to fortify body and spirit with a meal as proper as she.

It was a culinary fashion often dubbed "tearoom" dining; but the restaurants that specialized in ladies' lunch were frillier than dowdy English tearooms, their food more graceful than a cup and a crumpet. Yet the label tearoom distinguished these

citadels of femininity from the serious restaurants in town, as well as from ple-
beian coffee shops.

Only a cave dweller could misread the ethos of these "tearooms" as anything but feminine. The antithesis of the steak and martini joints frequented by
newspapermen and other types who like to scribble on tablecloths, they were
places in which ladies shared a common aura of *politesse*, in which food was
edible proof of the superiority of the feminine spirit. Tearoom cuisine asserted a
mannered ideal of femininity, forged into a definitive culinary style.

Mary Elizabeth, Virginia Allen, Mary Mac's, Mother Stouffer's, Patricia
Murphy's . . . the restaurants bore the names of their founders and guiding spirits, the ladies whose firm ideas about what was proper infused both menu and
decor. Men were welcome, and they came . . . but they knew to tread lightly, to
fasten loose collar buttons and snuff out cigars at the portal.

You don't have to be female to appreciate this cuisine of angel cakes and
ambrosia, of chicken swathed in creamy sauces, of muffin morsels sized to fit
just so between rouged lips.

Some ladies' tearooms, like the network of women's exchanges or restaurants nestled in the hearts of large department stores, served nothing fancier than
a club sandwich and a strawberry ice cream soda. But there were also bigger,
elaborate lunching rooms of a more serious ilk—places one went for a full hot
meal, where ladies could dine with assurance, waited on by other women in
black taffeta uniforms and starched white aprons. One could be sure there would
be no ogling salesman on his lunch hour, for these were safe isles of gentility,
where the morals were as high as the popovers.

Like a visit to the beauty parlor, lunch in one of these feminine restaurants
conveyed a sense of immunity. The dark things of the world would not dare
intrude into an edifice constructed on a sugary foundation of Lady Baltimore
cakes. After a meal of chicken à la king or creamed crab on toast points, the
jagged edges of life were nicely softened.

To get a full sense of lady food's charms, it is necessary to appreciate what
it meant to be a lady. Understand that there were once three sexes: men, women,
and ladies. Unlike women—who had sex, gave birth, cried, sweated, and often
got angry—ladies were creatures of a higher calling. While some might be to
high manners born, grand doyennes like Emily Post held out hope that with
proper effort, even those who crawled out from a grubby cabbage patch might
make it up through the ranks and enter the rarefied circle of polite society.

Would-be ladies studied the arts of charm and grace with the intensity scholars reserve for Proust. They emulated Emily Post's paragons from her book *Etiquette,* Mrs. Oldname and Mrs. Worldly. Their *bête noire,* Miss Not-From-Much, could always be counted on to pronounce *chaise longue* incorrectly as "cheese lung," and to spit her cherry pits somewhere they mustn't be. They crossed their legs (limbs, please!) at the ankle, and blotted their lipstick so as to not leave scarlet prints on the Spode. They knew that only a vulgarian would pick up an asparagus spear at the table, and they knew how to calmly and politely expire when a fish bone stuck in their throat.

Aspiring Mrs. Worldlys needed a stage on which to practice their act; so where better than the places ladies lunched? There they could be assured of an appreciative audience who (unlike husbands with their heads in the daily paper) could be counted on to admire them at their best. Among heart-shaped aspics, pink lemonades, shrimp wiggles, and desserts as palpitatingly sweet (and as proper) as Spring Byington, a lady was in her element.

Tearoom Lunch

THE BREAD BASKET

Frances Virginia Blueberry Gems • 10

Philadelphia Cinnamon Buns • 11

Quick Tea Rolls • 12

Banana Walnut Bread • 12

Orange Biscuits • 13

Corn Gems • 14

TEAROOM SALADS

Tomato Aspic in a Heart-Shaped Mold • 15

Waldorf Soufflé Aspic • 16

Lettuce Wedge with Poppy Seed Dressing • 16

Five Cup Salad • 17

TEAROOM ENTRÉES

Chicken à la King in a Potato Nest • 18

Cheese and Crab Delight • 20

TEAROOM DESSERTS

Ambrosia Layer Cake • 21

Chocolate Angel Food Cake with Butterscotch Sauce • 23

Dinner by Candlelight

Lemon Soup • 25

Victor's All-White Salad Platter • 25

Hawaiian Chicken and Pineapple Curry • 26

PINK PARTY BUFFET

Pink Ladies • 45

Queen of Muffins • 45

Lily Pons Party Salad • 47

Blushing Beetskis • 47

Pink Frosted Surprise Loaf • 47

Quivering Crab Apple Salad • 48

Pink Lady Baltimore Layer Cake • 49

Shower for Miss Alice Bride

"A Thousand Ways to Please a Husband" Molasses Puffs • 52

Candlelight Salad • 53

Cupid's Apricot Soufflé • 54

Gold Hearts • 54

Silhouette Cake with Harvest Moon Frosting • 55

BRIDESMAID LUNCHEON

Maid of Honor Iced Fruit Soup • 57

Sunbonnet Baby Salad • 58

Shrimp Wiggle • 58

Tipsy Trifle • 59

Tearoom Lunch

The queen of tearooms might well have been the Frances Virginia in Atlanta, Georgia. Mildred Huff Coleman, author of the Frances Virginia Tea Room Cookbook, remembers the clientele this way: "Even during the hottest July, Atlantans never went downtown in anything but their Sunday best. That meant a hat, perhaps puffs of pastel netting, or just a wisp of a veil brushing the brow. Makeup included a lot of loose powder, Navy Red or Cherries in the Snow lipstick, Pongee rouge, and perfume. Last but not least were gloves, white or tinted."

Like most of America's bastions of feminine dining, the Frances Virginia was born during the Depression as an oasis of breeding, good food, and value. Located on the third floor of the old Collier Building, marked by Frances Virginia Wikle Whitaker's silhouette in pink neon, it survived long past the halcyon days of ladies' lunch into the 1970s.

To dine there was a rite of passage, a little ceremony attesting to the fact that one belonged in polite society. Compared to urban lunching anywhere today, Frances Virginia was not of this earth. One imagines platoons of lost ladies searching cities in vain for one such last meal:

The Bread Basket

Any ladies' lunch is only as good as its bread basket. Ballooning popovers, minuscule vanilla gem muffins, or crisp tiny corn sticks, all warm and tucked into the folds of an immaculate linen napkin, are the overture to a Proper meal, and the keynote of mannered dining.

"In the progress of our great western peoples, bread has been a symbol of civilization," proclaims *Vitality Demands Energy,* a General Mills brochure of 1934. "The advance from savagery to the comforts and enlightenment of civilization has been accompanied by . . . an ever improving quality of bread." The pamphlet also notes that "motion picture stars take no chances with their diet; to insure the energy essential to glowing beauty and vitality, they include bread in every meal!"

If the dabs of sweet cream butter are molded in shapes of rosebuds or daisies, so much the better!

FRANCES VIRGINIA BLUEBERRY GEMS

"Gems" are an especially ladylike breadstuff—muffins miniaturized to please a dainty sense of proportion.

2 cups all-purpose flour	*1 cup buttermilk*
⅓ cup sugar	*¼ cup oil*
½ teaspoon salt	*1 cup fresh blueberries*
½ teaspoon baking soda	*1 tablespoon all-purpose flour*
2 teaspoons baking powder	*1 teaspoon grated orange or*
2 eggs	*lemon rind*

• Preheat oven to 425°.

Mix dry ingredients. Beat eggs with buttermilk and oil. Add to dry ingredients. Mix, leaving mixture slightly lumpy.

Mix blueberries with 1 tablespoon flour and rind. Add to muffin mixture. Fill well-greased gem tins two-thirds full. (A gem tin is a muffin pan designed to produce tiny replicas of muffins.)

Bake 15 to 20 minutes, until brown.

Makes 3 dozen gems.

PHILADELPHIA CINNAMON BUNS

Sticky buns—a must for the tearoom bread basket—from the *Royal Cookbook* of 1928.

6 tablespoons butter	*1 egg, beaten*
2 tablespoons plus ½ cup	*½ cup water*
granulated sugar	*2 teaspoons cinnamon*
2 cups all-purpose flour	*4 tablespoons raisins*
1 teaspoon salt	*2 tablespoons brown sugar*
4 teaspoons baking powder	

• Melt 4 tablespoons butter. Cool. Sift 2 tablespoons sugar with flour, salt, and baking powder. Add beaten egg and 2 tablespoons of the melted butter to water, and add slowly to dry ingredients to make soft dough. Knead lightly. Roll out ¼ inch thick on floured board; brush with remaining melted butter. Mix ½ cup sugar and cinnamon; sprinkle with raisins over dough. Roll as for jelly roll. Refrigerate 1 hour.

Cream 2 tablespoons butter with 2 tablespoons brown sugar. Spread this mixture on bottom and sides of a 9- or 10-inch cast-iron baking pan (or skillet), and heat just long enough for butter to melt. Cut dough into 1-inch pieces and place with cut edges up on pan, about ½ inch apart. Lots of cinnamon-sugar will fall out when you cut the buns. Sprinkle this on top of the pieces in the pan.

As oven heats to 400°, allow dough to stand 15 minutes.

Bake 25 minutes. Remove from pan at once, turning upside down to serve. Buns will expand to form a large cake.

There will be about a dozen buns. Pull apart to eat.

QUICK TEA ROLLS

A bread-basket staple, from *Mrs. Allen on Cooking* by Ida Bailey Allen, published in 1924. Mrs. Allen noted that "foods may be likened to the pipes of an organ—the homemaker to the organist. Press whatever keys you like—and *something* results—either bodily harmony or inharmony according to the skill and intelligence applied. When a quick bread is introduced, let it be with a reason!" These rolls, which Mrs. Allen calls "quick" even though they require a couple of hours to rise, are shaped like miniature pocketbooks, golden little pillows reminiscent of Parker House rolls, but not quite as sweet.

1 package dry yeast dissolved in
tepid (110°) water with
1 tablespoon sugar and
2 tablespoons flour
3 cups all-purpose flour

½ cup milk
2 tablespoons butter
½ teaspoon salt
2 tablespoons butter, melted

• Scald milk, add 2 tablespoons butter; cool until lukewarm. Blend with yeast mixture, which should be good and frothy at this point; add remaining flour and salt and knead thoroughly 5 to 8 minutes. Dough will be smooth and tough. Roll out ¼ inch thick, brush with some melted butter, cut out with 2- to 2½-inch-diameter biscuit cutter or floured glass, crease and fold circles in half.

Set rolls on buttered baking pan. Brush tops with remaining melted butter. Cover, set in warm place to rise for 2 hours. Rolls will double in size.

Preheat oven to 375°. Bake 12 to 15 minutes, or until light golden.

Makes about 18 rolls.

BANANA WALNUT BREAD

"Make it a rule to 'Just Add Walnuts' to at least one dish every day," advises *Menu Magic in a Nutshell,* a 1938 pamphlet put out by the California Walnut Growers Association. "Many a fine cook's reputation is based on a trick of kitchen magic—the little flick of the wrist that empties a cup of walnut kernels into some simple recipe."

1 cup sugar	2½ cups sifted all-purpose flour
8 tablespoons butter	1 teaspoon baking soda
2 eggs	½ teaspoon salt
1⅓ cups mashed bananas	¾ cup chopped walnuts

• Preheat oven to 375°.

Cream sugar and butter. Add eggs and bananas. Sift together flour, soda, and salt. Add to mixture, along with walnuts. Pour into greased 10-by-5-by-3½-inch loaf pan. Bake 1 hour. Cool and slice thinly.

ORANGE BISCUITS

Mild sweetened spirals from *The Household Searchlight*, written in the 1930s by a "family of specialists living in a seven-room house, whose entire time is spent in working out the problems of homemaking."

3 cups all-purpose flour	1 cup milk
4 teaspoons baking powder	2 tablespoons butter, melted
1 teaspoon salt	⅓ cup orange juice
3 tablespoons sugar	1 tablespoon grated orange rind
4 tablespoons cold butter	

• Sift flour, measure, and sift again with baking powder, salt, and 1 tablespoon sugar. Cut in butter. Add milk to form soft dough. Turn onto lightly floured board. Knead lightly. Pat into rectangular sheet ¼ inch thick. Spread with melted butter and 2 tablespoons sugar dissolved in orange juice, leaving aside about half the mixture. Sprinkle with orange rind.

Roll like jelly roll and cut in slices ½ inch thick. Place cut side down in well-oiled pan. Spread tops with remainder of orange juice and sugar mix. Cover and allow to stand 10 minutes.

Preheat oven to 450°.

Bake 15 minutes.

Makes 20 biscuits.

CORN GEMS

Submitted by "Aunt Liza" of Tennessee to the *D.A.R. Book of Recipes,* published in 1937 by the Stamford, Connecticut, chapter.

1 cup sifted all-purpose flour	*1 cup milk*
1 cup cornmeal	*¼ cup molasses*
2 teaspoons baking powder	*1 egg, well beaten*
1 teaspoon salt	*2 tablespoons butter, melted*

• Preheat oven to 400°.

Heavily grease gem pans (muffin pans designed to produce tiny replicas of muffins) or corn-stick pans. Put in oven to heat.

Sift flour; add cornmeal, baking powder, and salt. Sift together three times. Combine milk, molasses, egg, and butter; add gradually and beat. Pour into hot pan molds.

Bake 10 to 15 minutes, or until light brown.

Makes about 30 gems.

Tearoom Salads

At ladies' lunch, salads are seldom bowls of leafy garden vegetables—how untidy! Tearoom dining calls for a gelatinized salad, known in the South as "congealed salad," molded into a pretty shape, packed with copious amounts of miniature marshmallows, raisins, slivered nuts, and toasted coconut. Cool, refreshing, neat to eat, and far removed from nature's unkempt weedy tangle, molded salads are edible candied bouquets, always welcome when girls dine together.

TOMATO ASPIC IN A HEART-SHAPED MOLD

This tasteful tomato heart, suggested by *The Silent Hostess Treasure Book* of 1931, may be considered practically Bauhaus in spirit, such is its lack of frills, yet it is nonetheless appropriately feminine. "The silent hostess," by the way, is milady's refrigerator, which takes "an active part in the preparation and serving of her meals," allowing her to "appear calm and gracious, . . . free to entertain without having to excuse herself frequently to prepare refreshments."

2 tablespoons unflavored gelatin
¼ cup cold water
½ cup boiling water
1 28-ounce can whole
    tomatoes, with juice
1 tablespoon chopped onion
½ teaspoon celery seed

¼ teaspoon ground cloves
1 teaspoon salt
1 teaspoon sugar
2 teaspoons lemon juice
Lettuce leaves
Mayonnaise

• Soak gelatin in cold water, then add boiling water. Cook tomatoes, onion, celery seed, cloves, salt, and sugar for 15 minutes. Puree in food processor or blender. Add lemon juice and dissolved gelatin. Pour into 6 individual lightly oiled heart-shaped molds or a 4-cup mold. Chill until firm. Serve on crisp lettuce leaves with mayonnaise.

Serves 6.

WALDORF SOUFFLÉ ASPIC

A favorite from the Frances Virginia Tea Room, "Waldorf" suggests the height of elegance. It is a perfect companion for shrimp salad on a warm summer's day.

1 3-ounce package
lemon gelatin
Pinch salt
1 cup boiling apple juice
½ cup cold apple juice

¼ cup mayonnaise
¾ cup finely diced red apples
¼ cup finely diced celery
¼ cup chopped walnuts

• Dissolve gelatin and salt in boiling apple juice. Add cold apple juice. Cool until semicongealed. Add mayonnaise; whip until fluffy. When slightly thick, fold in apples, celery, and walnuts. Pour into 5 or 6 lightly oiled individual molds. Chill until set.

Serves 5 or 6.

LETTUCE WEDGE WITH POPPY SEED DRESSING

Not all salads need to be gelatinized to appeal to the feminine palate. But they'd better be sweet! Poppy seed dressing, customarily ladled on chunks of iceberg lettuce, is a Midwestern classic, still a favorite in the few Illinois, Ohio, and Wisconsin tearooms that continue to serve a respectable ladies' lunch.

⅓ cup white vinegar
1½ tablespoons onion juice
½ cup sugar
1 teaspoon dry mustard

1 teaspoon salt
1 cup vegetable oil
2 tablespoons poppy seeds
1 head iceberg lettuce

• In a small mixing bowl combine vinegar, onion juice, sugar, mustard, and salt. Stir vigorously by hand or with electric mixer set on low. Whisking constantly, pour in oil in a slow, thin stream, and continue to beat until dressing is smooth and thick. Stir in poppy seeds.

Cut lettuce into 6 wedges and lay each on a chilled salad plate. Ladle on 2 to 3 tablespoons dressing, or to taste.

Serves 6.

FIVE CUP SALAD

"Laugh if you will," wrote Carol Sama Sheehan, the Houston sophisticate who sent us the recipe for this ambrosial dish, "but the bowl is *always* licked clean." We mixed our first Five Cup Salad one Friday afternoon in anticipation of guests for Saturday lunch. By 10:00 P.M., Friday, with just the two of us in the house, it was gone. We learned two lessons from that delicious experience: first, although the recipe *ought* to be enough for four or even six dainty servings, you must beware of the sudden gluttony this salad induces. "Houstonians have been known to *fight* over the last miniature marshmallow," Carol had warned.

The second lesson is that it is ridiculously easy to make, so that when you polish off the first batch before your company arrives, it's only a matter of a couple of minutes to make some more . . . as long as you have plenty of ingredients on hand.

1 cup shredded coconut

1 cup mandarin
oranges, drained

1 cup crushed
pineapple, drained

1 cup sour cream

1 cup miniature marshmallows
(white only!)

• Combine all ingredients.
  Serves 4 to 6, maybe.

Tearoom Entrées

Small pieces of food, requiring no sawing with a knife or wrestling with bones, are perfectly suited to ladies' lunch. Chicken—on biscuits, waffles, or toast, or in nests or pastry shells—was the most popular tearoom entrée, followed closely by concoctions of crab, lobster, or shrimp.

CHICKEN À LA KING IN A POTATO NEST

Creamy, soft, and gentle, precut into bite-sized pieces, chicken à la king is warmingly substantial, yet never gross—an ideal entrée for ladies' lunch. Add a potato nest, and this dish is a favorite among visiting husbands or other men who frequent feminine dining rooms, namely those who earn their living lecturing women's clubs on flower arrangements—the ones who make Madam Chairman swoon with their chiseled profiles and fine old-family manners.

CHICKEN À LA KING

½ cup sliced mushrooms

½ cup green peppers, cut
   in strips

¾ cup diced celery

2 tablespoons butter

1½ tablespoons chicken fat
   or butter

1¾ tablespoons all-purpose flour

½ cup hot chicken stock

½ cup scalded milk

¼ cup scalded cream

½ teaspoon salt

1½ cups cold boiled
   chicken, cut in chunks

¼ cup canned pimientos

1 egg yolk, slightly beaten

1 teaspoon dry sherry

• Sauté the mushrooms, green peppers, and celery in butter. Set aside.

Melt fat, add flour, and stir until well blended; then add gradually, while stirring constantly, stock, milk, and cream. Bring to the boiling point and add salt, chicken, mushroom-pepper-celery mixture, and pimientos. Again bring to the boiling point, reduce heat, and add egg yolk. Stir until smooth and add sherry.

Serves 4.

POTATO NESTS

1 russet potato per nest

Vegetable shortening for frying

• This recipe requires a special kitchen device called a nest maker—two interlocking wire-mesh cages on a long handle. You will get approximately 1 nest from each medium-sized potato.

Wash, pare, and cut potatoes into thin strips. If using a food processor, use the julienne attachment. Soak potato shreds in cold water for 15 minutes, drain, and dry well between towels.

Heat fat to 375° in pot sufficiently deep to submerge nest maker. Dip nest maker in oil to coat it. Line the larger basket with a good ½ inch of shredded potatoes; attach the top basket, and fry in heated oil 3 to 4 minutes. Remove, drain, resubmerge in oil 1 minute. Do not overcook or nest will be brittle and hard to remove.

A ladleful of chicken à la king should be put into each potato basket just before serving. If potato nests do not appeal to you, substitute patty shells or toast points with crusts removed.

CHEESE AND CRAB DELIGHT

This recipe is from *Marye Dahnke's File,* published in 1938 by Kraft, where, according to Marye, "cheese cookery is a hobby as well as a business. For cooking with cheese is such a fascinating job one could scarcely call it work!" This "Delight" makes for a creamy plate of comfort in the midst of the shopping day.

2 tablespoons chopped green pepper	1 cup grated Kraft American cheese
2 tablespoons butter	1 egg, beaten
2 tablespoons all-purpose flour	¼ cup hot milk
Salt	1 cup crabmeat
Pepper	½ cup sliced mushrooms, sautéed in butter
½ teaspoon dry mustard	4 slices toast, trimmed of crust
1 cup cooked strained tomatoes	

• Cook green pepper in butter. Add flour, seasonings, and tomatoes, and cook slowly, stirring constantly, until thickened. Add cheese and mix well, then add beaten egg. Cook and stir constantly until slightly thickened. Add milk and crabmeat, mix and heat again. Top with mushrooms.

Serve on freshly made toast points.

Serves 4.

Tearoom Desserts

Portions may be demure, and place settings dainty, but when it comes to dessert at ladies' lunch, all restrictions are lifted. Tearoom bakeries were famous for their splendid selections of cakes and pies. To this day, some of the best, most cornucopian dessert menus in America will be found at Miss

Hulling's in St. Louis, Anna Maude in Oklahoma City, and Boder's on the River in Mequon, Wisconsin—each a bastion of feminine dining at its prettiest and most satisfying. (This day = 1984)

AMBROSIA LAYER CAKE

The essential distaff dessert—as white as a Sunday glove, and sweet as a whiff of lavender on lace. The term "ambrosia," whether applied to cake, pie, or gelatinized salad, always signifies the unmistakably feminine duo of coconut and oranges, Mandarin oranges preferred.

The New Coconut Treasure Book of 1934, from which this recipe is taken, says, "If you had been the wife of a clipper ship captain in the old days, you might have known the thrill of *discovering* coconut! Of having your husband bring you home one of those big brown coconuts that he saw natives in the tropics using for food." But then the *Treasure Book* beams, "Isn't it grand that you can have *your* coconut adventures, rejoice in coconut that the clipper ship era would have marvelled at—coconut shredded and ready—meaty and tender—for whatever treat you elect to make."

2¼ cups cake flour	*1 cup sugar*
2¼ teaspoons baking powder	*2 eggs, well beaten*
¼ teaspoon salt	*¾ cup milk*
1½ teaspoons grated lemon rind	*1 teaspoon vanilla extract*
1 tablespoon grated orange rind	*Mandarin oranges*
8 tablespoons butter	*½ can shredded coconut*

• Preheat oven to 375°.

Sift flour once, measure, add baking powder and salt, and sift together three times.

Add lemon rind and orange rind to butter, and cream thoroughly; add sugar gradually, and cream together until light and fluffy. Add eggs and beat well. Add flour, alternately with milk, a small amount at a time, beating after each addition until smooth. Add vanilla.

Bake in 2 greased and floured 9-inch layer pans 25 to 30 minutes. Cool thoroughly.

Spread Orange Coconut Filling between layers and Seven Minute Frosting on top and sides of cake. Arrange mandarin oranges on top of cake and sprinkle with shredded coconut.

ORANGE COCONUT FILLING

½ cup sugar	*2 tablespoons water*
2½ tablespoons cake flour	*1 egg yolk, lightly beaten*
Dash salt	*1 teaspoon butter*
¼ cup orange juice	*½ tablespoon grated orange rind*
1½ tablespoons lemon juice	*¼ can shredded coconut*

• Combine sugar, flour, and salt in top of double boiler; add fruit juices, water, and egg yolk, mixing thoroughly. Place over rapidly boiling water and cook 10 minutes, stirring constantly. Remove from heat; add butter, orange rind, and coconut. Cool and spread between cake layers.

SEVEN MINUTE FROSTING

2 egg whites	*1½ teaspoons light corn syrup*
1½ cups sugar	*1 teaspoon vanilla extract*
5 tablespoons water	

• Combine egg whites, sugar, water, and corn syrup in top of double boiler, beating with rotary beater until thoroughly mixed. Place over rapidly boiling water, beat constantly with rotary beater, and cook 7 minutes, or until frosting will stand in peaks. Remove from heat. Add vanilla and beat until thick enough to spread.

CHOCOLATE ANGEL FOOD CAKE
WITH BUTTERSCOTCH SAUCE

This mighty—but tender—confection, from *All About Home Baking,* published by General Foods in 1933, is called "the queen of cakes"; the sauce is from the Frances Virginia Tea Room.

CAKE

¾ cup sifted cake flour

4 tablespoons cocoa

1¼ cups egg whites (10 to 12 eggs)

¼ teaspoon salt

1 teaspoon cream of tartar

1¼ cups sugar

1 teaspoon vanilla extract

• Preheat oven to 275°.

Sift flour once, add cocoa, and sift four more times. Beat egg whites and salt; when foamy, add cream of tartar and continue beating until eggs are stiff enough to hold up in peaks, but not dry. Fold in sugar carefully, 2 tablespoons at a time, until all is used. Fold in vanilla. Then sift small amount of flour over mixture and fold in carefully; continue until all is used. Pour batter into ungreased 10-inch angel food tube pan.

Bake in slow oven at least 1 hour. Begin at 275° and after 30 minutes, increase heat slightly (to 325°) and bake 30 minutes longer.

Remove cake from oven and invert pan 1 hour, or until cold. Remove cake from pan; drizzle with warm Butterscotch Sauce. To serve, gently pull pieces of cake apart with two forks. Never cut an angel food cake!

BUTTERSCOTCH SAUCE

8 tablespoons butter

1 cup brown sugar

7 ounces evaporated milk

Pinch salt

Pinch baking soda

• Melt butter with brown sugar in top of double boiler. Add milk, salt, and soda. Cook until hot.

May be kept in refrigerator several weeks. Heat to serve.

Dinner by Candlelight

T here was a soigné version of lady food too, not lunch with the gals during a busy day of shopping, but a romantic dinner, with candles and flowers galore; an anniversary celebration, or any time a lady wanted to feel like Queen for a Day. For these occasions, Patricia Murphy's Candlelight Restaurant was just about perfect.

Starting during the Depression with a small tearoom in Brooklyn, Patricia Murphy built a reputation for good food and romantic atmosphere that spiraled over the decades until she became the reigning queen of feminine dining. She had a handful of restaurants, from Westchester County to Fort Lauderdale, all known for three things: flowers, candlelight, and popovers.

As a green thumb, she had no peers. The roses, floribunda, rare orchids, and pink-blossomed peach trees that decorated her dining rooms won countless prizes in horticultural shows. At Easter, her restaurants burst forth like living bonnets into pink, blue, and white hydrangeas and beds of perfumed lilies. When men took their wives to Patricia Murphy's, they were wasting their money on a predinner corsage. Her Rappaccini's Garden swallowed the effect like one tiny bud in a greenhouse.

The food at Patricia Murphy's was just as ladies liked it—delicate, and presented with a flourish of feminine taste and style. Nothing strident, no foul-smelling garlic or unbecoming showers of pepper or spice. Miss Murphy knew that, like the Princess and the Pea, the truly feminine soul was thrown out of whack by even a hint of overly robust cuisine. Guests in her restaurants dined on the mellowest versions of exotic food—curries that had left their fight back in India, soups with a pale but attractive piquancy.

Like a perfect flower arrangement, a Patricia Murphy's meal, lit by the glow of candles, was designed to make a woman feel cherished. How could life not look sweet with a pink champagne cocktail in one hand and a hot popover in the other?

Candlelight Dinners

Lemon Soup ◆ Victor's All-White Salad Platter ◆ Hawaiian Chicken and Pineapple Curry ◆ Patricia Murphy's Popovers ◆ Coffee Pearadise

LEMON SOUP

Inspired by a private recipe from the kitchen of "Kinsale," Patricia Murphy's home in Florida. She suggests it as an appropriate beginning for a formal meal. Not a wimpy soup, it is plush with egg yolks and the strong zest of lemon.

½ cup rice	*6 tablespoons lemon juice*
6 cups clear beef broth	*Watercress*
4 egg yolks	

• Simmer rice in broth until rice is very soft, about 30 minutes.

Beat egg yolks; combine with lemon juice. Remove broth from heat. Pour ½ cup broth into egg-lemon mixture, stir well, and combine with rest of broth. Stir for 1 minute over low heat. Serve immediately, topped with watercress.

Serves 6.

VICTOR'S ALL-WHITE SALAD PLATTER

"Kinsale would not be Kinsale," Patricia Murphy wrote, "without my cherished and devoted major domo, Victor de Leon"—who invented this visual blockbuster.

• On a large platter or silver tray arrange grapefruit sections, spears of canned white Belgian asparagus, water chestnuts, cauliflower, fresh pineapple chunks, peeled apple slices, hearts of palm, artichoke bottoms, cold braised hearts of celery, and white radishes. Sprinkle curls of fresh coconut over all. Serve with tart French dressing.

HAWAIIAN CHICKEN
AND PINEAPPLE CURRY

Most places where ladies lunched featured chicken curry as a house special-ty. Mary Elizabeth's Tea Room in New York built a reputation on it. Understand that tearoom curry is nothing like Indian curry. It is exotic food for the culinarily timid. This recipe, based on Patricia Murphy's version, is guaranteed not to scare even the most xenophobic palate, and is a happy, soothing dish in its own right.

2 cups Coconut Milk
½ cup minced onion
6 tablespoons butter
⅓ cup all-purpose flour
4 teaspoons curry powder
1 teaspoon salt

½ teaspoon ground ginger
2 cups chicken broth
3 cups diced cooked chicken
1 cup cubed fresh
  (or canned) pineapple

• Prepare coconut milk as directed below, if not obtainable fresh.

In deep pot, cook onion in butter until soft but not brown. Blend in flour, curry powder, salt, and ginger. Add coconut milk and broth. Cook over low heat, stirring constantly, until thickened. Add chicken and pineapple. Heat thoroughly.

Serve with fluffy rice and curry accompaniments, such as chutney, raisins, shredded coconut, macadamia nuts (or peanuts), etc.

Serves 6.

COCONUT MILK
2 cups hot milk
4 cups freshly grated coconut, or
  2 3½-ounce cans shredded coconut

• Pour hot milk over coconut. Let stand 30 minutes. Strain through double cheesecloth, pressing to remove all liquid.

Reserve coconut to toast and serve with curry. Chill coconut milk until ready to use.

Makes 2 cups.

COFFEE PEARADISE

A private recipe from the kitchen of "Sky High," Patricia Murphy's Manhattan penthouse—"suited to cosmopolitan palates," she advises.

1 tablespoon unflavored gelatin	*½ cup pear syrup*
2 tablespoons cold coffee	*5 or 6 canned pear halves*
6 tablespoons sugar	*1 cup heavy cream, whipped*
1 cup hot strong coffee	*½ teaspoon vanilla extract*

• Soften gelatin in cold coffee; add sugar. Pour hot coffee over all and stir until dissolved. Add pear syrup. Arrange pear halves in bottom of 10-inch lightly oiled ring mold. Add part of gelatin mixture to a depth of about ½ inch; chill.

Chill remaining gelatin mixture until slightly thickened. Whip cream and vanilla together; fold into remaining gelatin mixture. Spoon into ring mold; chill until firm.

Unmold on serving platter. Serve with additional whipped cream if desired.

Serves 5 or 6.

❧

To accompany the fine and fancy food served by the Candlelight restaurants, there were always popovers, the best-known dish in the house. "The recipe of the Patricia Murphy popover has remained standard through the depression, two World Wars, and the coming of the space age," Miss Murphy wrote in her autobiography, *Glow of Candlelight*. "Millions of these fluffy delicacies are eaten annually."

PATRICIA MURPHY'S POPOVERS

• Preheat oven to 450°.

Put ⅓ teaspoon butter or vegetable shortening in each muffin pan (or custard cup). Heat in oven 5 minutes while you are mixing batter:

1 cup sifted all-purpose flour   *1 cup milk*

¼ teaspoon salt   *1 tablespoon butter, melted*

2 eggs

• Sift flour and salt into a bowl. Beat eggs with rotary beater, add milk and butter, and sift in flour, beating only enough to make a smooth batter. Fill hot muffin pans one-third full of the mixture.

Bake 30 minutes at 450°, then reduce temperature to 350° and bake 15 minutes longer, or until firm, brown, and popped. Keep oven door closed while baking.

Makes 6 large popovers or 9 small ones.

Teatime —
Finger Sandwiches and Cakes

Primarily a woman's affair, afternoon tea is probably the most popular of entertainments with both husbands and wives. It gives the latter a chance to foregather with her kind and compare notes on topics dear to the feminine heart, and for the former, it keeps the dears amused without involving the tired businessman in any personal participation.

Culture and Good Manners, 1926

Whereas a husband or shanghaied male might feel at home in a tearoom or at a Candlelight Restaurant, a man at a tea party is like an overstuffed easy chair in a room full of Chippendale settees. Whether grand enough to compete with a debutante ball, or so modest that it is little more than friends gathered around a teapot nibbling watercress sandwiches, afternoon tea must always appear demure and the refreshments always be lady food at its ceremonious extreme. "Tea service must be complete, dainty, immaculate," advised *All About Home Baking*, a 1933 publication of the General Foods Consumer Service Department. "Remember that confusion and disorder are enemies to the good conversation and repose for which the tea hour stands, first of all."

The pouring of the tea is the domain of the hostess or her dearest *aide de camp*. As Emily Post details the situation in *Etiquette*, "The ladies who pour are always invited beforehand, and are always invited because they can be counted on for their gracious manners to everyone and under all circumstances."

A good tea pourer will customize the tea for each guest, knowing just the proper number of sugar lumps and the correct measure of cream or lemon peel. She knows that weak tea is made by quick dilution with a spare pot of boiling water. And if a guest throws her a double whammy by requesting hot chocolate, she will, without a blink, point graciously to another lady poised and ready at another steaming pot who, according to Miss Post, will exclaim, "How nice of you! I have been feeling very neglected. Everyone seems to prefer tea!"

In an autobiography called *Coffee and Waffles*, Alice Foote MacDougall, who ran a waffle shop in Grand Central Station in the 1920s, describes the "fateful moment" of choosing which tea one should serve. "Some of you, especially if you are of grandmotherly age, will be sure to ask for tea 'with that smoky flavour.' Alas, dear persons, that is no more."

Tea's decline is blamed on the fact that the men who load the tea onto sailing ships are no longer "gay and careless." They do not throw Souchong tea into a hold littered with "hides, hemp, and whatnot." Nowadays, tea is sanitary, hermetically sealed, without the magical flavors created by its intimacy with the other freight. It is now "just tea—*ni plus ni moins.*"

Of course, every lady knows the proper way to brew a pot of tea:

HOW TO BREW A POT OF TEA

• Bring a kettle filled with fresh cold water to a rolling boil.

Scald teapot with hot water.

Measure 1 rounded teaspoon of loose tea per cup into the emptied teapot; or place the tea in a wire-mesh tea infuser inside the pot.

Pour boiling water into teapot. Let tea steep for 3 minutes. Remove tea infuser, or pour tea through strainer to serve.

If you are an Oriental, Miss MacDougall suggests, tea is all you want—tea alone. "But if you are just Broadway/Fifth Avenue American," you will want tea plus: with cream. Or perhaps "a drop or two of lemon juice, a grain or two of sugar, and then, for the nonce, a dash of good Jamaica rum."

On a hot day, it is within the bounds of propriety to offer lady guests a glass of ice tea. *Coffee and Waffles* suggests this recipe:

ALICE FOOTE MACDOUGALL'S ICE TEA

• Squeeze juice of 3 lemons and 1 large orange. Set aside.

Fill a kettle with fresh cold water. Place 8 individual tea bags in a teapot. When kettle is boiling vigorously, pour on 1 quart boiling water; let tea steep 8 minutes. Press tea bags and stir, so essence will be thoroughly diffused through water. Drain at once into a pitcher filled with cracked ice. Let stand 3 minutes to chill.

Place lemon and orange juice in another pitcher filled with cracked ice, and pour in tea. Sweeten to taste and add, as garnishes, slices of lemon, pineapple, orange, Maraschino cherries, or mint.

Makes 8 to 10 cups.

The tea is brewed; then, the great moment, as portrayed by Alice Foote MacDougall:

We lift our tea cup—of course it is of the fine old India or Chinese porcelain (egg shell preferred)—to our lips. Rest—Peace—Ambrosia! We are at one with the gods. They of Olympus with nectar and damp clouds have nothing on us with our sparkling fire and tea inspiring and recreating us.

But even before this state of caffeinated nirvana is attained, a good hostess makes sure that her helpers supply the non tea drinkers with an appropriate beverage, such as this plush Reception Chocolate:

RECEPTION CHOCOLATE

Baker's Best Chocolate Recipes of 1932 calls this "a hot chocolate of extraordinary smoothness and rich flavor, especially suited for use at receptions, teas, and similar functions."

⅔ cup sugar

4 tablespoons all-purpose flour

2½ ounces Baker's unsweetened chocolate, cut in pieces

⅛ teaspoon salt

1 quart cold water

1 quart milk

½ teaspoon vanilla extract

• Combine sugar, flour, chocolate, salt, and water in upper part of double boiler. Place over direct heat and boil 15 minutes, stirring constantly. Add milk, place over hot water, and heat. Add vanilla and beat with egg beater until light and frothy. Serve immediately.

Serves 12.

By now, all assembled are hungry, but the genteel guest drops no hint, since she is much too busy with her obligations of commenting on the embroidery of the tea cloths and the perfection of the silver service.

Gentle sighs of relief heave from feminine bosoms as plates of dainties are brought forth to eat.

Nothing is quite so appropriate to the ritual of the tea party as lovely finger sandwiches—especially if they are filled with vanities such as flower petals. Ladies will be drawn to their delightful intricacies like honeybees to a hyacinth.

Tea Sandwich Fillings

"Bread," declared Emily Post in 1934, "is like dresses, hats and shoes—in other words, essential!" At a tea party, "unless the sweets and sours, the roes or the pates, the meat or fish or salad is put on top of, or in between bread, they are tabu according to the best conventions of social usage."

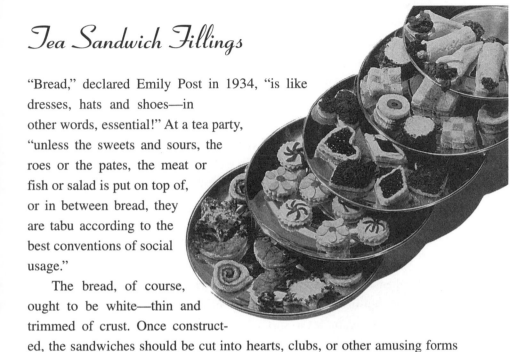

The bread, of course, ought to be white—thin and trimmed of crust. Once constructed, the sandwiches should be cut into hearts, clubs, or other amusing forms with a cookie cutter, or at least into slender wedges with a sharp knife.

WATERCRESS SANDWICHES

• With sharp knife, gently trim leaves from a clean bunch of watercress. In a blender or by hand, mix 2 tablespoons sweet butter with 1 teaspoon lemon juice until blended. Spread lightly on bread, trimmed of crust. Arrange watercress leaves on butter. Salt lightly. Top with bread slice.

SEWING SOCIETY SANDWICHES

• Finely cut 1 cup pitted dates, ⅓ cup seeded raisins, and ½ cup shelled walnuts. Moisten with mayonnaise, spread thinly on bread.

CUCUMBER SANDWICHES

• Slice seedless cucumber as fine as possible. Lay in pan and sprinkle with salt. Cover with paper towels for 1 hour. The cucumbers will yield much of their moisture, and any bitter taste. Place thin layer of cucumber slices between slices of bread spread with mayonnaise and butter.

WASHINGTON SANDWICHES

• Chop 1 cup candied cherries with ½ cup pecans, and mix with ¼ cup orange juice. Spread between bread slices brushed with sweet butter.

STRAWBERRY SANDWICHES

• Cream 4 tablespoons butter, then add 1 cup confectioners' sugar. When well blended, add 1 tablespoon lemon juice. Mix in 8 large, ripe (but firm) strawberries. The mixture should be the consistency of thick cream. If too stiff, add more berries; if too loose, more confectioners' sugar. Set in refrigerator 3 hours to harden. Spread on unbuttered bread.

PIMIENTO SANDWICHES

• Chop 1 small can pimientos fine, mix with 4 chopped hard-boiled eggs, ½ pound softened cream cheese, ¼ cup mayonnaise. Spread between slices of thinly cut nut bread.

GINGER FIG SANDWICHES

• In food processor, chop 1 cup dried figs and ½ cup crystallized ginger. Mix with grated rind and juice of ½ lemon and spread between buttered slices of brown bread.

HINDOO SANDWICHES

• Pit 2 ripe olives and mince with 1 small onion and 1 small sweet pepper. Add 2 tablespoons apple or mango chutney and 1 cup grated Cheddar cheese. If desired, add paprika for color.

LEMON PRUNE SANDWICHES

• To 1 cup cooked, mashed prunes, add grated rind of ½ lemon, 1 teaspoon lemon juice, 2 tablespoons crushed peanuts, and sufficient confectioners' sugar to make a paste. Spread on whole wheat bread with a thin layer of peanut butter that has been thinned with heavy cream.

KATE SMITH'S THREE CHEER SANDWICH

For heartier teatime nibbles, let's turn to *Kate Smith's Company's Coming Cookbook,* written in 1958. Kate was known not only for her stirring renditions of "God Bless America" and "When the Moon Comes over the Mountain," but for her ample girth, which she no doubt owed to favorite recipes such as The House That Kate Built—an architectonic mound of lady fingers and whipped cream. For tea parties she suggests this Dagwood version of the tea sandwich:

Whole wheat bread   *Ripe olives*

Pumpernickel bread   *Smoked salmon*

White bread   *Pimiento-stuffed olives*

Butter   *Watercress*

Cream cheese

• Cut slices of whole wheat bread into large rounds. Cut pumpernickel into rounds that are smaller in diameter by about 1 inch. Cut white bread into still smaller rounds. Mix butter and cream cheese, half and half, and spread all the rounds with plenty. Place one round atop another, three to a sandwich, with largest on bottom. Cut up ripe olives and arrange them around edge of bottom slice. Around pumpernickel slice, place thinly cut strips of smoked salmon. Around edge of top, place finely sliced stuffed olives. In center of top slice goes a small dab of cream cheese and a sporty leaf of watercress.

❧

"The little cakes and sandwiches which appear on the tea table spell sad temptation to the ambitious one who would fast to reduce," wrote Alice Foote MacDougall in *Coffee and Waffles.* "But happiness is more youth-ensuring even than slimness, so let's enjoy them all!"

To supplement crustless sandwiches, the conscientious hostess rounds out her tea with a variety of toasted crumpets, hot tea cakes, and cookies.

GINGER TEA CAKES WITH BUTTER FROSTING

"The progressive homemaker walks right up to Science and says, 'You tell me how to bake,'" advised *All About Home Baking,* in 1933. In the case of these deliciously spicy cupcakes, Science tells the homemaker to fill pans no more than two-thirds full, and that "butter frosting, delicately tinted, is one of the prettiest decorations for small cakes."

GINGER TEA CAKES

1½ cups cake flour	*4 tablespoons butter*
1½ teaspoons baking powder	*4 tablespoons brown sugar*
¼ teaspoon baking soda	*1 egg, well beaten*
½ teaspoon salt	*½ cup molasses*
½ teaspoon cinnamon	*½ cup boiling water*
¼ teaspoon ground cloves	*Sliced preserved ginger*
1½ teaspoons ground ginger	

• Preheat oven to 375°.

Sift flour once, measure, add baking powder, soda, salt, and spices, and sift together three times. Cream butter thoroughly, add sugar gradually, and cream together until light and fluffy. Add egg and beat well. Add flour mixture, alternately with molasses, a small amount at a time, beating after each addition until smooth. Add boiling water, mixing quickly to blend. Turn into small greased cupcake pans, filling them one-half full.

Bake 20 minutes. Cool in pans 5 minutes, then on rack. Make slit in cakes and insert slice of preserved ginger. Cover tops of cakes with butter frosting.

Makes 18 to 24.

BUTTER FROSTING

4 tablespoons butter	*1 teaspoon vanilla extract*
2 cups sifted	*Dash salt*
confectioners' sugar	*Food coloring (optional)*
3 tablespoons milk	

• Cream butter; add part of sugar gradually, blending after each addition. Add remaining sugar, alternately with milk, until of spreading consistency. Beat after each addition until smooth. Add vanilla and salt, and a dash of food coloring if desired.

Makes enough for about 2 dozen cupcakes.

CREAM SCONES

A crisp, elegant biscuit suggested for "over a friendly cup of tea" or a "smart serve-yourself supper," from *All About Home Baking*.

2 cups sifted cake flour	*1 egg plus 1 egg yolk,*
2 teaspoons baking powder	*well beaten*
½ teaspoon salt	*⅓ cup light cream*
1 tablespoon sugar	*1 egg white, slightly beaten*
4 tablespoons butter	*Sugar*

• Preheat oven to 450°.

Sift flour, measure, add baking powder, salt, and 1 tablespoon sugar, and sift again. Cut in butter; add whole egg, egg yolk, and cream, and stir until all flour is dampened. Then stir vigorously until mixture forms a soft dough and follows spoon around bowl.

Turn out on floured board and knead 30 seconds. Roll out to ½-inch thickness and cut in 1-inch triangles. Place on ungreased baking sheet. Brush tops lightly with egg white, and sprinkle with sugar.

Bake 10 to 12 minutes, until light brown.

Makes 12.

CURRANT TEA CAKES

From Royal Baking Powder's *Royal Cookbook,* 1928.

*2 cups plus 2 teaspoons
all-purpose flour*
3 teaspoons baking powder
½ cup sugar
¾ teaspoon salt

1 egg, beaten
2 tablespoons butter, melted
1 cup milk
½ cup currants

• Preheat oven to 375°.

Grease 2-dozen muffin tins and put in oven to heat.

Sift together 2 cups flour, baking powder, sugar, and salt. Add beaten egg and melted butter to milk and add to dry ingredients. Roll currants in 2 teaspoons flour, then add to batter and mix well. The batter should be stiff. Fill muffin tins one-half full.

Bake 20 minutes or until light brown. Cool on rack.

Makes 18 to 24.

PECAN DROP BISCUITS

"These biscuits are dainty for tea," advises *All About Home Baking.* Also, Science reminds us, they are "the easiest and quickest biscuit method," thanks to baking powder.

2 cups cake flour
2 teaspoons baking powder
4 tablespoons sugar
½ teaspoon salt
4 tablespoons butter

½ cup milk
1 egg, well beaten
½ cup finely cut pecan meats
⅛ teaspoon cinnamon

• Preheat oven to 425°.

Sift flour once, measure, add baking powder, 3 tablespoons sugar, and salt, and sift again. Cut in butter. Combine milk and egg, then add to flour mixture and stir until all flour is dampened. Add nuts and stir vigorously until mixture forms a soft dough that clings to sides of bowl. Drop from teaspoon in round balls onto ungreased baking sheet. Sprinkle with mixture of 1 table-spoon sugar and cinnamon.

Bake 10 to 12 minutes.

Makes 2 ½ dozen.

LADY FINGERS

From *The Boston Cooking-School Cook Book* by Fannie Merritt Farmer (1923 edition).

3 egg whites	*⅓ cup bread flour*
⅓ cup confectioners' sugar	*⅛ teaspoon salt*
2 egg yolks	*Confectioners' sugar, sifted*
¼ teaspoon vanilla extract	

• Preheat oven to 375°.

Beat egg whites until stiff and dry, add ⅓ cup confectioners' sugar grad-ually, and continue beating. Beat egg yolks until thick and lemon colored; add yolks and vanilla to whites. Sift together flour and salt; fold into egg mix-ture. Shape 4½ inches long and 1 inch wide on cookie sheet covered with parchment paper (a clean brown paper bag will do), using a pastry bag and tube. Sprinkle with sifted confectioners' sugar.

Bake 8 minutes. Remove from paper with a knife.

Makes about 1 dozen.

BANBURY TARTS

Fruit-filled miniature pastry crescents, suggested to *The Household Searchlight* (1941 edition) by Florence Taft Eaton of Concord, Massachusetts.

PASTRY

1½ cups all-purpose flour	*8 tablespoons butter*
½ teaspoon salt	*¼ cup cold water*

• Sift flour, measure, and sift again with salt. Cut in butter by hand or in a food processor until mixture is granular like cornmeal. Work water in until dough forms ball. Dust with flour and chill 1 hour.

FRUIT MIXTURE

2 tablespoons shortening (or butter)	**½ cup currants**
¼ cup sugar	**2 tablespoons cookie or biscuit crumbs**
1½ tablespoons minced candied orange peel	**⅛ teaspoon nutmeg**
1½ tablespoons minced candied lemon peel	**⅛ teaspoon cinnamon**
1½ tablespoons minced candied citron	**½ egg, slightly beaten**
	1 egg white, slightly beaten
	Sugar

• Preheat oven to 450°.

Cream shortening or butter with ¼ cup sugar. Add candied peels, citron, currants, crumbs, nutmeg, cinnamon, and beaten egg. Mix thoroughly.

Flatten pastry to ¼-inch thickness. Cut into 4-inch circles. Place 1 scant tablespoon fruit mixture into center of each round and fold over. Moisten edge with a bit of the beaten egg white, crimping to seal. Brush lightly with remaining beaten egg white and sprinkle with sugar. Set on greased baking sheet.

Bake 10 minutes or until light brown.

Makes 8 to 10.

Smart and Cunning Entertaining

"Parties? How I love to give parties!" said French-born coloratura Lily Pons in 1942. Miss Pons was a hostess who delighted in throwing "pink parties," at which the decor and all the food—right down to the dyed mashed potatoes—were pink.

How could mere tea parties be enough? Women sought new ways to flaunt their skills as hostess, often looking to social luminaries for inspiration. In 1935 General Mills published a slim volume with the odd title *How to Take a Trick a Day with Bisquick,* which contained a wealth of "novel ideas for quick delicious bridge luncheons, formal dinners, tea time treats, and evening snacks that men love and women envy."

To find her tricks, Betty Crocker (who in this incarnation was a slender bob-haired young thing) solicited opinions of America's "screen stars, society stars, home stars, and star homemaking editors." From the prim lips of Mrs. Phillip Cushing Hill, "one of Boston's outstanding hostesses of the younger group," Betty learned how to make a plate luncheon of curried chicken on a Bisquick biscuit. And she discovered that Mrs. Masten Gregory, "distinguished social leader of Kansas City, Missouri, is one of the smart women who are now serving Bisquick waffle lunches."

How to Take a Trick a Day is a mesmerizing fantasy world in which the humble housewife from Oshkosh finds herself joining up with Betty Crocker to swap fried chicken recipes over the backyard fence with Mrs. Thomas Jones Hilliard, of "the rambling country house she calls Ramblewood." Could it be that with a little imagination, a smart hostess might really serve a high-society meal in her bungalow?

Wouldn't that just make the girls green with envy!

Movie stars loved Bisquick. Bette Davis, "Warner Brothers' star of *Front Page Woman,* acclaimed for her fine interpretation of emotional roles, keeps her love of the simple homey things of her New England background." *How to Take a Trick a Day* shows La Davis seated on a white curvilinear couch, contemplatively pouring tea. Before her are plates of fresh-baked goodies: such a charming scene that one cannot help but find oneself saying, "Oh, thank you, Miss Davis. I would just love another London Bun."

TEATIME LONDON BUNS À LA BETTE DAVIS

1 egg	*4 tablespoons butter, softened*
⅔ cup milk	*4 tablespoons sugar*
2½ cups Bisquick	*1 cup currants*
baking mix	*½ cup candied orange peel*

• Preheat oven to 425°.

Beat egg; add milk, then stir in Bisquick, butter, and sugar. Add currants and orange peel.

Bake in small, greased muffin cups (gem pans) for 12 minutes.

Makes about 24 tiny buns.

The conscientious hostess, whether of a cozy tea party, bridge at four o'clock, or a committee meeting, needed to know how to be *smart.* Even the folks at Minute Tapioca concocted their own imaginary socialite to spread the word on how to do it—Miss Dine About Town. "I'm no cook and it's no use pretending I am," Miss D confesses. "Just a girl who's lucky enough to be invited to a lot of interesting places, to eat a lot of interesting food. Naturally, not every festive meal I sit down to contains tapioca (but a surprising lot of them do)." And there we see her, at a bridge club luncheon with three other party gals whose hats look like a fleet of Flash Gordon rocket ships. They're spooning up Duchess Soup, chock-full of tapioca, served in the best of homes.

MISS DINE ABOUT TOWN'S
DUCHESS SOUP

Be forewarned: this tasty culinary relic has the distinctively beady texture of tapioca.

2 tablespoons Minute Tapioca	*4 cups milk*
1 teaspoon salt	*2 tablespoons butter*
⅛ teaspoon pepper	*½ cup grated American cheese*
1 tablespoon minced onion	*2 tablespoons chopped parsley*

• Combine Minute Tapioca, salt, pepper, onion, and milk in top of double boiler. Place over rapidly boiling water and cook 10 to 12 minutes, stirring frequently. Add butter, cheese, and parsley, and cook until cheese is melted. Remove from heat and let cool 10 minutes to thicken.

Return to heat and warm over double boiler. Serve at once, garnished with parsley or a spoonful of whipped cream.

Serves 4 to 6.

❧

While Miss Dine About Town and her sisters in glamour epitomized *smart* dining, there were others—celebrities included—who preferred to be cunning, and spike their little get-togethers with an abundance of kitsch charms. Such was the pink party.

Pink parties were never smart. In fact, they were rather dumb—corny get-togethers whose success lay in how many dishes one could turn pink without making the guests ill (pink martini, anyone?).

When Lily Pons threw a pink party, she used her Gallic cunning to add an interesting wrinkle. Instead of inviting only giggly ladies to coo and bill over her masterful touch with red dye, she imported truckloads of G.I.'s from the local army base. Convoys of khaki jeeps arrived at her Connecticut mansion, where dogfaces found themselves among bowers of roses and pink candled centerpieces. Into hands accustomed to spit polishing boots or greasing tank axles were thrust pink plates. The men joined the buffet line, helping themselves to turkey salads dyed to match through the magic of pomegranate seeds; pink iced cakes; and pastry shells filled with strawberries, pink marshmallows, and pink whipped cream.

It was Lily's way of boosting morale; how could anyone not agree with a hostess who squealed, "It is fun to eat peenk food, is it not?" After recounting Lily's frolicsome life, including pink recipes and her proclamation that "I love cra-zee hats, and it is my luck that my husband is one of the few men who love cra-zee hats, too!" *American Cookery* magazine concluded, "Isn't it refreshing that people in the public eye should be so natural?"

Should you wish to emulate Lily and her hubby André, why not "go natural" yourself: buy a cra-zee hat, and serve your guests this gay menu for a rosy pink buffet.

Pink Party Buffet

Pink Ladies ◆ *Queen of Muffins* ◆ *Lily Pons Party Salad* ◆ *Blushing Beetskis* ◆ *Pink Frosted Surprise Loaf* ◆ *Quivering Crab Apple Salad* ◆ *Pink Lady Baltimore Layer Cake*

PINK LADIES

> **1 ounce light cream**   **1 shot gin**
> **Dash grenadine**

• Shake well with ice in cocktail shaker. Strain into martini or manhattan glass.

Makes 1 drink.

QUEEN OF MUFFINS

In St. Louis, a young girl named Florence Louise Hulling came to town in the early 1930s from an Illinois farm. She opened a small restaurant, which businessmen loved for its good, honest food, served in a pink-and-white dining room. They told their wives about it, and in no time at all, St. Louis women took Miss Hulling's place to heart. It's still there, all pink and pretty and gay, and if you go for lunch, it's likely you will find this blushing muffin among the cornucopian bread and roll selection.

4 tablespoons butter, melted
⅓ cup sugar
1 egg, well beaten
1½ cups sifted all-purpose flour
2½ teaspoons baking powder

½ teaspoon salt
½ cup milk
¾ cup chopped sour red cherries
(drained, if canned or frozen
are used)

• Preheat oven to 400°.

Cream butter and sugar. Add egg and blend. Sift dry ingredients and add alternately with milk. Mix only enough to combine. Fold in cherries with last amount of flour.

Bake in greased muffin pan 20 to 25 minutes, until golden. Let cool in pan 10 minutes.

Makes 12 muffins.

LILY PONS PARTY SALAD

"It sounds frilly and feminine. . . . But then, why do he-men in uniform fight for it?"

4 cups diced cooked turkey	*2 tablespoons cream*
2 cups chopped celery	*Mayonnaise*
Seeds from 2 large pomegranates	*Salt to taste*
2 cups blanched shredded almonds	*Lettuce*

• Lightly toss turkey, celery, pomegranate seeds, and almonds together. Add cream, sufficient mayonnaise to moisten, and salt. Serve on lettuce leaves.
    Serves 12.

BLUSHING BEETSKIS

Lily Pons was married to Russian-born maestro André Kostelanetz. As a salute to "Kosty," who *American Cookery* says "holds strong allegiance to his native cookery," we include these pinko beets.

4 bunches beets (about 16 medium-large beets)	*2 tablespoons butter*
	2 teaspoons salt
2 cups sour cream	*1 teaspoon pepper*

• Cut tops off beets, leaving about 1-inch stems. Cook until tender. Remove stems, skin and chop coarsely.
    Warm sour cream, butter, salt, and pepper in saucepan over low heat; add to beets. Serve warm or at room temperature.
    Serves 8.

PINK FROSTED SURPRISE LOAF

Sandwich loaves, once a great favorite of clever hostesses, belong to the *trompe l'oeil* school of gastronomy: a club sandwich with delusions of grandeur, impersonating a layer cake. Frosted loaf fillings are as open to imagination as a Dagwood sandwich, but this pretty pink one was suggested by *Marye Dahnke's File* of "Favorite Recipes," published by Kraft in 1938.

3 8-ounce packages cream cheese, softened to room temperature
3 tablespoons milk
Few drops red food coloring
1 unsliced pullman-size loaf of day-old bread

Mayonnaise
2 to 3 large tomatoes, peeled and sliced
2 cups minced ham salad (or deviled ham)
Lettuce

• Whip together cream cheese, milk, and food coloring until it forms a pretty pink frosting. Set aside.

Remove crusts from all sides of bread loaf. Cut 4 *lengthwise* slices. Place bottommost slice on party platter and spread with mayonnaise; cover with slices of peeled tomato. Spread another slice with mayonnaise, and place dressing side down on tomatoes. Spread top of this slice with ham salad, and cover with third slice of bread. Spread with mayonnaise and cover with lettuce. Spread fourth slice of bread with mayonnaise and put dressing side down on top of lettuce.

Frost entire loaf with cream cheese, swirling as if frosting a cake. To serve, cut 1½-inch slices from end of loaf, as if cutting a pound cake.

Serves 8 to 10.

QUIVERING CRAB APPLE SALAD

Delicate, shimmering gelatin—so pretty and bright—was always welcome, in a variety of guises, This congealed salad, from the ever-popular *Joy of Jell-O*, has a nice tart flavor.

1 3-ounce package cherry Jell-O gelatin
1 cup boiling water
1 14-ounce jar spiced apples

½ cup sour cream
1 tablespoon grated orange rind
Lettuce

• Dissolve gelatin in boiling water. Drain apples, measuring ¾ cup syrup. Add water if necessary to make ¾ cup. Add apple syrup to gelatin and chill until thick but not congealed. Beat thickened gelatin in bowl of mixer with sour cream until frothy. Cut apples and fold into gelatin along with orange rind. Pour into oiled 3-cup mold. Chill until firm. Unmold on lettuce leaves.

Serves 6 to 8.

PINK LADY BALTIMORE LAYER CAKE

A wonderfully goocy, classically feminine dessert, originated in Charleston in the early 1900s at the Lady Baltimore Tea Room. This recipe comes from the *Woman's World Book of Cakes and Desserts,* published in 1927.

CAKE

8 tablespoons butter	*2 teaspoons baking powder*
1 cup sugar	*¾ cup milk*
5 eggs	*Tiny pinch salt*
2 cups all-purpose flour	*1 teaspoon vanilla extract*

• Preheat oven to 350°.

Cream butter until pale yellow, add sugar and blend until smooth. Separate 4 eggs. Beat 4 egg yolks and 1 whole egg and add to butter and sugar mixture. Sift flour twice with baking powder and add alternately with milk, by spoonfuls, to egg and sugar mixture. Beat egg whites stiff but not dry with pinch of salt, add vanilla and fold lightly into batter.

Bake in 3 greased and floured 9-inch cake pans 20 minutes. Cool on wire rack.

FILLING

1 cup sugar	*½ cup chopped Maraschino*
5 tablespoons water	*cherries*
1 egg white	*½ cup chopped seeded raisins*
1 teaspoon lemon juice	*½ cup chopped walnuts*

• Boil sugar and water, uncovered, until mixture reaches 240°. Beat egg white until it holds soft peak, add lemon juice, then add sugar-water mixture and heat until creamy. Add chopped cherries, raisins, and nuts and mix gently. The cherries will tint the filling a tantalizing red.

FROSTING

1½ cups sugar
1 teaspoon almond extract
⅔ cup water
Pecan halves
2 egg whites
1 teaspoon lemon juice
2 tablespoons Maraschino cherry juice, or 4 drops red food coloring

• Cook sugar and water together until a little lifted from a spoon forms a thread (230° on a candy thermometer). Beat egg whites until they hold soft peaks; pour hot syrup over them. Add lemon juice, cherry juice, and extract, and continue beating until frosting is thick enough to spread.

To assemble cake: Put filling between layers; frost thickly; decorate with a circle of pecan halves.

A Shower for Miss Alice Bride

The bridal shower is the ultimate feminine party, an event at which men are absolutely forbidden. Sneak one into a tea party or a pink party, and you will get a titter or two, but the sight of a man at a bridal shower is like finding a dead halibut on your vanity table.

Our favorite shower is detailed in *A Thousand Ways to Please a Husband,* published in 1917. It's a kitchen shower, given for Alice:

> As soon as Alice appeared in the living room, a small table was drawn up
> before the open fire. Two girls appeared, wearing gingham aprons and
> carrying overflowing market baskets.
>
> "This is a kitchen shower for you, Alice," Ruth explained. "But if
> you are willing, we will use the utensils in serving the luncheon and
> afterwards present them to you. May we unpack the baskets?"

Oh, lucky Alice! Her bounty is enough to make the reader run out and marry the first jerk on the street: twelve white enameled plates, twelve crossbarred tea towels, a glass rolling pin filled with stick candy, an earthenware mixing bowl, a large enameled coffee pitcher, fragrant baked apples in two enamel pans, forks and spoons and measuring cups of all sizes, and Molasses Puff Muffins heaped high in a small basket.

"A THOUSAND WAYS TO PLEASE A HUSBAND" MOLASSES PUFFS

MUFFINS

¾ cup molasses

¾ cup sugar

½ cup hot water

6 tablespoons butter, melted

1 egg, well beaten

2 teaspoons ground ginger

1 teaspoon cinnamon

3 cups all-purpose flour

2 teaspoons baking soda

• Preheat oven to 375°.

Mix molasses and sugar. Add hot water and butter, and beat well. Add egg and mix thoroughly. Sift ginger, cinnamon, flour, and soda together, and add to molasses. Mix well. Fill well-buttered muffin pans three-quarters full.

Bake 25 minutes.

Makes 12 muffins.

MOLASSES PUFF ICING

2 cups confectioners' sugar

½ cup water

2 egg whites

1 teaspoon lemon extract

• Cook sugar and water together until candy thermometer reaches 240°. Whip egg whites until frothy and slightly stiff. Add syrup in thin stream, beating constantly with electric hand mixer set on high. When fully combined and frosting is thick and glossy, add lemon extract.

~⌒

After her kitchen shower, Alice was lucky enough to have a handkerchief shower—a custom that must have disappeared at the dawn of the Age of Kleenex. This is but another occasion for the girls to get together to eat something light and feminine while exchanging gifts.

In popped little Marjorie carrying a huge bouquet of handkerchiefs folded like white roses, fastened somehow to long stems with green leaves attached, tied with streaming yellow satin ribbon. Making a low bow to Alice she recited in a baby voice:

A handkerchief posie to carry each day
We trust they will not come amiss.
In fact, we are sure that no other bouquet
Was ever so useful as this!

The ladies then sat at a table bedecked with purple and yellow pansies for their bridal shower lunch of Candlelight Salad, Cupid's Apricot Soufflé, and Gold Hearts.

CANDLELIGHT SALAD

The most notorious of all the affectations of feminine dining, repudiated by sophisticated cooks as tasteless and spurious, Candlelight Salad is a paradigm of *cunning* cuisine. For each serving:

1 slice canned pineapple	*Shred of coconut and pimiento bit*
1 thick, short banana	*Lettuce for garnish*
Mayonnaise	

• Set pineapple slice on individual salad plate. Cut off top of banana so it will stand in the hole in the center of the pineapple slice. Dribble a tad of mayonnaise atop the banana candle to simulate wax. Insert coconut and pimiento in mayonnaise at top to simulate wick and fire.

CUPID'S APRICOT SOUFFLÉ

"Say 'soo-flay,'" advises *A Thousand Ways to Please a Husband* about this yolkless meringue puff.

¼ pound dried apricots
½ cup sugar
⅛ teaspoon salt
1 teaspoon lemon juice

3 egg whites
1 teaspoon baking powder
¼ teaspoon vanilla extract

• Wash dried apricots and soak for 3 hours in sufficient water to cover them. Cook slowly until tender, about 10 minutes, in the same water in which they soaked. Drain well, then press through a colander or puree in food processor. Add sugar and cook over low heat for 2 minutes, stirring constantly to prevent burning. Add salt and lemon juice. Allow to cool.

Preheat oven to 325°.

Beat egg whites until stiff but not dry; fold in baking powder, apricots, and vanilla, folding together lightly, just enough to mix. Pour into buttered 8-cup soufflé dish. Place dish in a pan of hot water.

Bake 35 minutes, Serve at once.

Serves 6 to 8.

GOLD HEARTS

Little melting butter cookies, these fragile hearts break easily!

8 tablespoons sweet butter
1 cup sugar
2 eggs
2½ cups all-purpose flour
½ teaspoon salt

2 tablespoons baking powder
½ cup milk
1 teaspoon lemon extract
1 tablespoon grated lemon rind

• Preheat oven to 375°. Grease 2 large baking sheets.

Cream butter and sugar until fluffy. Add eggs, one at a time, beating well. Sift flour, add salt and baking powder, sift again. Add flour mixture to egg mixture, alternating with milk. Add lemon extract and rind. Scrape bowl and place dough on wax paper. Roll tightly and place in refrigerator to chill for at least 1 hour.

Divide dough in half, roll out on lightly floured board, and cut with heart-shaped cookie cutter. Place cookies on greased baking sheets.

Bake 8 to 10 minutes. Cool on cookie rack.

Makes 24 to 30.

Alice now has more pots and pans and hankies than anyone needs, but she is in store for more—at perhaps a "pair shower," at which she gets things that come in pairs—salt and pepper shakers, "his and her" towels, sugar bowl and creamer, or a brace of Highland Terriers.

She might have a green-and-white luncheon at which, Alice Foote MacDougall assures, lilies of the valley and maidenhair "give distinction to corned beef and cabbage."

If Alice is very lucky, her friends will give her a hosiery shower, as detailed in the 1948 book *Showers and Engagement Parties:* "All the guests sit in a circle, except the hostess. She stands in the middle and tosses a stocking into the air. As she does so she starts laughing, giving it everything she has. All the others must laugh with her until the stocking touches the floor, when there must instantly be perfect silence. Anyone who laughs after the stocking touches the floor must leave the circle." This game is called "Hosiery Ha Ha."

If she is an autumn bride, she will have a harvest party, the centerpiece of which is this spectacular three-layer, two-tone cake:

SILHOUETTE CAKE WITH HARVEST MOON FROSTING

From *All About Home Baking,* a General Foods book first published in 1933.

CAKE

2⅓ cups cake flour

2¼ teaspoons baking powder

¼ teaspoon salt

8 tablespoons butter

1 cup sugar

1 whole egg plus 2 egg yolks,
well beaten

¾ cup milk

1 teaspoon vanilla extract

CHOCOLATE MIXTURE

2½ ounces unsweetened
chocolate, melted

½ teaspoon baking soda

3 tablespoons sugar

2 tablespoons butter, melted

¼ teaspoon salt

¼ cup boiling water

HARVEST MOON FROSTING

2 egg whites

1 cup firmly packed brown sugar

Dash salt

¼ cup water

1 teaspoon vanilla extract

2 ounces semisweet chocolate

2 teaspoons butter

• Preheat oven to 375°.

Sift flour once, measure, add baking powder and salt, and sift together three times. Cream butter thoroughly, add sugar gradually, and cream together until light and fluffy. Add egg and egg yolks and beat well.

Prepare chocolate mixture by combining melted unsweetened chocolate, soda, sugar, butter, salt, and water, and mix well.

Combine flour, baking powder, and salt with light-colored mixture, alternately with milk, a small amount at a time. Mix thoroughly after each addition. Add vanilla.

Pour one third of batter into greased and floured 8-inch layer pan. Add chocolate mixture to remaining batter, blend, and pour into 2 greased 8-inch layer pans.

Bake 20 minutes, or until sharp knife inserted in cake comes out clean.

To make frosting, combine egg whites, sugar, salt, and water in top of double boiler, beating with an electric hand mixer or egg beater until thoroughly mixed. Place over rapidly boiling water, and beat constantly for 7 minutes with mixer until frosting stands in peaks. Remove from boiling water, add vanilla and beat until thick enough to spread.

To frost, arrange light layer between dark layers, spread each layer and sides of cake with Harvest Moon Frosting. Pile frosting on top.

Melt 2 ounces of semisweet chocolate with 2 teaspoons butter. When frosting on cake has set, pour chocolate mixture over cake, letting it trickle down sides,

Serve within 2 or 3 hours of frosting. This frosting toughens overnight.

As the wedding nears, Alice will want to throw her own party, this one for the bridesmaids, who have by now worn their hands raw hemming tea towels for her. At this party, just before she takes the plunge into married life, the food should be the most feminine of all:

Bridesmaid Luncheon

Maid of Honor Iced Fruit Soup ♦ *Sunbonnet Baby Salad* ♦ *Shrimp Wiggle* ♦ *Tipsy Trifle*

MAID OF HONOR ICED FRUIT SOUP

A blushing bridal-pink appetizer, inspired by a cool soup recipe in *Electric Refrigerator Recipes and Menus,* published in 1927 to promote use of the "Aladdin's Lamp" of appliances . . . the owning of which "is a form of health and happiness insurance which every homemaker in America should have the privilege of enjoying."

8 ounces fresh raspberries
1 10-ounce package frozen
   strawberries
2½ cups buttermilk

4 ounces plain yogurt
Juice of ½ lemon
Fresh mint

• In blender or food processor, puree raspberries and strawberries together. Add buttermilk, yogurt, and lemon juice. Blend until smooth. Serve garnished with fresh mint. Serves 4 to 6.

SUNBONNET BABY SALAD

Although this recipe comes from *A Thousand Ways to Please a Husband*, it is strictly for distaff palates—a contender for the prize of Most Inappropriate Food to Feed a Man. For the full effect, wheel out the tiny tots on a miniature cart strewn with nasturtium petals.

5 canned pear halves	*10 blanched almonds*
5 leaves lettuce	*15 thin slices pimiento*
10 whole cloves	*5 tablespoons mayonnaise*

• Arrange the halves of canned pears, round side up, on lettuce leaves that curl closely about the pear and have the effect of a hood. Place cloves in the pear for eyes and blanched almonds for ears, and slip thin slices of canned pimiento into cuts made for nose and mouth. The expressions may be varied. Put mayonnaise around the outside of the pear to represent hair, and arrange a bow of red pimiento under the chin of each Sunbonnet Baby.

Makes 5 Babies.

SHRIMP WIGGLE

A magic brew of bygone flavors—creamy, feminine, reassuring. Shrimp Wiggle is a breeze to make, which is why, according to James Beard, it was for years "in the repertoire of every coed with a chafing dish and every girl who had a beau to cook for." But this is a dish that transcends simplicity.

4 tablespoons butter	*1 cup tiny cooked peas*
2 tablespoons all-purpose flour	*½ teaspoon salt*
1½ cups light cream	*1 teaspoon paprika*
2 cups cooked, cleaned shrimp	*8 slices white toast, buttered*

• In large skillet, melt butter over low heat; gradually add flour, stirring constantly for 3 to 5 minutes. Slowly add cream; cook and stir until mixture begins to thicken. Add shrimp, peas, salt, and paprika. Stir well. Heat until shrimp are warm, Serve on toast.

Serves 4.

TIPSY TRIFLE

Trifle was, according to the *Frances Virginia Tea Room Cookbook,* "as close as a Southern lady would come to consuming liquor in public—unless she was ill or about to faint." It is a classic Southern dessert—pretty and sweet, ladylike in looks and taste, delightfully intoxicating. This recipe comes from the Olde Pink House in Savannah, Georgia.

POUND CAKE

½ pound butter
1⅔ cups sugar
5 eggs
2 cups cake flour

¼ teaspoon salt
1 tablespoon brandy
1 teaspoon vanilla extract

• Preheat oven to 300°.

Cream butter and sugar together and beat in eggs, one at a time. Beat well. Add flour and salt. Stir in brandy and vanilla, mix thoroughly, and pour into a greased and floured 9-by-5-by-2 3/4-inch pan.

Bake 1½ hours.

CUSTARD

1½ quarts milk
1½ cups sugar
5 tablespoons cornstarch
6 eggs

½ cup sherry
2 cups heavy cream
Raspberry or
strawberry preserves

• Pour milk into top of double boiler. (Unless you have an enormous double boiler, this must be done in two batches.) In a mixing bowl, beat together sugar, cornstarch, and eggs until smooth. Add to milk and heat until mixture is thickened, stirring constantly. Set aside to cool.

Add sherry to cooled custard.

Whip cream. Arrange ½-inch cake slices in a 13-by-9-by-2-inch baking pan. Spread with preserves, then top with a layer of custard and a layer of whipped cream. Repeat until all ingredients are used, about 3 layers' worth. Chill.

Serves 6 to 8.

To bid farewell to Alice, we offer her one last bridal gift, a cheerful poem to launch her from the role of bride, sweet as a candied violet, to full-blown housewife. This verse is from a 1962 book entitled *To the Bride,* a chapter called "The Care and Feeding of Young Husbands."

TO THE BRIDE

A juicy, red steak
   Or a tender fish fillet
Done to a turn
   In a bright copper skillet,

Will smooth the rough edges
   Of tempers, no fooling!!!
And leave the man happy
   Contented and drooling.

LUNCH COUNTER COOKING

For those of us who grew up facing three wholesome home-cooked meals a day, hot lunch at a lunch counter was a walk on the wild side of the culinary world, away from the moral rectitude of Mom's roast beef dinners to the cheap thrill of a Kresge's lunch counter hot roast beef sandwich. Ribbons of beef piled next to a volcano of mashed potatoes with gravy bubbling in the crater and flowing down from the peak onto fields of pink meat and cushions of white bread: there's a square meal for you, with an extrathick chocolate malt—three full glasses in a silver container—on the side.

Understand there is a big difference between hot lunch and warm dinner. Warm dinner is home food. Hot lunch you get only at a lunch counter—at the dime store luncheonette, the Automat, a school cafeteria, soda fountain, or roadside diner.

Lunch counter meals always fit on a single plate, sometimes a portioned plate to keep the lima bean juices from running into the mashed potatoes. You might get a little no-account withered salad on the side, and a roll and a pat of butter; and of course you'll want a wedge of pie later, on another plate, but lunch counter aesthetics demand that hot lunch arrive on one plate, or in one bowl.

You know Lunch Counter Cooking by its institutional aroma—the smell of fish sticks on a steam table, of onions sizzling on a grill, of warm giblet gravy for roast tom turkey dinner.

Lunch counter chow is a kick precisely because it is so different from home, gloriously institutional, prepared with exotic machines no home kitchen ever has—wide, oily grills, triple-wanded malted machines, and awesome implements like the mighty bacon flattener, or the silver manacle that binds hash browns in a tight, buttery circle.

The lunch counter is an all-American, yet romantically alien culinary netherworld, fraught with ritual folderol: putting quarters in slots at the Automat; a fancy squirt of scarlet syrup to make a cherry Coke; trading wisecracks with the hashslinger; mounting a lonely counter stool in a roadside diner to contemplate a cup of java, black, wedge of pie on the side.

If you are in thrall to the world of blue plates and black cows, you know that luncheonettes, diners, coffee shops, and soda fountains are on the endangered species list of American eateries. And so if you want that hot roast beef sandwich or the egg cream of your dreams, it is likely you will have to do it yourself.

But even with a home blender, how could one hope to compete with the fabulous choreography of the professional soda jerk? And what English-speaking home cook is fluent in the exotic patois of the hashslinger, doling out "Adam and Eve on a raft" (poached eggs on toast); "First Lady" (ribs); "Christmas BLT" (bacon, lettuce and tomato, Noel—No L: hold the lettuce);

or a "whiskey radio, seaboard" (tuna—tune it down, as in radio, on rye, as in whiskey; to go)?

It *is* possible to work a bit of lunch counter sorcery in your own home kitchen, however. What you must do, for starters, is to get out that old blender (the kind you used before the food processor) and heavy, uncoated cast-iron skillet, buy yourself a good ice cream dipper, roll up your sleeves, and twirl a wooden toothpick in your mouth. If you have a set of heavy blue plates, so much the better.

Diner Classics

Lunch Counter Liver

Burger and Fries

Blue Plate Noodles

Soda Fountain Treats

MILK SHAKES

Vanilla Shake ("White Cow") • 95

Chocolate Shake • 96

Vanilla Malt • 96

Chocolate Malt • 96

Double Chocolate Malt ("Burn One All the Way") • 96

Peppermint Smoothie • 97

Choco-Peppermint Smoothie • 97

Banana Frosted Shake • 97

Banana Almond Frappe • 98

Banana Date Shake • 98

Cream Nogg ("Make It Cackle") • 98

Egg Cream • 98

ICE CREAM SODAS

Black-and-White • 99

Bodacious Black-and-White • 99

Canary Island Special • 101

Black Cow • 101

Brown Cow • 101

Strawberry Soda ("In the Hay") • 101

Hoboken • 101

Boston Cooler • 101

Catawba Flip • 101

Diner Classics

I n the hierarchy of food values, diner grub is far below home cooking; but at least diner food *is* hot, and a hot lunch always tops a cold one. Compared to the hoi polloi who eat sandwiches, those who feast on hot lunch at noon are living the life of Riley.

Roadside diners are home to a particular genre of hot lunch: meat loaf, liver and onions, and mountains of mashed potatoes.

Let us make it clear here and now that we are not bleary romantics about diner grub. Ninety-nine percent of it is awful, and it probably always has been awful, myths about savvy truck drivers notwithstanding. But there is that 1 percent—the singular beanery where not only is the patter snappy and the coffee strong, but the meat loaf is incomparably delicious.

Great Diner Meat Loaf is different from home-cooked meat loaf. Its *je ne sais quoi* is partly the hash house ambience in which it's served, partly a matter of side dishes (nobody at home bothers to put craters of gravy in their mashed potatoes), but mostly the difference is in the loaf itself.

We've worked long and hard perfecting a Diner Meat Loaf for home kitchens. It's the centerpiece of this paradigmatic hash house meal, which we call . . .

De Gustibus Gearjammer

Cream of Tomato Soup ◆ *Diner Meat Loaf* ◆ *Highway Patrol Succotash* ◆ *Mashed Potatoes with Crater Gravy* ◆ *Crumb Top Apple Pie* ◆ *Black Coffee*

CREAM OF TOMATO SOUP

A bowlful, with a tuna sandwich, is practically a Nice Hot Lunch. A cup is a perfect appetizer for Diner Meat Loaf, since
the loaf is light on tomatoes. You can, as
many lunch counters do, open a can of
Campbell's, add milk, heat, and serve. Or for
a touch of luxury you can mix a can of tomato
soup with a can of Cheddar cheese soup, add water, heat, and serve.

Or you can make your own! It's really not too difficult, and it is actually—believe it or not—better than Campbell's.

1 onion, chopped fine
1 carrot, chopped fine
4 tablespoons butter
3 tablespoons all-purpose flour
1 quart chicken broth
6 fresh, ripe large tomatoes,
*   peeled and chopped coarse*

1 clove garlic, crushed
6 scallions, chopped fine
4 white peppercorns (whole)
1 teaspoon salt
1 tablespoon sugar
1 cup light cream

• In a deep pot, sauté onion and carrot in butter until onion turns slightly
brown. Add flour; mix well. Slowly add broth, tomatoes, garlic, scallions,
peppercorns, salt, and sugar. Cover and cook over low heat 1½ hours.

Blend in blender or food processor and add cream. Garnish with a sprinkle of basil, oregano, or toasted croutons.

Serves 4 to 6.

DINER MEAT LOAF

You have a lot of leeway making Diner Meat Loaf. You can use all beef, or a
combination of beef and pork. You can extend the meat with either instant
Quaker Oats or softened bread. You can add sage or savory, marjoram or mustard or MSG. You can salt and pepper to taste. There are a few rules, however,
that cannot be broken, lest the essential dinerhood of the dish be compromised.

- Do not use lean meat or fancy sirloin. Ground chuck, 20 percent fat, will ensure the loaf is juicy.
- Do not skimp on oatmeal or bread crumbs. Extenders give the loaf that distinctive pulpy texture that soaks up gravy so well. All-meat meat loaf has no place in the world of diner food.

- Do not undercook. A pink-centered meat loaf would humiliate any true diner chef. Gray-brown is the color, through and through.

1¼ pounds ground beef	*1 onion, minced*
½ pound ground pork	*1 tablespoon*
¾ cup instant oatmeal	*Worcestershire sauce*
2 eggs, beaten	*1 teaspoon salt*
½ cup milk	*¼ teaspoon pepper*
½ cup tomato juice	

- Preheat oven to 350°.

Mix beef, pork, oatmeal, and eggs. Blend in milk, tomato juice, onion, Worcestershire, and seasonings. Pack firmly into 9-by-5-inch loaf pan, shaping a rounded top.

Bake 1½ hours. Let stand 10 minutes before slicing. Drain off any excess juice at bottom of pan.

Serves 8.

MASHED POTATOES WITH CRATER GRAVY

Mashed potatoes are potatoes that you mash. They don't get whipped or riced, or colcannoned or chantillied. They must be mashed by hand with a potato masher. There is no substitute for this hard work. And there is nothing in the world better than a mound of fluffy white spuds, running rivulets of melting butter.

The art of mashing potatoes is simple, if you know these few tricks of the trade:

• From the time they get tossed in the water, never let the potatoes cool.

• Always preheat the milk.

• Never try to hurry up the boiling by cutting the potatoes into smaller pieces.

• And finally, remember that they are a last-minute dish: the sooner you serve them after cooking, the better they will be.

6 russet potatoes	*Salt and pepper to taste*
6 tablespoons sweet butter	*¾ cup warmed milk*

• Peel potatoes and boil until tender, about 20 to 25 minutes. Drain, then return to pot over medium heat, tossing and stirring the potatoes to thoroughly expel all moisture. Mash potatoes with a masher, adding butter and salt when they are clear of lumps (or do you like a few lumps?). While mixing vigorously with a heavy whisk, add the warm milk. At this point, the more you beat, the fluffier the potatoes.

Serve immediately, garnished with pepper and pats of butter.

Note: If they are accompanying Diner Meat Loaf or any other lunch counter entrée, serve the potatoes with an ice cream dipper. Plop a scoopful on the plate next to the meat, then flip the scoop over and use its rounded surface to indent a crater in the top of the potato globe. This indentation will hold the gravy.

Serves 4 to 6.

The lifeblood of diner lunch, Crater Gravy is for blanketing meat loaf, liver and onions, hot roast beef sandwiches, and potatoes of all kinds, but especially mashed. There is no question that it is better when made from pan stock retrieved from a roast (the recipe for which is in the Sunday Dinner chapter), but if you don't have pan drippings, this alternative is a close approximation to what you will get in diners all across America.

CRATER GRAVY

3 tablespoons butter	*¾ cup water*
3 tablespoons flour	*1 10-ounce can condensed cream*
1 10-ounce can beef broth	*of mushroom soup*

• Melt butter and blend in flour. Add broth and water and cook until thickened, 10 to 15 minutes. Add mushroom soup, stirring constantly until fully blended. Cook another 15 minutes, stirring occasionally.

Makes 3 cups.

HIGHWAY PATROL SUCCOTASH

Did you ever eat succotash made from fresh ingredients? It's unlikely you ever will in a diner, which is one reason succotash has such a bad rep among vegetable lovers. For this recipe, you can use canned corn and beans and exactly duplicate diner chow, or you can create a *trompe l'oeil* by using kernels of corn just off the cob, and garden-fresh lima beans. Add a few chopped pimientos and it will *look* just like deluxe succotash at the Acme Diner . . . but watch your guests' faces turn from grouchy reluctance to astonished pleasure when they dip into it and discover otherwise!

1 thick slice bacon or blanched	*¼ cup cream*
salt pork	*Salt and pepper to taste*
2 cups cooked lima beans	*4 tablespoons chopped pimientos*
2 cups corn kernels	*(optional)*
4 tablespoons butter	

• Dice bacon and cook in large skillet until crisp. Add drained lima beans and heat in bacon fat. Add corn and stir. Add butter and cream. Stir over low heat 5 minutes. Add salt, pepper, and pimiento.

Serves 4 to 6.

CRUMB TOP APPLE PIE

For reasons we have yet to fathom, apple pie à la diner is often topped with crumbs instead of a second crust. With all that butter and sugar up top, it's certainly heartier, and a fitting finale to a manly meal.

Crumb top pie, with strong coffee, is also a favorite afternoon pick-me-up at cafés all around the country. We know travelers whose little black books list nothing but pie-and-coffee stops. If they can have a wedge and a cuppa java as the sun sets, they're content, wherever they wind up for dinner.

This apple pie is a reconstruction of one we fondly remember from a long-gone truck stop in New England. It was served warm with a chunk of store cheese on the side.

APPLE PIE

½ cup brown sugar	*Unbaked pastry for 1-crust*
¼ teaspoon nutmeg	*9-inch pie*
½ teaspoon cinnamon	*6 apples, peeled, cored, and cut*
½ teaspoon salt	*into chunks*
1 teaspoon grated lemon rind	*1 tablespoon lemon juice*

• Preheat oven to 450°.

Mix sugar, nutmeg, cinnamon, salt, and lemon rind. Line a pie plate with pastry and fill with a few apple chunks; sprinkle on some of the sugar mixture and a bit of lemon juice. Add more apples, more sugar mixture and lemon juice; continue until the pie pan is full, making sure the top layer of apples is liberally covered with sugar and seasonings. Sprinkle top with crumb mixture.

CRUMB TOP

½ cup sugar	*Dash salt*
¾ cup flour	*8 tablespoons cold butter*
½ teaspoon cinnamon	

• Combine sugar, flour, cinnamon, and salt. Cut in butter by hand or in food processor until mixture is crumbly. Sprinkle on top of apple pie.

Bake crumb-topped pie 15 minutes; reduce heat to 350° for 30 minutes, until crumbs are golden brown and apples sizzle.

Serve warm, with Cheddar cheese or a scoop of vanilla ice cream.

Lunch Counter Liver

There aren't too many people who will tell you they love beef liver, us included. It's an unpopular dish we are never tempted to order unless we are sitting in a Naugahyde-upholstered booth, surrounded by pink Formica and silver stainless steel. The way we see it, lunch counters and liver are like ball parks and wieners: even if you'd never eat a tube steak anywhere else, it is *right* to have one at the ball park; and because it is right, it tastes good. Ditto liver.

Liver tasted great at Larry's Diner, a once-glorious beanery not too far from our house. For years, Larry's was a tradition. A delicious one.

But Larry's hit the skids, and we knew that if we ever wanted good lunch counter liver again, we were on our own. So it was back to our spotless test kitchen (with a detour to the butcher), where we devised this liver-centered meal, in homage to a grand old diner:

Liver at Larry's

Split Pea Soup ♦ Blue Plate Liver and Onions ♦ Hashslinger Potatoes ♦ Creamed Spinach ♦ Boston Cream Pie

SPLIT PEA SOUP

Float it with disks of frankfurter or (for gourmets) small cubes of ham and, with a chunk of bread on the side, a bowl of Split Pea Soup is a meal. For an appetizer, you'll want only a cup, hold the franks.

1 pound yellow split peas
½ pound diced salt pork
½ cup diced onion
2 cloves garlic, minced
1½ quarts water (or, if possible,
   the broth in which a ham has
   been boiled)
2 cups milk
1 ham hock (or leftover ham
   bone)

1 bay leaf
2 teaspoons salt (omit if ham
   broth is used)
½ teaspoon pepper
2 tablespoons butter
2 tablespoons flour
Croutons for garnish

• Cover peas with water and soak overnight; or bring to boil for 2 minutes, and let cool in water 1 hour.

In a deep kettle, sauté salt pork until crisp. Remove pork and save. Add onion and garlic to fat. Sauté until onion is soft.

Drain peas and put in kettle with fat. Cover with water (or ham broth) and milk; add ham hock. Add bay leaf, salt, and pepper. Simmer 2 hours, or until peas are tender.

Strain soup through colander. Remove bay leaf and ham hock or bone. Place cooked peas in food processor or push through fine sieve until pureed. Return pea puree to liquid.

In a small saucepan, melt butter. Stirring constantly, add flour. Add this to soup. Simmer 15 minutes. Add reserved diced pork and serve, garnished with croutons.

Serves about 12.

BLUE PLATE LIVER AND ONIONS

Only beef liver will do. If the grown-up stuff is too scary, you can get something called baby beef liver, which isn't quite as dark and coarse; but under no circumstances is calf's liver suitable. It is too fine and fancy, without the sturdy character that makes diner liver special. For each serving:

3 strips bacon
2 tablespoons butter
1 large onion, sliced

1 3- to 4-ounce slab of beef liver, cleaned of all membrane and external gristle

• In a well-seasoned cast-iron skillet, cook bacon. Remove strips, pour off grease, but do not wipe out pan. Toss in butter and melt over moderate heat. Toss in onion slices. As they cook, use a fork to separate slices into individual rings. When onions begin to brown, move them to side of pan, turn up heat, and slap on the liver. Give it only 2 to 3 minutes, then flip over. Shovel onions on top as other side cooks, another 2 to 3 minutes.

Serve garnished with bacon.

HASHSLINGER POTATOES

A diner standard, with more pizazz than ordinary hash browns, our cottage-fried Hashslinger Potatoes are great to accompany any meat entrée or even a breakfast omelette, if it's a gutsy one.

In most diners, spuds are simply fried and put on plates. You can do that with these ingredients, but we think the extra step of baking them makes an ordinary dish spectacular.

4 large russet potatoes	*1 tablespoon finely*
1 clove garlic	*chopped onion*
6 tablespoons butter	*Salt and pepper to taste*

• Preheat oven to 450°.

Peel potatoes and slice into ¼-inch-thick disks. Dry disks between paper towels.

Rub large cast-iron skillet with cut edge of garlic clove. Melt 3 tablespoons butter. Add onion. Toss in potatoes and sauté over high heat for about 3 minutes, flipping and separating disks to coat evenly. Arrange disks in an overlapping pattern in pan. Dot with remaining butter, salt, and pepper, and sauté over high heat another 2 minutes, without stirring.

Transfer to oven and bake 30 minutes, or until rims of disks are golden brown.

Serves 4.

CREAMED SPINACH

1½ pounds fresh spinach, washed	*⅔ cup heavy cream*
and trimmed of stems	*Salt and pepper to taste*
4 tablespoons sweet butter	*Nutmeg or cooked bacon*
	for garnish

• In a large pot of boiling water, cook spinach 4 to 5 minutes. Drain, squeezing out all water. Chop leaves coarsely.

Melt butter in large skillet, add spinach. Cook over medium heat, stirring constantly, about 5 minutes, until all butter is absorbed. Stir in cream, cover, and cook approximately 15 minutes, stirring occasionally. Add salt and pepper. Garnish with dash of nutmeg or bits of bacon.

Serves 4.

BOSTON CREAM PIE

Of course you know this legendary dessert isn't a pie at all. It's a custard-filled cake, allegedly invented at the Parker House in Boston. From such lofty beginnings, it has become a lunch counter classic, apparently too gloppy to be popular in fine restaurants.

For the cake part, any good pound cake or sponge cake recipe will do, so long as the cake isn't so heavy that the top layer squeezes out the custard filling.

CAKE

1¾ cups sifted cake flour
2 teaspoons baking powder
½ teaspoon salt
6 tablespoons sweet butter
1 tablespoon vegetable
shortening

1 cup sugar
3 eggs
⅔ cup milk
1 teaspoon vanilla extract

• Preheat oven to 375°.

Butter 2 8-inch cake pans and line bottoms with wax paper.

Combine flour, baking powder, and salt.

Cream butter and Crisco with all but 2 tablespoons sugar. Beat until fluffy.

Beat eggs thoroughly, 3 to 5 minutes; add remaining sugar and beat again.

Combine butter and egg mixtures, and beat thoroughly. Add dry ingredients, alternately with milk, beating after each addition. Add vanilla. Pour into cake pans and smooth tops.

Bake 10 minutes, then reduce heat to 350° and bake 15 minutes more, or until cake is golden brown and cake tester comes out clean.

Cool on wire racks. Remove wax paper carefully. Prepare filling.

FILLING

½ cup plus 3 tablespoons sugar	1 package unflavored gelatin
2 eggs, separated	(1 tablespoon) dissolved in
¼ cup all-purpose flour	2 tablespoons cold water
1 cup scalded milk	½ cup heavy cream
1 teaspoon vanilla extract	

• Combine ½ cup sugar and egg yolks in heavy saucepan, stirring over low heat. When mixed, stir in flour. Continue cooking and stirring 5 minutes; gradually add milk and vanilla, stirring and cooking another 15 to 20 minutes, until mixture thickens enough to hold the trail of a spoon.

Stir softened gelatin into custard, mix, and cool, stirring as it cools. When cooled to room temperature, set in refrigerator to chill.

While custard chills, beat cream until it begins to peak. Separately, beat egg whites until they begin to thicken, adding 3 tablespoons sugar gradually. Continue beating until you have a shiny, firm meringue.

Custard should be starting to set. Remove from refrigerator and beat in meringue. Fold in whipped cream. Chill again until quite thick—about 15 minutes.

Put one cake layer upside down on a serving plate; pile on filling in a mound. Put second layer right side up atop mound, pressing it down just enough to spread custard to edge. Refrigerate. Prepare icing immediately.

CHOCOLATE ICING

3 ounces semisweet chocolate	¼ cup cream
2 tablespoons sweet butter	1 teaspoon vanilla extract
¼ cup sweetened condensed milk	

• Melt chocolate and butter in top part of double boiler. Mix in condensed milk and cream. Cook 10 minutes over boiling water, stirring occasionally. Remove from heat, stirring and beating until mixture is room temperature. Blend in vanilla.

Remove cake from refrigerator. Gently and slowly pour icing onto center of top, allowing it to drip down sides.

Chill cake 3 hours, or until filling is completely set.

Burger and Fries

In New York, at Prexy's luncheonettes, you used to be able to eat a "hamburger with a college education." What actually made Prexy's burgers more educated than other loutish clods of grilled ground beef is a matter lost in the oily mists of hash house history. The point is that the humble burger was considered worthy of an education (it was depicted on the menu in horn-rimmed glasses and a mortarboard). That faith in its natural nobility belongs to the Golden Age of the Lunch Counter, before fast food ignoramusburgers and elitist epicurean burgers.

For an honest sandwich, with no more pretense than a squirt of ketchup or a Bermuda onion slab, there was—and still is—no beating a burger and fries, pickle on the side.

Educated or not, here is a portrait of that vanishing, but once proud pillar of the culinary community, the classic lunch counter hamburger. It's a flattened patty, cooked on a hot grill, where onions and bacon have sizzled. This hunk of meat is luscious, with a bit of a crust, and never so thick that the center is brighter than pale pink. Usually, in fact, it's gray-brown—but still dripping moist. It is served peeking out from the edges of a domed spongy bun that got toasted alongside the meat on the grill, and it might be topped—if there is a bit of panache in your soul—with a square slice of American cheese.

To make this kind of hamburger at home, you must remember there are certain characteristics of most home-cooked burgers that automatically brand the patties, however tasty, as impostors. Lunch counter burgers are never thick and round like crushed softballs. Unlike home hamburgers, the meat is never doctored with Worcestershire or garlic powder or cream. And they must not be too lean, lest they dry out so much that their juices don't permeate the bun.

And speaking of buns, lunch counter hamburgers are never served on good French bread or any other highfalutin roll; even a hard roll or toasted whole wheat is leaning away from classic form toward the baroque.

There are a couple of choices in selecting burger meat. You can . . .

• Buy ground chuck at the supermarket, either in bulk or patties. Don't get extra lean, or ground round. You want choice chuck steak, 20 to 25 percent fat content, with a dash of pulverized gristle among the meat—just like at the corner luncheonette. The preformed patties are aesthetically superior, perfectly round, but so thin that it will be impossible to cook them any less done than "medium." They are closer in form and quality to most lunch counter hamburgers than you could ever get grinding your own beef. We like them for double burgers or double chili cheeseburgers, where you don't want too oozy a hunk of meat.

• Grind your own chuck steak, in a meat grinder or food processor. If you use a processor, don't pulverize the meat; and fluff it up with your fingers before you flatten it into patties. We prefer a meat grinder—and patties formed from the little red worms of meat it extrudes.

HOW TO COOK A HAMBURGER

Hamburger patties are best formed with as little handling as possible. Your goal is to create a perfect circle of meat, about ½-half inch thick, 3 to 5 inches in diameter.

Assuming you do not have access to a diner-style grill, the next best bet for a cooking utensil is a cast-iron skillet—the biggest and best-seasoned one you have. Do *not* use a Teflon or otherwise coated skillet. It cannot "seize" the meat, nor does it yield up the bouquet of flavor imparted by a venerable hunk of cast iron. As Joanne McDaniel of Jo-Mac's Hamburger Shop in Houston says, "It's the grill that makes them good."

And what makes the grill good is *use*; so, assuming your cast-iron pan is clean, what you must do is give it a patina of savory grease. The best way to do that is to sauté a diced onion in about 2 tablespoons of butter, over medium heat. When the onion bits soften and just barely begin to brown, scoot them to the side of the pan. Flip the burner up to *high*, and turn on your exhaust fan (or turn off all smoke detectors). You are now ready to cook hamburgers.

When the pan is hot (but not yet smoking), slap on the patties. Salt the tops. Cook one minute, then, very carefully, slide your spatula beneath the burgers and flip them. They will want to stick, but by pressing the spatula hard to the pan, you should be able to lift them without tearing the crust-in-the-making. Salt again. (This helps seal in the juices.) Cook approximately 2½ minutes. Flip them again and cook another 2½ minutes. (A ½-inch-thick burger should be about medium-rare at this point.) Remove burgers from pan directly to prepared buns (see below).

For cheeseburgers, have individual American cheese slices prepared in advance. Put them on the patties after they've been flipped for the last time, and to help the cheese melt, cover the pan for the last 30 seconds. Cheeseburgers can also be made by spreading Cheez Whiz on toast, which may seem eccentric; but in fact, this is the way it's done at Louis Lunch in New Haven, Connecticut—where the hamburger was invented 100 years ago.

The onions you pushed to the side of the pan will have turned into luscious black-and-brown squiggles, perfect for spooning atop the patty.

THE BUN

Store-bought buns are fine; they are, after all, a lunch counter staple. You can eat them straight from the package, or toast them in a toaster oven, or best of all—if there is room—warm them on the oniony skillet, right along with the grilling hamburgers. The trick is to have the buns done first, so You can get them ready to receive the burgers.

For the classic arrangement, as practiced by Jo-Mac's, the bottom half of the bun is smeared with mayo, then topped with lettuce (a leaf of iceberg, *not* shredded) and a slice of tomato. The top half is squirted with mustard, then garnished with pickles and onion. If desired, ketchup goes on top, too.

For a "White Castle effect" (those bite-sized novelties that you buy by the sack, a dozen at a time) steam rather than toast your buns. Slice them, sprinkle the insides with finely diced onion, wrap each bun tightly in foil, and bake at 350° for about 10 minutes. They will come out spongy and aromatic. (For the full White Castle treatment, make your meat patties as thin as a dime, cut them into 2-inch squares, cook them, insert into buns with onion, and steam the whole kaboodle.)

We admit that even though store-bought rolls are more authentic, we occasionally indulge our gourmet selves and make our own. This recipe turns out a nice, fluffy bun, slightly sweet, perfect for burgers, Sloppy Joes, minute steaks, or bacon-and-egg sandwiches:

1 package dry yeast dissolved in	*6 tablespoons butter, melted and*
2 cups of tepid water (110°)	*cooled to lukewarm*
with 1 tablespoon sugar	*5 to 6 cups all-purpose flour*
¼ cup sugar	*1 egg yolk dissolved with*
½ cup dry skimmed milk	*1 teaspoon water*
2 teaspoons salt	*Sesame seeds*

• In a large bowl, add dry milk, ¼ cup sugar, salt, and melted butter to yeast mixture. Add 5 cups flour, 1 cup at a time, stirring after each addition, until dough is soft and sticky. Turn out onto floured board. Let rest while you clean and butter the bowl.

Knead dough about 10 minutes, adding up to a cup of flour, until it is resilient. Return to buttered bowl, cover tightly with plastic wrap, and let rise in a warm place until doubled in bulk (about 1 hour).

Punch down dough, turn onto floured board. Divide into 15 to 20 equal pieces, each about half the size of the buns you want to wind up with. Roll each piece into a smooth ball and place on greased baking sheets. Cover and let rise again, until doubled in bulk.

Preheat oven to 375°. Brush tops of rolls with watered-down egg yolk and sprinkle on sesame seeds.

Bake 20 minutes. Cool on rack.

Makes 15 to 18 buns.

CONDIMENTIA

We have seen Screaming Pigburgers in Knoxville, Ambrosia Burgers in Big Sur, and Awful Burgers in Phoenix. We have seen recipes for hamburgers topped with carrots, peanut butter, curry, and coriander . . . not to mention the ignominy of sprouts and imported cheese. Fine, go ahead, dude it up; it is a credit to the innate *truth* of the hamburger that it can bear any and all condiments creative chefs can conceive.

But when it comes to genuine lunch counter burgers, the list of options, however long, is a classic repertoire: ketchup, mustard, relish, onions, mayo, lettuce, tomato, pickles. Take your pick; we won't quibble. Cheese, or double cheese, is good, too—as long as it's yellow American.

Bacon is wonderful on a cheeseburger, if you're careful not to overcook the bacon. You want it soft, so it presses into the cheese atop the meat, curving to fit the patty without crumbling.

One of the great toppings for a hamburger is chili, especially the kind served in Cincinnati's five-way chili parlors or in Los Angeles at Tommy's or Pink's (yes, Pink's sells burgers, too, and they're not so good, but the chili topping is sensational). Chili on a burger (known, inexplicably, in some parts of the country as "chili size") is beanless and hot, *con carne*. It makes a hamburger impossible to eat with any decorum at all.

This recipe for chili topping is a variation of Cincinnati-style chili, customarily ladled onto burgers and hot dogs; or you can spoon it as is on buns (and top it with grated cheese)—a souped-up Sloppy Joe.

CHILI SIZE

1 pound chuck steak,
    ground very fine
1 medium onion, diced fine
1 clove garlic, minced fine
1 8-ounce can tomato sauce
½ cup water
1 tablespoon red wine vinegar
1 tablespoon chili powder

1 teaspoon dry mustard
½ teaspoon ground cuminseeds
¼ teaspoon ground
    coriander seeds
1 teaspoon salt
1 teaspoon freshly ground pepper
½ bay leaf, crumbled fine
3 to 6 ounces tomato juice

• Salt a large cast-iron skillet; add beef, onion, and garlic. Cook over medium heat until beef is browned.

Add all other ingredients except tomato juice. Simmer over low heat at least 1 hour, periodically stirring and tasting. Adjust seasonings to taste. Add enough tomato juice to keep it sloppy.

Makes enough to heavily blanket 6 to 8 hamburgers. Tastes even better when refrigerated and reheated.

∾

The ultimate, and about as far as we are willing to go in dressing up hamburgers, is a deluxe sandwich we first tasted at the Beacon Drive-In in Spartanburg, South Carolina: the Double Chili Cheeseburger with Bacon. Here is how to stack it up:

For each sandwich, fry three slices of bacon. Remove from pan when cooked but not yet crisp, and drain on paper towels.

Heat up your Chili Size.

Grill two fairly thin meat patties per sandwich, topping each with a slice of cheese. (For an extra thrill, fry them in your bacon pan, pouring off—but not wiping out—the grease.)

While the meat is grilling, slice the biggest hamburger bun you've got, Spread the bottom with mayonnaise and layer on a lettuce leaf and a slice of tomato. Leave the top dry.

Remove one cheeseburger patty from grill, and put it, cheese side up, on the prepared bun bottom. Lay the bacon slices across the cheese, which will have been softened by heat from the pan. Take the other cheeseburger and— here's the good part—lay it *cheese side down* atop the bacon.

Ladle on as much chili topping as you dare, capping the whole mess with the top of the bun.

FRENCH FRIES

French fries are some trouble to cook at home, but they are worth it—an irresistible companion to a good hamburger.

The choice of potato is a matter of taste. If you like thick, starchy french fries, choose Idahos—baking potatoes. For thinner "shoestring" potatoes, or curly "Suzy Q's," russets or boiling potatoes work better. Count on at least one large potato per person.

Potatoes (1 per person)   *Salt*
Vegetable oil for frying

• Peel and cut potatoes into strips of desired size, between ¼ inch and ½ inch thick. Soak in cold water for 1 hour, changing water twice.

Heat oil to 380°, with a frying basket in the oil. (Or you can use a deep skillet.) Drain and blot potatoes thoroughly dry. Lift out basket, quickly throw in only enough potatoes to cover bottom (you don't want the basket to cool), and carefully reimmerse in fat. Lift and shake basket a bit if potatoes seem to be sticking together. The thinnest fries will take no more than 3 or 4 minutes to brown, thick ones up to 10.

Reheat basket in fat, and throw in next batch. Continue, always making sure the oil stays up to temperature. Salt potatoes just before serving.

Once fries are cooked, they can be made into *Philadelphia Cheese Fries* by putting them in a large paper cup and ladling on a molten sauce made of Cheez Whiz warmed in the top of a double boiler.

POTATO CHIPS

Cut potatoes into slices of desired thinness. After they have soaked 1 hour in cold water, as above, drain and plunge into boiling water for just 1 minute. Drain, blot completely dry, and proceed as with French fries.

Blue Plate Noodles

At school cafeterias across America, Friday means macaroni and cheese: wads of overcooked noodles, glued together with happy yellow Cheddar, splatted onto waiting plates.

But not all servings are the same. You've got to be shrewd to get the macaroni you want. If you are a soft, creamy type of person, you prefer the center of the casserole, where everything is pillowy rich. You position yourself in line to come after the blackened cheese is skimmed off the top, but well before the serving lady hits bottom and starts grazing the sides of the pan for hardened, stuck bits of noodle. If, on the other hand, your tastes are rugged, you rush to the head of the line for those first skimmings of chewy cheese, or hold back until the last serving is scraped onto a plate.

At swanky school cafeterias, macaroni and cheese might be accompanied by tuna salad or fish sticks. But we like it all by itself, with chocolate milk on the side. It is austere and intensely focused, yet one of the most satisfying things on earth. Like meditation, or a long, lonely marathon.

SCHOOL CAFETERIA MACARONI AND CHEESE

This recipe comes from a home ec textbook, *Adventuring in Home Living,* a 1959 guide for teens that covers everything from problem perspiration to making popcorn balls. The last step of broiling the casserole ensures generous amounts of chewy top as well as creamy center. You can soup it up with Tabasco sauce; you can enrich it by using cream instead of milk; or you can dot it with bits of Canadian bacon—but the crucial decision will be the choice of cheese. Being average folks, we like a mild Vermont Cheddar, but if you like it blander than that, use Velveeta; for more zest, choose New York State coon cheese or Oregon Tillamook.

1 8-ounce package macaroni	*1 teaspoon salt*
4 tablespoons butter	*Pepper to taste*
2¼ cups grated cheese	*Buttered crumbs or crumbled*
1 cup milk	*potato chips*

• Preheat oven to 300°.

Cook macaroni 5 to 8 minutes in boiling salted water, until just tender; drain.

Stir butter into noodles. Add 2 cups cheese, milk, salt, and pepper, and pour into 2-quart casserole.

Bake 30 minutes, until cheese is well set. Sprinkle on remaining ¼ cup of cheese and crumbs or chips, then broil 1 minute, or until brown on top.

Serves 4 to 6.

FISH CAKES AND SPAGHETTI

Come if you will to Horn & Hardart, citadel of lunch counter noodles, home of fish cakes and spaghetti. 'Cakes and spaghetti are a classic noontime combo, seemingly incompatible, yet undeniably right when savored in alternate forkfuls.

In 1983 we visited the remaining Automat on 42nd Street in New York, and there it was, behind glass, stacked in a vertical row alternating with plates of baked macaroni. Sadly, like the Automat itself, the fish cake and spaghetti plate was a shadow of its former self (or had our taste buds lost their innocence?). In any case, our recipe is guaranteed to recapture the fish cake glory that once was. Made with real mashed potatoes and a silky fish such as lemon or grey sole, it is an elegant dish.

The point of fish cakes and spaghetti, cooked at home, is to make a new meal out of yesterday's fish and mashed potato dinner. Not that Horn & Hardart does it that way; in fact, we haven't dug up their famous recipe. But we found the following good one in *500 Delicious Dishes from Leftovers,* published in 1940 by the Culinary Arts Institute of Chicago.

The spaghetti recipe is from *Adventuring in Home Living.* You may use your own favorite meatless spaghetti recipe to accompany the fish, but for authenticity's sake, be sure to use thick, round noodles, thoroughly cooked, three to five minutes past *al dente.* One way to ensure this is to cook the spaghetti first, and let it float in hot water while you prepare the fish.

FISH CAKES

1 cup flaked cooked fish (sole or	*Pepper*
some other fine-grained	*1 egg, slightly beaten*
flatfish is best)	*1 cup cold mashed potatoes*
1 tablespoon minced onion	*2 tablespoons flour*
1 teaspoon lemon juice	*¼ cup fat or shortening*
¼ teaspoon salt	

• Combine fish, onion, lemon juice, seasonings, egg, and potatoes. Form into small (2½-inch-diameter) cakes, coat with flour, and sauté in hot fat about 5 minutes, turning once. Drain on paper towels.

Makes 6 to 8 cakes.

SPAGHETTI

1 tablespoon shortening	*1 cup water*
1 small onion, minced	*½ teaspoon plus 1 tablespoon salt*
1 sprig parsley, cut fine	*Dash pepper*
1 small clove garlic, minced	*1 8-ounce package spaghetti*
2 stalks celery, minced	*2 quarts boiling water*
1 cup ketchup	

• Melt shortening in skillet. Add onion, parsley, garlic, and celery. Cook 10 minutes. Add ketchup, water, ½ teaspoon salt, and pepper. Simmer until sauce is thickened—30 to 60 minutes.

Add 1 tablespoon salt to boiling water in large saucepan. Add spaghetti gradually. Boil until tender, stirring occasionally. Drain off excess water. Mix with sauce.

Serve on plate with one or two fish cakes. Serves 6.

BAKED SPAGHETTI

It used to be a lunch counter staple, but we found only one restaurant, Mary Elizabeth's in New York City, that still had the audacity (or, more likely, the culinary anility) to serve baked spaghetti, It is a dish so outré that it took some digging to find an authentic recipe. We turned up this one in *The Practical Cookbook* of 1910, written by Elizabeth O. Hiller ("Principal of the Chicago Domestic Science Training School"). Ms. Hiller didn't give exact amounts in her recipe, so we've modernized it, keeping all her ingredients and approximate proportions. It's a real taste of the past.

1 8-ounce package spaghetti	*Cayenne pepper to taste*
(4 servings)	*1 onion, grated*
1 medium onion	*4 strips barely cooked*
4 whole cloves	*bacon (optional)*
2 tablespoons butter	*¼ cup buttered bread crumbs (or*
1 8-ounce can tomato sauce	*pulverized potato chips)*
½ cup grated Parmesan cheese	

• Break spaghetti into 2-inch pieces. Cook with whole onion, stuck with cloves, in 2½ quarts boiling salted water, until *al dente*. Drain. Remove onion, and butter noodles.

Preheat oven to 350°.

Butter a baking dish and add alternate layers of spaghetti and tomato sauce, sprinkling each layer with Parmesan cheese, cayenne pepper, and grated onion. Cover with strips of bacon (optional) and crumbs.

Bake until crumbs are browned—approximately 20 minutes.

Serves 4.

CINCINNATI FIVE-WAY CHILI

No one who loves to eat can visit Cincinnati without falling in love with the most eccentric and delicious noodle dish of all—Five-Way Chili. Invented by Greek immigrants in the 1920s, it is unique to southern Ohio, and served only in chili parlors, most of which are fluorescent-lighted luncheonettes that haven't changed much since 1950.

Nobody in Cincinnati gives out their recipe. It is a dish of startling complexity, so dizzyingly spicy that we never even considered we could approximate it at home. Like Carolina barbecue, Cincinnati chili seemed so secret, ritualized, and local in spirit that it would be sacrilege to eat it anywhere other than at a counter stool in the Queen City.

But one day, while browsing through *Women's Household* magazine, among the ads for bed dolls and crocheted bathroom tissue covers we spotted a tiny classified ad for a "genuine" Cincinnati Chili recipe. Curiosity piqued, we sent away and tried it. Not quite, but we were close. About six batches later, we hit our stride and turned out a chili that comes about as near as our taste buds can remember to our favorite local variation on the theme, the one served at Camp Washington Chili Parlor.

Five-Way is a one-plate lunch, readily prepared in advance, fun to serve, and once you get the hang of it, easy to adjust to your own taste. One thing is certain—there is no *wrong* way to make it. Starting with beef, garlic, chili,

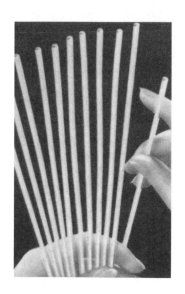

cumin, cinnamon and allspice, you can quickly turn it into your own—hot, sweet, thick, however you like it. Cincinnati chili is always accompanied by bowls of oyster crackers, and for the robust of appetite, a couple of chili-and-cheese-smothered wieners (called "Coneys" in Cincinnati).

Despite an avalanche of bizarre ingredients, the chili itself is actually an easy one-pan preparation. Remember, though, it is only one of five layers that compose the dish. The layering is crucial for authenticity; and if you want to make a Cincinnatian homesick, construct the chili on a small oval plate. Make the chili first, and as it simmers, the other four ingredients can be prepared. The following recipe will make enough for 4.

1 pound chuck, ground fine   *½ teaspoon ground cumin*
    (twice in a meat grinder)   *½ teaspoon turmeric*
2 medium onions,   *½ teaspoon marjoram*
    chopped fine   *½ teaspoon allspice*
2 cloves garlic, minced   *¼ teaspoon nutmeg*
1 cup tomato sauce   *½ teaspoon cinnamon*
2 tablespoons ketchup   *¼ teaspoon ground cloves*
1 cup water   *¼ teaspoon mace*
1 tablespoon red wine vinegar   *¼ teaspoon ground coriander*
1 tablespoon chili powder   *¼ teaspoon ground cardamom*
1 tablespoon paprika   *½ dry bay leaf, crumbled*
1 teaspoon ground black pepper   *1 teaspoon salt*
1 teaspoon honey
½ ounce unsweetened chocolate,
    grated

• Salt a large cast-iron skillet. Turn heat to medium and add meat, onions, and garlic. Cook until all meat is browned. Add tomato sauce, ketchup, water, and vinegar. As mixture begins to boil, add everything else. Adjust spices to taste, adding more salt if it needs perking up, turmeric and cumin for a sweatier chili flavor, cinnamon, cloves, and mace if you want it sweeter, cardamom for more bang, unsweetened chocolate for body.

Cover and simmer at very low heat for about 1 hour, stiffing and tasting occasionally, adding tomato juice if it is getting too dry to ladle up easily.

CONSTRUCTING THE CHILI

8 ounces spaghetti   *1 pound Wisconsin Cheddar*
1 16-ounce can red   *cheese, grated fine, as fluffy*
    kidney beans   *as you can make it*
2 onions, chopped

1. The bottom layer is always spaghetti, the thickest you can find. In fact, we found none in our supermarket that was thick enough, so we got perci-

atelli—long, thin macaroni. We broke it into 4-inch pieces and boiled it in salted water to which 2 tablespoons of olive oil were added. For a touch of swank, melt a stick of sweet butter into the just-cooked noodles before you dish them out.

You will need about 2 to 3 ounces per serving. You want them soft enough to cut easily with a fork, but not so soft they lose their oomph. Remember, they are the support layer for four other ingredients. Spread them out to cover the bottom of a small plate (preferably oval).

2. Next comes the chili. Ladle on enough to cover the noodles.

3. Kidney beans. One 16-ounce can. Wash, heat with 2 cups water, then drain. Don't season them or do anything fancy, though. They're here more for texture than taste. Spoon a sparse layer atop the chili.

4. Chopped onions. Spread them out, to taste, over the beans.

5. Quickly now, so it melts a bit, spread the grated cheese to cover everything. Don't skimp. Cheese should completely blanket the plate, enough so that you can pat it into a neat mound with your hands, just the way they do in Cincinnati.

You may, if desired, omit either the beans or onions, or both, for Three-Way or Four-Way Chili.

Soda Fountain Treats

The soda fountain is an enchanted world in the galaxy of lunch counter cookery. It is a place where movie stars were discovered, where Archie and Veronica settled their spats, where the lead singer of the Shangri-las met the hero of her tragedy, "The Leader of the Pack."

It is a world colored with Crayolas—green rivers and strawberry banana boats, brown cows and pink elephant punch. And Maraschino cherries everywhere, most of them bright red; but occasionally, atop a coconut snowcapped whipped cream mountain, you will find the rarer, more exotic Maraschino—the green one, brighter than a lime Chuckle.

Perhaps, in a small Iowa town or a candy store in the Bronx, you might happen upon an authentic soda fountain complete with fudge vat, malt dispenser, and silver-bottomed cups for holding paper inserts, with a repertoire of Broadway flips, double-cherry Cokes, and licorice whip-garnished black cows. But all around America, silver milk shake pitchers stand empty—monuments of a forgotten pleasure that few adults ever return to savor.

It is easy to recreate the reliquiae of the soda fountain world at home, but

before you do, you must know that no matter how exactly you replicate your favorite malt or egg cream or banana split, it will never taste the way it did when it was manufactured and served at a genuine fountain. You don't have the right equipment—no nozzle to dispense a furious stream of seltzer into a buxom fountain glass, no trough large enough to contain a Harlequin Royale.

Even if you do get the right stuff, and learn to dive-bomb scoops of ice cream into the milk shake pitcher, it still won't taste the same. But that's okay, because in a way, it's better. After all, you aren't sixteen years old anymore; you cannot down a milk shake and fries and a double cheeseburger with impunity. Even most health-conscious kids don't eat that stuff anymore.

It just isn't done! Maybe that's why it tastes so especially wonderful.

Milk Shakes

Any blender will make a milk shake, although the kind with large blades at the bottom tends to pulverize the ice cream quickly, making for a thin shake. Don't overmix! Good vanilla ice cream and very cold milk are crucial for that velvety texture.

(*Note:* There are parts of New England where "milk shake" means milk shook up with flavoring. Where we come from—New York and Chicago—it means milk, flavoring, *and ice cream*, so this recipe is for what Rhode Islanders call a "cabinet" and Down-Easters a "velvet" or "frappe.")

Each of the following recipes yields 2 to 3 glasses of milk shake; any less would be untrue to the soda fountain silver pitcher tradition. Consider the measurements starting points, and adjust ice cream, milk, and flavorings to taste. With very high quality ice cream, less flavoring is required.

VANILLA SHAKE ("WHITE COW")

4 scoops vanilla ice cream *1½ cups milk*
1 tablespoon vanilla extract

• Mix just enough to blend ingredients.

CHOCOLATE SHAKE

4 scoops vanilla ice cream
1½ cups milk

4 tablespoons chocolate syrup
1 teaspoon vanilla extract

• Mix in blender.

VANILLA MALT

4 scoops vanilla ice cream
1½ cups milk
1 tablespoon vanilla extract

2 tablespoons Carnation or
   Horlick's malted
   milk powder

• Mix in blender.

CHOCOLATE MALT

4 scoops vanilla ice cream
1½ cups milk
2 to 3 tablespoons
   chocolate syrup

1 teaspoon vanilla extract
2 tablespoons malted milk powder
   (do not use chocolate malted
   milk powder)

• Mix in blender.

DOUBLE CHOCOLATE MALT ("BURN ONE ALL THE WAY")

4 scoops chocolate ice cream
1½ cups milk
2 tablespoons chocolate syrup (less, or none, if using
   high-quality dark chocolate ice cream)

1 teaspoon vanilla extract
2 tablespoons malted milk powder

• Mix in blender.

PEPPERMINT SMOOTHIE

4 scoops peppermint ice cream   *2 drops peppermint extract*
1½ cups milk   *1 teaspoon vanilla extract*

• Mix in blender.

CHOCO-PEPPERMINT SMOOTHIE

4 scoops peppermint ice cream   *1 teaspoon vanilla extract*
1½ cups milk   *4 tablespoons bittersweet*
2 drops peppermint extract   *chocolate syrup*

• Mix in blender.

BANANA FROSTED SHAKE

From *Bananas—How to Serve Them,* a
1941 publication of the fruit industry.

1 banana
1 cup milk
3 to 4 scoops vanilla ice cream
1 tablespoon vanilla extract

• Pulverize banana in blender, then add
remaining ingredients. Mix.

BANANA ALMOND FRAPPE

1 banana
1 orange, peeled
1 cup milk

3 scoops vanilla ice cream
1 tablespoon honey
3 drops almond extract

• Pulverize banana and orange in blender, then add remaining ingredients. Mix.

BANANA DATE SHAKE

6 pitted dates
1 banana

4 scoops vanilla ice cream
1½ cups milk

• Pulverize dates and banana in blender, then add remaining ingredients. Mix.

CREAM NOGG ("MAKE IT CACKLE")

To any milk shake or malt recipe, add 1 raw egg.

EGG CREAM

An inexpensive soda fountain drink, made without ice cream, the egg cream got its name because it tastes as rich as eggs. You will still find thriving egg cream parlors on the Lower East Side of New York and in the Bronx. In Chicago, egg creams made without milk (soda and syrup only) are called phosphates.

2 tablespoons chocolate syrup
(preferably a thin one; Fox's
U-Bet brand is preferred)

⅓ cup cold whole milk
⅔ cup ice-cold charged
seltzer water

• Put chocolate syrup in the bottom of a large soda fountain glass. Add milk and stir, blending, but don't worry if a few streaks of unblended chocolate are visible at the bottom of the glass—that's traditional. Add seltzer and stir vigorously. Of course, the best way to add seltzer is to squirt it in. But it's okay if you don't have a squirter, so long as the seltzer is very bubbly. A foamy head will rise. Drink immediately.

For more tingle and a higher head, use ¼ cup milk and ¾ cup seltzer. For a richer egg cream, go the other way, half milk, half seltzer.

Ice Cream Sodas

Traditionally, an ice cream soda is flavoring, charged water, ice cream, and possibly a nice dab of whipped cream. The technique is 1-2-3: put 2 tablespoons of syrup or flavoring in the bottom of the largest glass you have. Add seltzer water, stirring as you pour, to within 2 inches of the lip of the glass. Add one large scoop of very firm ice cream, trying to get it to straddle the rim of the glass, yet still submerge in the seltzer enough to begin reacting with the bubbles to create a foamy head. If the ice cream is too deep in the flavored seltzer, the soda will overflow. If it doesn't touch the seltzer at all, you don't have a soda. With a little practice, you will reach a perfect balance. Top the soda with a hefty squirt of whipped cream.

The possible combinations are unlimited—black-and-whites (chocolate syrup, vanilla ice cream), Canary Island specials (vanilla syrup, chocolate ice cream), double chocolates, mochas, etc. Here are a few soda fountain standards:

BLACK-AND-WHITE

• Chocolate syrup, seltzer, vanilla ice cream.

BODACIOUS BLACK-AND-WHITE

• Chocolate syrup, seltzer, French vanilla ice cream.

CANARY ISLAND SPECIAL

• Vanilla syrup, seltzer, chocolate ice cream.

BLACK COW

• Root beer afloat with vanilla ice cream; hold the whipped cream.

BROWN COW

• Coca-Cola, 1 tablespoon chocolate syrup, and vanilla ice cream.

STRAWBERRY SODA ("IN THE HAY")

• ¼ cup strawberry syrup, a splash of milk, seltzer, and vanilla or strawberry ice cream.

HOBOKEN

• ½ cup pineapple syrup, a splash of milk, seltzer, and chocolate ice cream.

BOSTON COOLER

• For the sophisticate. Dry ginger ale with a scoop of vanilla; no whipped cream.

CATAWBA FLIP

An antique-tasting soda that dates back to the 1860s, made without whipped cream. The traditional flavoring is grape syrup, but Welch's Concord Grape Juice is powerful enough to do the job just fine.

1 scoop vanilla ice cream   *Shaved ice*

2 ounces grape juice   *Seltzer*

1 egg

• Put all ingredients except seltzer into blender and mix thoroughly. Strain into tall glass, then fill with seltzer.

Sundaes and Banana Splits

The most free-form of all soda fountain delicacies. Like a pro wrestling Battle Royale, all rules are suspended, no ingredients barred. Use your favorite kind of ice cream and top it with your favorite syrup, topping, nuts, sprinkles, jimmies, candy bits, marshmallow sauce, and whipped cream.

Creativity is part of the sundae ethos; crazy-named stupendous mountains of ingredients are what make an ice cream sundae pig-out fun. But no serious soda jerk attempts to create new combos of syrup and sauce until he or she has mastered certain classic forms.

Limber up your technique with variations of the ever-popular *harlequin* theme. Begin with alternating scoops of vanilla and chocolate ice cream, add perhaps one scoop of coffee to balance the stark black-and-white pattern, then dollop each scoop with an opposite-colored topping—marshmallow on the chocolate ice cream, fudge on the vanilla, perhaps a bold streak of raspberry on the coffee. Garnish the whole tastefully designed tableau with sprinkles of chocolate jimmies and fluffy coconut.

For Fauvist sundaes, consider tinting your whipped cream—easy to do with a drop or two of food coloring.

A basic repertoire should include:

HOT FUDGE SUNDAE

• Vanilla ice cream, hot fudge, whipped cream, and a cherry. Chopped nuts are optional.

C.M.P.

• Vanilla ice cream topped with both chocolate and marshmallow sauce, and coarsely chopped peanuts. (C.M.P. means chocolate-marshmallow-peanuts.)

TIN ROOF

• Vanilla ice cream, chocolate (not fudge) sauce, and whole Spanish peanuts (the little red-skinned ones); hold the whipped cream.

Advanced Sundaes

CHOP SUEY SUNDAE

Once the basic sundaes are mastered, the soda jerk should try his or her hand at more inventive fare, such as this relic suggested by an old recipe from *The National Soda Fountain Guide.*

my *¼ cup sugar*

¼ cup water

¼ cup raisins

¼ cup dates

2 scoops vanilla ice cream

¼ cup flaked coconut

¼ cup chow mein noodles

• Boil sugar and water together 5 minutes. Mix in raisins and dates. Pour over ice cream in a bowl. Top with coconut and chow mein noodles.

DIONNE SURPRISE

Sundaes are a freewheeling art, ready to respond to whatever whim or popular fancy drifts past the door of the soda fountain—like this quintuple-scoop cribful from the 1930s named after the Dionne quints.

5 scoops vanilla ice cream

Whipped cream

5 Maraschino cherries

¼ cup crushed pineapple

¼ cup crushed strawberries

• Line up the ice cream scoops in a troughlike dish. Top each with a dab of whipped cream and a cherry. Spread pineapple along one side of the ice cream, strawberries on the other.

THE ALL-AMERICAN

A 1942 invention of the Ice Cream Merchandising Institute, part of their World War II "Victory Sundae" campaign.

¼ cup marshmallow syrup

2 scoops vanilla ice cream

2 tablespoons crushed
  Maraschino cherries

2 tablespoons blueberries

• Put half the marshmallow syrup in bottom of tulip glass. Add ice cream and top with remainder of marshmallow. On one side of the top, lay on the cherries. Leaving a stripe of white in the middle, lay the blueberries on the other side.

BANANA SPLIT

When appended to the name of any soda fountain specialty, the word *royale* means that the ice cream has been given a touch of class by the addition of that dress-up fruit, bananas.

A traditional banana split, or *houseboat,* looks best in a glass trough, with the bananas cut lengthwise (not into disks), forming a "fence" for two or three scoops of ice cream. The best banana split we ever had was at a place called Ames Ice Cream in Maine, where they featured a *Battleship.* (Note the nautical motif again.) The ship began with two big bananas, each cut in half, the halves laid out to form a square railing in a small tub. Inside the banana rail was a cargo of nine scoops of various-flavored ice cream topped with chocolate, marshmallow, and strawberry sauces and a cloud of whipped cream, plus chopped peanuts and a half-dozen Maraschino cherries.

In *The Great American Ice Cream Book,* we discovered these historical and patriotic variations on the banana split theme:

SKYSCRAPER BANANA SPLIT

A recipe printed in *The Ice Cream Review*, July 1936, described as "especially popular among the college crowd."

½ ounce chocolate syrup
1 scoop vanilla ice cream
1 banana, cut lengthwise, then in
* half (quartered)*

1 scoop chocolate ice cream
1 ounce strawberry syrup
Whipped cream
Maraschino cherry

• Pour chocolate syrup into a tall tulip sundae glass. Add vanilla ice cream. Place quartered banana into glass like columns, round side up, cut side out. Add chocolate ice cream, strawberry syrup, whipped cream, and cherry.

WASHINGTON MONUMENT SUNDAE

A specialty of Weile's soda fountain in Washington, D.C., found in the 1947 Dairy Training and Merchandising Institute's book called *Let's Sell Ice Cream.*

¼ cup chocolate syrup
6 scoops ice cream,
   different flavors
¼ cup raspberry syrup
1 banana, cut into disks
¼ cup nuts in syrup

1 banana, cut in half, across
   its width
Whipped cream
Candy sprinkles (blue and red)
Maraschino cherries
5 small American flags on toothpicks

• Into your tallest glass, put 1 tablespoon chocolate syrup and 1 scoop vanilla ice cream. Add 1 tablespoon raspberry syrup and a few banana disks. Continue, adding ice cream, nuts, syrups, topping them with ½ banana, placed upright, held in place by a mound of whipped cream. Sprinkle blue and red candy over whipped cream, and arrange a few Maraschino cherries around the edge of the glass. Insert small paper American flags.

Sundae and Banana Split Toppings

The chocolate syrup that comes closest to soda fountain syrup is Fox's U-Bet, at room temperature. (Refrigerated, it thickens too much.) Hershey's is good, too; or you can make your own. Here's how:

CHOCOLATE SYRUP

6 ounces semisweet chocolate   *½ cup evaporated milk*

• In top of double boiler, melt chocolate over hot but not boiling water. Gradually stir in evaporated milk and, if a thinner sauce is desired, ¼ cup water. Stir over hot water until sauce is smooth and fully blended.
   Makes 1 cup.

BITTERSWEET CHOCOLATE SAUCE

4 ounces unsweetened chocolate   *¹⁄₄ cup brown sugar*

¹⁄₃ cup sour cream   *¹⁄₃ cup milk*

¹⁄₄ cup granulated sugar   *1 teaspoon vanilla extract*

• Melt chocolate in top of double boiler. Stir in sour cream, sugars, and milk. When fully blended, stir in vanilla.

Makes 1½ cups.

SWEET SHOP HOT FUDGE

One day in 1983 we returned to what was, for Michael, the basal lunch counter—the Sweet Shop of Winnetka, Illinois. Here a growing boy could stop for after-school snacks of cheeseburgers, a Coke, and—if feeling rich as Mr. Plushbottom—a hot fudge sundae.

The Sweet Shop was famous for serving their sundae in a special way: the ice cream, topped with whipped cream, chopped nuts, and a Maraschino, came in one large tulip glass; and the hot fudge came separately, in its own little pitcher. It was an agonizing presentation, a moment of truth in the formation of youthful habits concerning self-indulgence and thrift. The problem was that the hot fudge was so delicious that you had to decide what to do with it. Do you pour it all on the ice cream at once, enjoying it bit by bit, hoping to wind up with a final spoonful that has a fudge-to-ice cream ratio equal to the first? Or do you put on just a little fudge at a time (it stays warmer that way), winding up with an empty ice cream dish and a couple of spoonfuls of pure fudge to savor? Or . . . pure hedonistic evil! . . . do you eat all the ice cream, then *drink the hot fudge?*

On our return trip to the Sweet Shop in 1983, we were faced with the same delicious dilemma. We won't tell you which technique we used, but we will say that the fudge was the exact superior stuff it used to be a quarter century ago: wonderfully grainy, not too thick or sickeningly chocolaty, just perfect. Steve Poulos, the Sweet Shop fudgemaster (and a registered pharmacist as well), told us he uses his father's recipe, unchanged since 1924, which makes 5 gallons at a time and requires 20 pounds of glucose.

QUICK HOT FUDGE

If 5 gallons of hot fudge seems like a lot, or if, like us, you find it impossible to locate large quantities of glucose, we recommend this comparatively easy fudge sauce. The only problem is that when you make it yourself, its preciousness is diminished, because there is always plenty. Serve warm, in a little pitcher.

½ cup unsweetened cocoa	*1 tablespoon sour cream*
½ cup sugar	*4 tablespoons sweet butter*
⅓ cup light corn syrup	*1 teaspoon vanilla extract*
½ cup evaporated milk	

• Combine cocoa, sugar, corn syrup, milk, and sour cream in heavy saucepan. Heat over medium flame, stirring constantly, until mixture begins to boil. Immediately turn off heat; stir in butter and vanilla. Serve warm.

Makes enough for 4 good-size hot fudge sundaes.

ROCKY ROAD

6 ounces semisweet chocolate   *Dash salt*
½ cup sour cream   *1 cup miniature marshmallows*
1 tablespoon water

• Melt chocolate in top of double boiler. Mix in sour cream, water, and salt. Turn off heat. Fold in marshmallows.

Makes enough for 4 sundaes.

MARSHMALLOW SAUCE

8 ounces marshmallows   *¼ cup milk*
2 tablespoons water   *1 tablespoon light corn syrup*
¾ cup sugar   *1 teaspoon vanilla extract*

• In top of double boiler, melt marshmallows with water. Leave in double boiler and set aside.

In a heavy saucepan, combine sugar, milk, and corn syrup. Bring to boil, reduce heat, and simmer 5 minutes. Pour this liquid over marshmallows and, with a hand-held mixer, whisk, or egg beater, beat until smooth. Sauce will thicken as it cooks.

Remove from heat. Add vanilla. Serve at room temperature. Makes enough for 4 to 6 sundaes.

GOLDEN MARSHMALLOW SAUCE

¼ cup boiling water
1 cup dark brown sugar
1 cup miniature marshmallows
or quartered large
marshmallows

½ teaspoon vanilla extract

• Add boiling water to sugar and cook until a little less than the very soft ball stage is reached (about 220°). Pour in marshmallows, beating steadily with electric beater over low heat until smooth. Remove from heat; add vanilla. Serve warm or at room temperature.

Makes enough for 4 sundaes.

BUTTERSCOTCH SAUCE

1 cup packed dark
brown sugar
⅔ cup light corn syrup
4 tablespoons butter

½ cup heavy cream
¼ cup milk
1 teaspoon cornstarch

• Boil sugar, corn syrup, and butter in saucepan. Bring to 230°. Mix cream and milk with cornstarch; add to syrup, mix until smooth over lowered heat. Sauce will thicken as it cools.

Makes enough for 4 sundaes.

CARAMEL SAUCE

30 caramel squares

¼ cup water

• Melt caramels and water in top of double boiler, stirring occasionally. Serve warm.

Makes enough for 4 to 6 sundaes.

POLLY'S PANCAKE PARLOR HURRICANE SAUCE

3 tablespoons butter
2 cups pure maple syrup

3 cups unpeeled, thinly sliced tart
apples

• Simmer butter and syrup together in deep saucepan. Add apples. Cook very gently so as not to break up slices for 1½ to 2 hours, until apples are transparent and liquid is syrupy. Serve warm over vanilla ice cream.

Makes enough for 6 to 8 sundaes.

PINEAPPLE SAUCE

1 cup crushed pineapple
with juice

½ cup light corn syrup

• Combine ingredients in deep saucepan over low heat; mix well. Chill.
Makes 1½ cups.

RASPBERRY TOPPING

10 ounces red raspberries
(fresh or frozen)
1½ teaspoons cornstarch
dissolved in ¼ cup water

½ cup currant jelly or
raspberry jam
1 tablespoon grenadine (if using
fresh berries)

• Mix raspberries, cornstarch, jelly, and grenadine in a saucepan. Cook over low heat, stirring until sauce begins to thicken. Cool.

Makes 1½ cups.

CHERRY COKE

This most awful and decadent soda fountain treat is something we had almost forgotten until one day, while mixing manhattans for soigné company, we plucked the last of the Maraschino cherries from the jar. "What are you going to do with that juice?" asked a suave gentleman guest. He explained that his refrigerator is filled with jars of dry Maraschino cherries . . . because he uses the liquid in which they're packed to make cherry Cokes! (The man is in his fifties, and in perfect health.)

His authentic-tasting recipe calls for 1 tablespoon of Maraschino cherry juice, mixed quickly with about 8 ounces of Coke.

For vanilla Coke, use ½ tablespoon of vanilla extract.

For chocolate Coke, we discovered that the thinner syrups such as Fox's U-Bet or Bosco are better than Hershey's. Start with ½ tablespoon.

SUNDAY DINNER

There was a time when "come for Sunday dinner" was a gilt-edged guarantee of a square meal. It meant a feast of pot roast or plump roasted chicken; it meant constellations of white china plates, filled with biscuits and whipped yams and steaming peas, circling the table as each diner dipped in with a hearty ladle.

Mother rose at dawn to prepare the rolls for their leisurely rise. Into a pot of apples would go a handful of cinnamon sticks, cloves, and brown sugar—on their way to becoming applesauce. Later, Granny was on the porch shelling peas, Sis was setting the table, dreaming of the day her children would eat off this same china with the blue willow pattern. Dad and Junior were polishing their shoes and brilliantining their hair with lavender-scented gunk.

If this picture seems a bit less than authentic, so be it. The American dinner table was an icon, an ideal to be strived for if never perfectly attained. Even if Granny was nipping at the bottle of rye and Junior pocketing a few pieces of family silver to trade for a car horn that played "Chantilly Lace," at least everybody had an image of what was normal and healthy and upright. And a pot roast was a nice solid object on which to hang one's dreams.

The fantasy of such square meals may be only a dim memory, but with pots and pans and good recipes, it is possible to go back in time and retrieve them.

For the recipes, we have searched our own family files, as well as musty old books with such titles as *Gifts from Your Kitchen* and *Housewifery: A Manual of the Womanly Arts.* These guides paint a picture of ladies industriously making their farmhouse or honeymoon bungalow into a hollyhock-rimmed paradise; they are bibles of unabashed pride in the beauty of a perfectly made bed, or the goodness of turning yesterday's meat scraps into today's scrumptious meal.

Homemaking was a respected, full-time occupation. According to Elizabeth O. Hiller's 1913 recipe book, *Fifty-two Sunday Dinners,* "To the modern wide-awake, twentieth-century woman, efficiency in household matters is quite as much a problem as efficiency in business is to captains of industry."

From formidable home economists with ample bosoms and pince-nez glasses, the unprepared homemaker learned all she needed to know. If your angel cake deflated like an old tire or your jelly wouldn't jell, they had the answer. Some media mentors, such as Betty Crocker, were imaginary; others were as solidly flesh and blood as Ida Bailey Allen, host of "The Radio Homemakers Club" in the 1930s.

According to a 1926 cookbook called *Feed the Brute,* "the well-fed man is a happy man"; but Ida Bailey Allen's philosophy of homemaking went deeper than simply pulling the roast out of the oven at the right time. She believed that a well-run kitchen was the heart of a happy home. Listeners were instructed to keep pots of flowers or a chirping canary on the win-

How's That, Grandma?

dowsill. "Bright cushions on the chairs, stenciled sash curtains of checked gingham, a braided rug, inexpensive shining copper, stenciled oilcloth trays"—each was "a small brick in the structure of Home—the Centre for which civilization exists."

Ladies tuned their radios to "Sara and Aggie," two good old girls from Monticello, Illinois, who gossiped over an imaginary party line about hometown cooking, interspersing recipes with recommendations for their sponsor, Dr. Caldwell's Syrup Pepsin Laxative. Among their advice was this homily for domestic bliss:

Three Domestic Spices

THE FIRST SPICE: A definite dependable mealtime.
THE SECOND SPICE: A snow white cloth on a neatly arranged table.
THE THIRD SPICE: The housewife's sweet and friendly expression, that like the sun, will dispel the small clouds of discontent and irritation that sometimes threaten the domestic sky.

The conscientious homemaker studied technique with Sara and Aggie and Ida Bailey Allen and Betty Crocker; she pored over manufacturers' brochures to learn about wondrous products like Crisco and Royal Baking Powder that promised she could be a better cook; and she read earnest tomes like *The American Home Diet: An Answer to the Ever-Present Question, WHAT SHALL WE HAVE FOR DINNER?* And if she was good at her job, the reward was nothing less than a lifetime of happiness.

Like the rubber dolls with which we played in the second grade (including a dad whose rubber fedora and briefcase were glued solid to his body), it all seems so *ordained,* the role models as mythic as the gods of Mt. Olympus.

It is a rendering to make Betty Friedan cringe.

But let's face it—who doesn't love the stroke of a freshly pressed bed-sheet, or the smell of steam rising from a blackberry pie? What husband—or wife—wouldn't like to come home from work on Washington's Birthday to find a cunning table arrangement of a black tricornered hat filled with dark sweet cherries? Oh, to be able to crawl into the frame of a 1930s movie and be the lady of the house after the boss has come for dinner and left, happily patting his belly and puffing his dollar cigar. Remember the look on hubby's face?

So, return with us if you will to a blissful past that never was. Come to our house for Sunday dinner.

Sunday Dinner on the Farm

Roast Pork with Sinner Stuffing • 119
Iowa Pea Salad, White Way Style • 120
Farmhouse Corn Cakes • 121
Celery Seed Cole Slaw • 122
Old-Fashioned Devil's Food Cake • 123

Front Porch Sunday Supper

Maggie's Coca-Cola Basted Ham • 125
Country Pan-Fried Chicken • 126
Best Cook in Town Spoonbread • 127
Watermelon Rind Pickles • 128
Fresh Peach Shortcake • 129

Mother's Sunday Dinner

Mom's Best Pot Roast • 131
Pot Roast Gravy • 133
Perfect Mashed Potatoes • 133
Minted Carrots and Peas • 134
Anadama Bread • 134
Deep Dish Apple Pie • 136

Prosperity Sunday Dinner

Roast Chicken with Peacemaker Herb
    and Fruit Stuffing • 138
Spinach Timbales with Cheese and Horseradish Sauce • 140
Perfection Salad • 141
Cloverleaf Rolls • 142
Squash Pie with Maple Cream Topping • 143

Sunday Dinner on the Farm

Roast Pork with Sinner Stuffing ♦ *Iowa Pea Salad, White Way Style* ♦ *Farmhouse Corn Cakes* ♦ *Celery Seed Cole Slaw* ♦ *Old-Fashioned Devil's Food Cake*

Our first menu is inspired by an automobile breakdown we had near Walnut, Iowa. We were far from the highway, exploring a countryside straight out of Grant Wood—soil black as pitch, rolling fields plowed with geometric precision.

We found a farmhouse, prim and white, and although it was a brisk October day, we were shaky and flushed with anxiety about our abandoned car.

"Phone's in the kitchen," said the farmer, pointing us toward a profoundly delicious aroma. We lingered longer than was necessary to make the call, fumbling through the pamphlet-slim yellow pages as we became enthralled with this farm kitchen and with the lady of the house, who was preparing a pork roast for dinner.

It was a perfect *tableau vivant,* as if the Smithsonian Institution had commissioned a diorama entitled "Sunday Dinner at the Farm, 1946": porcelain stove, well-worn but immaculate linoleum decorated with bluebirds, blue-speckled pots and pans, and the lady herself, pulling the roast from the oven time and again, basting it with great seriousness.

"That smells wonderful," we said, trying to strike up a

conversation with the silent cook. But her attention was on the roast, and although she smiled faintly, she ignored our chatter. She must have known we were trying to wangle a dinner invitation.

"Smelled good, didn't it?" said the grubby tow-truck driver as we headed away toward our car.

"You bet," we said hungrily. "If you had been any longer coming, maybe we would have tried some of it."

"Just as well you didn't." He chuckled. "Or you would have had to climb over them just to get out the door."

He grinned at our puzzled expressions, then explained.

"The reason that ol' pork smells so good is that she stuffs it with fruit that's crocked to its eyeballs in whiskey. She puts whiskey in everything; by the time pie's on the table, they're out cold."

Our car was towed and fixed. The only thing around to eat was snacks from our motel vending machine. We thought about driving back to the farm in Walnut, but figured that the two sinners had by now devoured their pork roast and were, as the tow-truck driver put it, out like lights.

ROAST PORK WITH SINNER STUFFING

1 cup pitted prunes, halved
½ cup dried apricots, halved
1 cup bourbon
1 teaspoon grated lemon rind
1 teaspoon grated orange rind
½ apple, peeled and cut into
    ½-inch chunks
1 tablespoon honey
1 5- to 6-pound pork loin roast,
    boned and butterflied

Salt and pepper
1 clove garlic
4 tablespoons sweet
    butter, softened
1 tablespoon dried thyme
2 tablespoons flour
1 cup apple cider

• Put prunes and apricots in a bowl. Pour bourbon over them and let them soak 2 to 3 hours or until fruits have absorbed most of the whiskey. Add lemon and orange rinds, chopped apple, and honey and mix gently. Reserve extra liquor.

Preheat oven to 325°.

Open boned and butterflied pork loin and sprinkle with salt and pepper. Lay boozy fruits in a strip a few inches from end of loin. (Make sure fruit strip stops about 1½ inches from ends of meat, to prevent fruit from falling out when meat is rolled.) Gently roll meat up around fruit. Tie with butcher twine securely at 2-inch intervals. (If loin has been halved by butcher, untie it and stuff boozy fruits between halves into center and retie.)

Cut garlic into slivers, and with a sharp knife, punch deep slits in roast and insert them. Rub softened butter on outside of roast, then sprinkle on thyme. Dust with flour.

Place roast on rack in roasting pan. Pour cider and reserved bourbon over meat, cover with foil, and place in center of oven.

Roast 25 minutes per pound at 325°. After first hour, remove foil and increase oven to 375° to finish. Baste frequently, adding cider if necessary.

When done, remove roast from pan and let sit covered loosely with foil before cutting. Spoon pan juices over each slice.

Serves 6 to 8.

IOWA PEA SALAD, WHITE WAY STYLE

This Midwestern specialty is an extremely rich "salad" of peas and cheese and eggs, all bound together in old-fashioned boiled dressing (not mayonnaise!). The recipe comes from Mr. Carroll Marshall, owner and chef at the White Way Cafe in Durant, Iowa—one of our favorite *Roodfood* restaurants, a bastion of Midwestern farm cuisine. (If not using Miracle Whip salad dressing, make boiled dressing ahead.)

16 ounces fresh or frozen peas
2 stalks celery, sliced fine
4 ounces sharp Cheddar cheese, grated coarse
½ cup diced sweet pickle chips

2 hard-boiled eggs, chopped
1 teaspoon salt
1¼ cups boiled dressing (recipe follows) or Miracle Whip salad dressing

• If using fresh peas, cook until just tender, then cool under running water. If using frozen peas, do not boil. Just soak peas in warm water until defrosted; then drain.

Combine peas, celery, cheese, pickle chips, eggs, and salt in mixing bowl. Make boiled dressing as follows:

BOILED DRESSING

1 tablespoon all-purpose flour   *¾ cup milk*

1 teaspoon dry mustard   *¼ cup white vinegar*

3 tablespoons sugar   *1½ tablespoons butter,*

2 egg yolks   *melted and cooled to*

Pinch cayenne pepper   *room temperature*

• In a heavy-bottomed saucepan, combine flour, mustard, and 1 tablespoon sugar. Add egg yolks, cayenne pepper, milk, vinegar, and melted butter. Place over low heat. Stir constantly and gently until thickened and smooth (20 to 25 minutes).

Remove from heat and stir in remaining 2 tablespoons sugar. Let cool. Dressing will thicken further.

When dressing is cool, add gently to pea salad, and stir until combined. Salt to taste. Serve cold.

Serves 6 to 8.

FARMHOUSE CORN CAKES

Corn compliments pork. Pigs eat it to grow fat, and we eat it along with pork roast, grunting happily too. If it is corn season when you make the cakes, it is worth scraping kernels fresh from the cob. But frozen or canned nuggets are an adequate substitute. Serve with sweet butter; and if you are not serving Sinner Stuffing, side the cakes with applesauce or apple butter.

1½ cups all-purpose flour   *3 eggs*

½ cup yellow cornmeal   *¾ cup milk*

3 tablespoons sugar   *4 tablespoons butter, melted*

2 teaspoons baking powder   *2½ cups corn kernels*

2 teaspoons salt

• Sift dry ingredients together. Mix eggs, milk, and butter, and add to flour, stirring gently. Add corn and stir.

Pour in 4-inch-diameter circles onto a well-buttered, heated skillet. Cook 3 to 4 minutes or until golden. Flip cakes; cook 3 minutes more.

Makes 10 to 12 corn cakes.

CELERY SEED COLE SLAW

Sunday dinner on the farm wouldn't be complete without cole slaw—not the creamy kind that accompanies hamburgers and hot dogs on Fourth of July picnics, but a sweet-and-sour relish slaw, freckled with celery seeds. Use red cabbage along with the familiar green head. It makes a lovely accompaniment to the pork.

½ cup cider vinegar	*1 teaspoon caraway seeds*
½ cup sugar	*1 teaspoon celery seeds*
½ teaspoon turmeric	*1 ½ pounds cabbage,*
1 teaspoon salt	*shredded fine*
3 tablespoons salad oil	*1 small onion, grated*
3 tablespoons water	*1 large carrot, grated fine*
½ pound fresh green beans, cut	
into ½-inch lengths	

• Place vinegar, sugar, caraway seeds, celery seeds, turmeric, salt, salad oil, and water in saucepan. Cook 2 to 3 minutes over moderate heat until mixture boils and sugar dissolves. Remove from heat and let cool.

Cook beans in salted water about 5 minutes, until just barely tender. Drain and rinse under cool water.

Combine cabbage, onion, carrot, and beans. Add dressing and toss to mix. Cover tightly and refrigerate overnight.

Serves 8.

OLD-FASHIONED DEVIL'S FOOD CAKE

"*Cake*—this is a word to conjure with," says *Here Are the Cakes America Loves*, a Royal Baking Powder booklet of 1950. "Cake calls up memories of happy family dinners, gay holiday home-comings, children's parties fun of fun and laughter, old fashioned church suppers." What could be more intoxicatingly nostalgic than this black velvet devil's food beauty, its frosting swirled and sensuous, decorated in the center with one perfect red cherry.

Such a cake is a fitting end to Sunday dinner. Serve it on a pretty plate on a blue-and-white gingham tablecloth.

2½ cups cake flour	*1 cup granulated sugar*
½ cup cocoa	*1 cup firmly packed dark brown*
½ teaspoon baking soda	*sugar*
2 teaspoons baking powder	*3 eggs*
½ teaspoon salt	*½ cup light cream*
8 tablespoons butter	*⅔ cup sour cream*
2 teaspoons vanilla extract	

• Preheat oven to 350°. Butter and flour 3 8-inch cake pans.

Sift flour, measure, and sift again with cocoa, soda, and salt.

Cream butter; add vanilla and both sugars, beating well. Beat in eggs one at a time, until thoroughly mixed.

While beating slowly, add half of dry ingredients. Add light cream. Add remaining dry ingredients, then sour cream. Mix thoroughly.

Pour into prepared cake pans and bake 25 to 30 minutes, or until knife inserted in center comes out clean. Do not open oven while baking.

Cool in pans 5 minutes, then on rack. When completely cooled, frost layers with Chocolate Cream Frosting.

CHOCOLATE CREAM FROSTING

8 tablespoons butter	*3 egg whites*
⅛ teaspoon salt	*4 ounces unsweetened chocolate,*
1½ teaspoons Vanilla extract	*melted and cooled*
5 cups sifted confectioners' sugar	*3 to 4 tablespoons milk*

• Cream butter, salt, and vanilla together. Add sugar alternately with egg whites, beating well after each addition. Pour in melted chocolate and mix, gradually adding 3 tablespoons milk and beating until smooth and thick. Add more milk if necessary to achieve spreading consistency.

Spread on layers, top, and sides of triple-layer cake.

Front Porch Sunday Supper

Maggie's Coca-Cola Basted Ham ◆ *Country Pan-Fried Chicken*
◆ *Best Cook in Town Spoonbread* ◆ *Sliced Tomatoes* ◆
Watermelon Rind Pickles ◆ *Fresh Peach Shortcake*

MAGGIE'S COCA-COLA BASTED HAM

When Jane was ten years old, a housekeeper named Margaret came to work for her family. "Maggie" was a tiny black lady from Mobile, Alabama, four foot ten in her size two pumps, her bobbed hair topped by a straw hat ringed with cherries.

She was a fount of exotic culinary wisdom, spinning tales about biscuits so light they floated from the plate, sweet peaches from her father's tree, speckled eggs still warm from the nest, and honey stolen from the hive. But no tall tale was as wondrous—or as delicious—as the Coca-Cola ham that Maggie made.

As she explained it, this ham takes a full quart of Coke, half for the basting, and half to drink as the ham turns a spectrum of hues from tender pink to glistening mahogany.

*1 10-pound precooked (not cured
  or canned) ham
6 cups Coca-Cola
1 cup dark brown sugar*

*1 tablespoon dry mustard
2 tablespoons prepared
  sharp mustard
2 cups fine dry bread crumbs*

• Preheat oven to 325°.

Place ham fat side down in a shallow pan. Pour Coke into pan to ½ inch deep. Bake 2 to 3 hours, or until ham can be easily pierced with a fork, basting with Coca-Cola every 15 to 20 minutes. (Center of ham will read 140° on a meat thermometer when properly cooked.)

Remove ham from pan and cool. Cut away rind and fat with a sharp knife. Combine sugar, mustards, bread crumbs, and enough Coke to form a thick paste. Place ham on roasting rack in pan and pat all over with paste. Add remaining Coke to bottom of pan.

With oven increased to 375°, bake 45 minutes longer, basting every 10 to 15 minutes, until sugar-mustard paste has melted into a dark glaze. Let stand at room temperature 30 minutes before slicing.

Serves 12 to 15.

COUNTRY PAN-FRIED CHICKEN

Maggie waxed grandiloquent when telling tales of the Sunday supper bounty her family enjoyed down in Mobile. Tables groaned, belts and girdles were loosened, and the feast continued through the day. It wasn't until we traveled South ourselves that we realized she was no embroiderer. Southerners love to eat, and Sunday supper is a time to wallow in abundance. It is not at all unusual for the ham to be accompanied by platters of pan-fried chicken.

3 pounds chicken breasts	*½ teaspoon cayenne pepper*
and legs	*1 teaspoon black pepper*
1 egg	*Brown paper bags*
⅔ cup buttermilk	*1 cup lard*
3 cups all-purpose flour	*1 cup Fluffo shortening*

• Let chicken warm to room temperature. Wipe with damp cloth.

In a wide bowl, beat egg with buttermilk. Place flour and peppers in a brown paper bag.

In a large skillet (preferably cast-iron) heat lard and shortening. (Any shortening will produce equal results, but Fluffo gives the chicken a yellow hue that is the Southern preference.)

Dip each piece of chicken in buttermilk-egg mixture and place in brown paper bag. Close top of bag and shake until piece is well coated. Remove, and repeat for each piece.

When shortening is hot (375°), ease chicken into pan and cook over high heat, turning so both sides cook evenly. Do not crowd more than a few pieces of chicken in pan at one time. When chicken is light golden on both sides, turn down heat to low and partially cover skillet. Cook 15 minutes, turning chicken once.

Remove chicken and drain on brown paper bags. Serve warm or cool.

Serves 6 to 8.

BEST COOK IN TOWN SPOONBREAD

Spoonbread is the best possible thing to eat with ham or chicken or both. If you have never had it, you may be surprised to learn it is not bread at all. It is a countrified soufflé, a creamy puff of fine white cornmeal mixed with egg whites and cream. Like any soufflé, it has to be timed precisely. Once it is out of the oven, serve it right away with a dollop of honey on the side.

1¼ *cups light cream*	*3 tablespoons butter*
½ *cup white cornmeal*	*3 eggs, separated*
½ *teaspoon salt*	

• Preheat oven to 375°.

Heat cream in a deep saucepan. When hot—but not boiling—slowly pour in cornmeal, stirring constantly, and cook over very low heat until very smooth. *Do not boil.* Add salt and butter; mix well.

Remove from heat. Add each egg yolk separately, beating well after each addition.

Beat egg whites until stiff. Slowly and gently add egg whites to cornmeal mixture, folding together without deflating whites.

Pour mixture into a buttered 1-quart casserole or 4-cup soufflé dish. Smooth top.

Bake 30 minutes, or until golden brown. Serve at once from soufflé dish with a large spoon.

Serves 4.

WATERMELON RIND PICKLES

We usually stock up on watermelon pickles at roadside stands and country fairs. It's a bit of trouble to make them at home—three days of soaking and waiting and boiling—but there is no better way to get in the spirit of a real old-fashioned Southern porch supper. This zesty recipe is Grace Hartley's, from Atlanta, printed in a 1952 edition of *Favorite Regional Recipes of America.*

2 quarts watermelon rind	*1 quart vinegar*
2 quarts limewater (1 tablespoon	*1 tablespoon allspice*
slaked lime per 1 quart water)	*1 tablespoon whole cloves*
or saltwater (4 tablespoons	*1 stick cinnamon*
salt to 1 quart water)	*2 tablespoons chopped gingerroot*
4 to 6 cups sugar	

• Trim flesh from large pieces of thick, firm watermelon rind. Soak in limewater 4 hours, or overnight in saltwater. Limewater makes a crisper pickle.

Drain, rinse, cover with fresh water, and boil 1½ hours. Cool, then cut into small pieces. Trim off green skins.

Boil 2 cups sugar, 1 quart fresh water, 1 cup vinegar, and spices for 5 minutes. Add rind. Simmer 30 minutes.

Let stand overnight.

Add remaining sugar and vinegar, and boil gently about 1 hour until syrup is thick and rind is clear. Add boiling water if syrup becomes too thick before rind is translucent.

If not serving right away, pack into sterile jars. Seal at once.

Makes 4 to 5 pints.

FRESH PEACH SHORTCAKE

New Englanders, who figure that fruit and whipped cream are frivolous enough, take their shortcake sugarless, like a biscuit. But down in Dixie, where lilies are always sweetly gilded, the recipes are gay and saucy—like this charmer of a peach shortcake. It *looks* homemade, a sort of rough layer cake, split and heaped generously with fresh peaches and cream.

The recipe is from *What Shall I Cook Today?,* a Spry brochure published in the 1930s that promises guests will rave if you cook with Spry. In fact, an illustration shows two dapper gentlemen in the process of raving:

"Say, you should taste my wife's pie. It's a dream!"

"So is my wife's! She's using Spry, too!"

SHORTCAKE

3 cups sifted all-purpose flour	*¾ cup Spry shortening*
4½ teaspoons baking powder	*¾ to 1 cup milk*
3 tablespoons sugar	*1 egg, beaten*
1½ teaspoons salt	

• Preheat oven to 450°.

Grease a 9-inch layer pan with Spry.

Sift dry ingredients together. Cut Spry in by hand or with a food processor (using the metal blade). Add milk and egg and blend or knead until well blended. Put into greased pan.

Bake 30 minutes.

Remove from oven and turn out onto wire rack to cool. When cool, cut in half (horizontally) with a serrated knife,

FILLING

8 fresh ripe peaches   *Whipped cream*
⅓ cup sugar

• Peel and section peaches. Sprinkle with sugar.

Cover bottom layer of shortcake with half the peaches. Top with second layer and remaining peaches. Serve topped with whipped cream.

Serves 6 to 8.

Mother's Sunday Dinner

Mom's Best Pot Roast ♦ Gravy ♦ Perfect Mashed Potatoes ♦ Minted Carrots and Peas ♦ Anadama Bread ♦ Deep Dish Apple Pie

MOM'S BEST POT ROAST

There isn't a food in creation cornier or dowdier than pot roast. It's a mother's dish, and every mother does it a little bit dfferently. Moms whose culinary expertise peaked in the 1950s cannot make a pot roast without reaching for the Lipton's Onion Soup Mix; ethnic moms go heavy on the tomato sauce, or the beer, or garlic.

But there is one goal all moms share. A good pot roast must emerge from the stove (or from atop it) a deep, glistening russet brown. It should be fall-apart tender, cooked long enough so that all the meat's resistance has been overcome and the vegetables used to enhance the juice have surrendered their sweetness.

This recipe, which turns out a dark roast crowned with soft caramelized vegetables, borrows from a few moms. There will be enough pan juice to use as the base for gravy to ladle atop the accompanying mashed potatoes. It has a long-simmered flavor that makes it even better reheated, the next day.

½ tablespoon salt	*3 large carrots, sectioned into*
½ tablespoon pepper	*2-inch pieces and halved*
4 pounds center-cut	*6 ounces fresh green beans,*
chuck steak	*trimmed to 1-inch pieces*
3 tablespoons all-purpose flour	*1 16-ounce can*
1 medium onion, chopped	*stewed tomatoes*
1 clove garlic, minced	*1 bay leaf*
3 tablespoons shortening	*2 tablespoons Kitchen Bouquet*
1 cup boiling water	

• Salt and pepper meat and rub with flour. In a heavy roasting pan or skillet, sauté onion and garlic in shortening until translucent but not browned. Add meat and brown on both sides. This will take about 15 minutes. Add boiling water, carrots, beans, tomatoes, bay leaf, Kitchen Bouquet, and additional salt and pepper if desired.

Cook on top of stove over low heat, tightly covered with aluminum foil. Cook 20 minutes, unwrap foil, baste, and reseal. Continue slow cooking and basting every 15 minutes, turning meat over once during cooking. (This will be difficult as the meat becomes more tender. Use two spatulas, making sure you scrape all the caramelized bits of onion and garlic from the bottom of the pan. You may also need to add water when you baste to keep meat moist.) Cook 2½ to 3 hours, until meat is fall-apart tender.

Remove meat from roasting pan with vegetables, but leave drippings in pan to make gravy. Discard bay leaf.

POT ROAST GRAVY

Pot roast gravy is made by adding 4 to 6 tablespoons of flour, bit by bit, to the drippings in the roasting pan, stirring as you add. When the flour is browned, add 1 to 2 cups boiling water, and salt and pepper to taste. Stir over low heat until slightly thickened. Serve over roast and mashed potatoes.

PERFECT MASHED POTATOES

Mashed potato lovers divide into pro-lump and anti-lump people. Pro-lumpers view the little nubs of unmashed potato in the same light as the small flaws that Renaissance artists consciously put into their masterpieces—symbols of humility, a nod to the imperfection of man's handiwork.

To the anti-lumpers, any such imperfection is a red flag that the potatoes have been made by a slattern, a slugabed with no respect for domestic science.

We admit that we are pro-lump. Too-smooth potatoes remind us of giant noisy kitchen appliances, whereas lumps conjure up the rickety-rack of a spoon hitting the side of a bowl.

You can make this recipe lumpy or smooth.

2 pounds all-purpose potatoes, peeled and halved	*¼ cup heavy cream*
½ cup milk	*3 tablespoons butter*
	Salt to taste

• Boil potatoes in rapidly boiling salted water until tender enough to be pierced easily with a fork. Discard water and return potatoes momentarily to cooking pot. Turn on heat and let any moisture in potatoes evaporate.

Remove potatoes from heat and transfer to mixing bowl. With a handheld mixer, potato masher, heavy wire whisk, or wooden spoon, mash the potatoes well. Stop mashing sooner if you like them lumpy, later if you like them smooth.

Combine milk and cream, and warm. Pour in a slow stream into potatoes, while you continue to mash. Add butter and salt to taste, and combine until well blended. Serve immediately with gravy.

Serves 4 to 6.

MINTED CARROTS AND PEAS

12 ounces frozen or fresh peas	*2 tablespoons butter*
3 carrots, peeled and cut into	*½ cup chopped fresh mint*
½-inch disks	*Salt and pepper to taste*

• Toss peas into boiling water and cook until just tender. Splash with cold water to stop cooking. Boil carrots until tender, drain, and place with peas in saucepan. Add butter, and stir gently until vegetables are lightly coated. Combine with mint, salt, and pepper, and stir until mint leaves are tender.

Serves 4 to 6.

ANADAMA BREAD

The reason we recommend Anadama Bread with this dinner is that it is the perfect choice for pot roast sandwiches the next day. The bread is alleged to have gotten its name when an irate husband cursed his wife, "Anna—damn her!" Here, obviously, was a man with a problem, and without a Sunday dinner.

This recipe yields two endearingly old-fashioned loaves of hearty, grainy bread that is delicious warm from the oven, slathered with sweet butter.

½ cup yellow cornmeal	*½ cup molasses*
2½ cups water	*1 package dry yeast*
1 teaspoon salt	*1 teaspoon sugar*
3 tablespoons butter	*5 cups all-purpose flour*

• Mix cornmeal into 1 cup water. Bring a second cup water to a rolling boil. Pour cornmeal mixture into boiling water; return to boil. Reduce heat, and continue cooking and stirring until mixture is very thick—5 to 8 minutes. Add salt, butter, and molasses. Remove from heat. Cool to tepid.

Dissolve yeast and sugar in ½ cup warm (110°) water. Let stand 5 to 10 minutes, then add yeast to tepid cornmeal mixture. Gradually stir in enough flour to make a stiff dough—about 5 cups.

Knead for 10 full minutes. Place dough in buttered bowl, cover, and let rise in a warm place until doubled in size, 1 to 2 hours.

Preheat oven to 400°.

Punch down dough and divide into two pieces. Shape each piece into a loaf, and put into well-buttered 8-inch bread pan. Cover pans and let rise in warm place until doubled again, about 30 minutes.

Bake 20 minutes. Reduce heat to 350°, bake 30 to 40 minutes longer, or until loaves sound hollow when slid from pans and tapped on the bottom.

Remove bread from pans and bake directly on rack of oven 5 minutes, then cool.

Makes 2 loaves.

DEEP DISH APPLE PIE

> "But Aunt Jenny, I'm scared stiff of pastry making! And Jack's boss is coming to dinner. Gee, I wish I could make pie like you do."
>
> "Helen, I'll show you how easy a pie can be with my *can't fail method*. Just follow my pointers, and you'll get topnotch pastry every time."
>
> *That afternoon:* "Each step's so easy! From now on I'll give my husband home-made pies often."
>
> *Later that night:* "What a swell pie, hon. And did you see how the boss praised your cooking!"

Another meal, another job, another marriage saved by Aunt Jenny! This lovely lady was the young homemaker's fictional friend from Lever Brothers; her job in fife was to enlighten the innocent about Spry shortening. Unlike Betty Crocker, who at the time was quite svelte, Jenny was a cushiony old thing, like Uncle Ben if he had been white and female.

Aunt Jenny's 1949 book, *Enjoy Good Eating Every Day,* intersperses recipes for pies and cakes with turgid household melodramas in which nervous wives learn the secrets of winning compliments from husbands, in-laws, bosses, and even children. ("Shortcake for me, mom!" . . . "Man, you should taste my wife's French fries!" . . . "Why, Helen, Jack didn't tell us you were such an expert cook.")

From the gleaming white Spry kitchens ("set off by vibrant color accents of aquamarine and maroon"), where a staff of trained home economists test and retest recipes with scientific precision, comes Aunt Jenny's best recipe for deep dish apple pie. "So digestible you can eat all you want!"

PIE SHELL (for a top crust only—this pie is bottomless; for a two-crust pie, double measurements)

1¼ cups sifted all-purpose flour	*½ cup Spry shortening*
½ teaspoon salt	*2½ tablespoons ice-cold water*

• Mix flour and salt. Cut in two-thirds of the Spry, using a food processor or by hand, until mixture is as fine as meal. Cut in remaining Spry to size of large peas. Do not overmix.

Sprinkle water over mixture. Mix thoroughly with food processor or fork just until all particles cling together in a dough. Take up in hands and shape into smooth ball. Chill 30 minutes.

Remove dough from refrigerator and place on floured board. Roll into rectangle 10 by 6 inches, ⅛ inch thick, or large enough to cover baking dish.

Preheat oven to 425°.

PIE

6 cups pared and cored thin apple slices	*2 tablespoons all-purpose flour*
	¼ teaspoon nutmeg
⅔ cup granulated sugar	*½ teaspoon cinnamon*
⅓ cup brown sugar	*1 teaspoon lemon juice*
½ teaspoon salt	*2 tablespoons butter*

• Mix apples with sugars, salt, flour, nutmeg, cinnamon, and lemon juice. Place in 10-by-6-inch baking dish and dot with butter. Lay prepared dough over dish, and cut a few decorative openings in rectangle of dough for steam to escape. Turn under edge, flute rim.

Bake 45 to 55 minutes. Serve with ice cream or light cream.

Serves 6.

Prosperity Sunday Dinner

Roast Chicken with Peacemaker Herb and Fruit Stuffing ◆ Spinach Timbales with Cheese and Horseradish Sauce ◆ Perfection Salad ◆ Cloverleaf Rolls ◆ Squash Pie with Maple Cream Topping

ROAST CHICKEN WITH PEACEMAKER HERB AND FRUIT STUFFING

Turkeys and geese mean Thanksgiving and Christmas; but a chicken is a chicken. Bubbling in a pot or cooking slowly in a gentle oven, it stands for home and hearth and family dinner more than any other food.

"It isn't easy to say what makes the difference between good cooking and just plain all-right cooking," Sara and Aggie say in their *Party Line Cook Book,* and that is especially true of roast chicken. "Sometimes I think it's butter," Sara suggests, which certainly helps this chicken; but the big difference is more in the stuffing.

For years we battled over stuffing. One of us liked corn bread, fruit, and a generous jigger of brandy. The other insisted on a stuffy New England mélange of white toast, herbs, and nuts. It was stalemate, each of us so immovable that the only possible choices were Stove Top or marriage counseling. The stuffing crisis was resolved one Sunday when we roasted two chickens, each stuffed with our best, and let the dinner guests decide.

To our horror, the corn bread stuffing was declared too fruity; the white bread too prim. "I have an idea," announced one friend never known for kitchen expertise. "Let's lump them together and see what we get."

From that day we have lived happily ever after, with a perfect stuffing recipe, this cornucopian compromise:

THE BIRD

1 roasting chicken   *Butter*
   (4 to 6 pounds)   *Salt and pepper*
1 lemon

THE STUFFING

Giblets from chicken   *½ tablespoon ground rosemary*
¾ cup chopped onion   *¼ cup diced apple*
8 tablespoons butter   *¼ cup diced dried apricot*
½ cup chopped celery   *¼ cup diced fresh kumquat or*
1 clove garlic, minced fine   *   grapefruit wedges*
2 cups day-old toast cut in   *½ cup chopped pecans*
*   ½-inch cubes, or store-bought*   *1 tablespoon Worcestershire*
*   white bread stuffing mix*   *   sauce*
1 cup crumbled corn bread   *3 tablespoons brandy*
1 teaspoon salt   *3 tablespoons dry vermouth*
½ tablespoon ground sage

• Remove and reserve giblets from chicken. Clean chicken with a damp cloth, inside and out. Pat dry and squeeze juice of a lemon inside roasting cavity. Butter inside of bird and sprinkle with salt and pepper. Refrigerate while you make stuffing.

Place giblets in saucepan, cover with water, and bring to simmering boil. Cook until done. Dice giblets. Reserve stock.

Sauté chopped onion in butter; add celery and garlic. Cook until onion is transparent but not brown.

Place all other ingredients in a large mixing bowl. Pour onion mixture over, and gently blend together. Add diced giblets, and mix again. If mixture seems dry, slowly add just enough giblet stock to dampen, but don't let stuffing become soupy.

Preheat oven to 325°.

Stuff neck and belly of bird, but don't pack it in—stuffing expands. You can truss the cavity for beauty's sake, but it isn't necessary. (If you are cooking a small bird, you will have leftover stuffing. Place it in a small pan, cover pan with foil, and bake with chicken.) Rub exterior of bird with butter and an extra dash of rosemary or sage.

Place chicken on roasting rack in oven. Roast 20 minutes per pound, basting frequently with pan juices.

When chicken is fully cooked, allow it to sit for 10 minutes loosely covered with foil before serving.

> The carving will of course be done at the table, and the homemaker will do well to see that the carver does not give all the choicest pieces to the rest of the family while keeping the least attractive scraps for himself. Not infrequently, fathers are quite as unselfish as mothers!
>
> —"The Family Dinner," from *The Art of Cooking and Serving,* by Sarah Field Splint, 1926

SPINACH TIMBALES WITH CHEESE AND HORSERADISH SAUCE

One of our favorite books is called *Balanced Recipes,* published in 1933 by Pillsbury's "home-type experimental kitchen, maintained entirely for service to the women of America." What we love is the book itself—bound in metal like a small refrigerator, illustrated with a photo of earnest white-uniformed home economists stirring and measuring and taking notes, "constantly developing new recipes, new ways to improve the flavor of food and the value of meals." One such recipe combines old-fashioned spinach timbales with a horseradish cream sauce.

2 pounds fresh spinach, or 2
   8-ounce packages frozen
   chopped spinach
4 tablespoons butter
2 tablespoons finely
   chopped onion
Salt and pepper to taste

1½ cups light cream
4 eggs, beaten
½ cup grated mild
   Cheddar cheese
½ cup heavy cream
3 tablespoons
   prepared horseradish

• Wash spinach and remove stems. Boil 5 minutes or until tender.

Melt butter in saucepan, and cook onion in butter until soft, Stir in cooked spinach, and when spinach has been coated with butter, add salt, pepper, cream, and beaten eggs. Mix well. Add grated cheese; mix again.

Preheat oven to 325°.

Boil a pot of water. Butter eight ½-cup timbale molds (or one large 4-cup) mold). Pour spinach mixture into molds, and arrange molds in a large pan. Pour boiling water into pan, high enough so that water reaches halfway up the sides of the molds.

Bake 20 to 30 minutes, or until cake tester inserted in spinach comes out clean.

While spinach cooks, whip cream until stiff. Fold in horseradish.

Unmold timbales and dollop with horseradish cream.

Serves 8.

PERFECTION SALAD

Mrs. John Cooke of Pennsylvania won third prize (a new sewing machine) for her entry of Perfection Salad in a 1905 Knox gelatin cooking contest. Since then, homemakers all over America have invented thousands of regional and personal variations of the cabbage and gelatin theme. In the 1960s radio cook Mike Roy traced this vivid version back to his North Dakota church-social days:

1 package unflavored gelatin	*½ cup chopped celery*
¼ cup sugar	*¼ cup chopped green pepper*
½ teaspoon salt	*¼ cup chopped pimiento*
¾ cup cold water	*1 cup small carrots, cut into thin*
¾ cup boiling water	*disks and cooked*
¼ cup lemon juice	*French dressing*
3 stuffed olives, sliced	*Ripe olives*
1 cup shredded cabbage	

• Blend gelatin, sugar, and, salt. Add ¼ cup cold water and let stand until gelatin softens. Add boiling water, stir until gelatin dissolves. Stir in remaining cold water and lemon juice; cool.

Place stuffed olives in an even design on bottom of a 3½-cup ring mold. Add cabbage, celery, green pepper, and pimiento to gelatin, and turn into mold. Chill until set.

Unmold, fill center with carrots marinated in French dressing. Garnish with ripe olives.

Serves 4 to 6.

CLOVERLEAF ROLLS

"It is possible to liven the plainest sort of meal by the addition of homemade rolls," Ida Bailey Allen notes, in *Mrs. Allen on Cooking*.

There is something especially out of date—and irresistibly delicious—about cloverleaf rolls, those buttery bread triplets that complement any good dinner, but especially on Sunday.

1 package dry yeast dissolved in	*1 tablespoon sugar*
¼ cup tepid water (110°) with	*3 to 3½ cups all-purpose flour*
1 teaspoon sugar	*1 teaspoon salt*
1 cup light cream	*Melted butter*
3 tablespoons butter	

• Scald cream but do not boil. Add butter and 1 tablespoon sugar to cream, stirring until butter melts.

Sift 3 cups flour and salt into a large bowl. Add yeast and cream mixtures. Stir to create a sticky dough. Turn out on floured board and knead 10 minutes, adding more flour if necessary to create a smooth dough. Clean bowl, butter sides, put dough in it, and cover. Set in warm place until double in bulk, 1½ to 2 hours.

Punch down dough, knead it 1 minute into a ball. Let it rest, covered with a cloth, 10 to 15 minutes.

Butter 20 muffin pans or cups, (If you don't have enough, you will have to do this in stages. If so, keep the risen dough covered and cool.) Pinch off 1-inch balls of dough, roll round, and press 3 into each muffin cup so that cups are crowded, but not full. Cover muffin pans and let dough rise 30 minutes. It ought to reach tops of cups.

Preheat oven to 400°.

Brush tops of rolls with melted butter, put in oven, and spray water inside oven with a plant atomizer. Bake 15 to 20 minutes, or until light brown. Humidify oven twice more with atomizer, after 5 minutes and after 10 minutes.

Remove rolls from pans to wire rack immediately when done. Serve warm.

Makes 15 to 20 rolls.

SQUASH PIE WITH MAPLE CREAM TOPPING

Squash pie was suggested to *Favorite Regional Recipes of America* in 1952 by the Extension Service Nutritionist at the University of Connecticut. It is a fanciful twist on traditional New England pumpkin pie, crowned with a cloud of maple-sweetened whipped cream. Use 100 percent pure maple syrup and this pie will sing.

SQUASH PIE

1 unbaked piecrust, homemade or
frozen (but thawed)
3 eggs, well beaten
¾ cup brown sugar
1 teaspoon salt
½ teaspoon cinnamon

½ teaspoon nutmeg
½ teaspoon ground ginger
2 cups light cream, scalded
2 cups cooked, strained
yellow squash

• Preheat oven to 450°.

Line 9-inch pie pan with pastry. Make a fluted standing rim.

Combine eggs, sugar, salt, and spices. Gradually stir in hot cream, then add strained squash. Mix, and pour into pastry-lined pan.

Bake 10 minutes, then reduce heat to 325° and continue baking 30 minutes more, or until firm.

Cool pie. Just before serving, cover with Maple Cream Topping.

Serves 6 to 8.

MAPLE CREAM TOPPING

1 cup heavy cream

¼ cup maple syrup

• Whip cream until stiff. Pour maple syrup in a fine stream over cream, folding it in carefully. Cover surface of pie with topping, swirling to give an attractive appearance.

NURSERY
FOOD

How nice it is, in a world filled with mean, scary people like landlords, motor vehicle bureau personnel, and headwaiters, to set aside time for milk and cookies.

Everybody has some special food that makes them feel taken care of, a culinary escape from danger: noodles and pot cheese, Mom's chicken soup, rice pudding with raisins, or a tall glass of chocolate milk with vanilla wafers on the side.

Nursery food is the supreme comfort. No wonder, because however abysmal it really was, childhood looks so appealing the farther away it gets. You remember warm farina served in a bowl decorated with dancing bunnies, or the ritual cup of cocoa after school. Compared to grown-up worries like earning a living, developing a double chin, or thermonuclear war, the childhood horror of spilling grape juice doesn't seem all that awful.

In fact, one of the great things about being an adult is that grape juice drinking isn't confined by house rules to the tile-floored kitchen. You can now gulp it with impunity while gallivanting about the white living room rug.

As an adult, you've got a little cash, too, and the fabulous, unattainable rich man's foods of childhood—pecan candy turtles, chocolate-covered cherries, and gold foil-wrapped truffles—are yours on a whim. You can mash every chocolate in the box to find just the center you want; you can eat the white stuff in the Oreos and cavalierly throw the chocolate disks away; you can put five spoonfuls of Bosco in your milk, and no one will cut off your allowance for the crime.

It's great being grown up! Just so long as you don't have to eat ghastly grown-up food like fish with their heads on or pâtés made of nameless entrails and viscera.

We contend that the more emotionally evolved a person is, the higher his required intake of baby food. Not exactly pablum and gruel, but *nice* food that takes the edge off a not-so-nice world—like pudding and Horlick's malted milk powder.

Most people eat their nursery food in small moments eked out of a busy schedule—after midnight, or when dinner guests cancel and you breathe a long sigh of relief. But sometimes life is too tough to wait for one of those accidental moments to find comfort. When you've had an especially difficult day or week, a bowl of Kadota figs in heavy cream is not enough. You need to make plans, set aside a block of time, take the phone off the hook, and arrange a full-scale nursery supper.

The Nursery Supper

Gentle Noodles

Toast and Cereal

Nursery Snacks: Bananas and Prunes

Primary Puddings

What Nice Children Drink

The Nursery Supper

At nursery supper, you are allowed to talk to yourself in silly voices, cavort higgledy-piggledy in front of the mirror, and eat with your hands, or holding the spoon in an infantile fist. You can gurgle through a straw and make funny shapes with your mashed potatoes.

Any day can be nursery day, but we have always been partial to drizzly winter afternoons, when the sky is the color of a muddy elephant's skin, when steam hisses from the radiator and the house smells of Ivory soap and pressed sheets, when cat and dog are sleeping intertwined and breathing gently in sync.

The time for nursery supper is 5:00 P.M., so you can eat and be in bed by 7:00. One does not eat nursery food in front of the TV watching the 6 o'clock news, nor in a candlelit dining room.

For the full, comforting effect, everything must be correctly choreographed.

First, take a bath. A bath, not a shower. Showers are for grown-ups, as are scratchy loofah cloths and exotic bath oils. Ivory soap's the ticket; or maybe juvenile-scented bubble bath. When your fingertips have shriveled like prunes, you are clean enough to get dressed in fresh pajamas. Pajamas with feet are preferred, but slippers are acceptable. Only hooligans run around the house barefoot.

Since people clad in bathrobes do not dine at a formal table, set a place for yourself in the kitchen, or on a small tray with legs. This is not the time to bring out lucite place mats or all-black art deco china. You want small plates and mugs, pale ivory china patterned with tiny chicks and bunnikins. Only an ogre would serve Paddington Bear on Fritz and Floyd dinnerware. Likewise, candles are out, as are light dimmers or even vaguely romantic music.

Nursery food is customarily solitary fare for adults; the nursery gourmet is both nanny and child. It is, however, possible to share this very private pleasure; to do so is the most intimate, yet most asexual of dining experiences.

Alone or with a dear close friend, cozy is the word. Every effort must be made to induce snuggliness. Here is a menu that cannot fail to ease even the grumpiest crosspatch into a nursery mood:

Rinktum Tiddy on Toast Snippets ◆ *Warm Applesauce* ◆
Mary Jane's Rice Pudding with Cream ◆ *Cambric Tea*

RINKTUM TIDDY ON TOAST SNIPPETS

From *Good Housekeeping's Book of Menus, Recipes, and Household Discoveries,* published in 1942. Rinktum Tiddy is an aleless Welsh rabbit, with a blush of tomatoes, suitable for children or upset adults. It is suggested that each slice of toast be cut into small pieces, and then rearranged neatly to resemble an uncut piece of toast. "Then the toast is very easily eaten by the child or invalid."

1 35-ounce can tomatoes, drained (about 2 cups)	½ pound mild Cheddar cheese, cut into bits
1 teaspoon salt	1 tablespoon butter
1 teaspoon sugar	1 egg, beaten
⅛ teaspoon pepper	Hot buttered toast (4 to 6 slices)
1 tablespoon chopped onion	

• Chop tomatoes coarsely, then heat in saucepan; add seasonings and onion. When hot, melt in cheese over low heat, stirring constantly. When smooth, add butter, then egg, stirring well. Pour over toast.

Serves 2.

WARM APPLESAUCE

8 tart apples	Dash cinnamon or nutmeg
¾ cup water	1 tablespoon lemon juice
½ to ¾ cup sugar, depending on desired sweetness	

• Pare and core apples. Slice thin. Put in sauceepan, add just enough water to cover, and bring to boil. Lower heat to simmer, cover, and cook for 20 minutes, or until apples are soft.

Drain apples well and put through food mill, or process in blender or food processor. Add sugar, spice, and lemon juice. Blend again,

Serves 4.

MARY JANE'S RICE PUDDING WITH CREAM

If you are feeling especially tantrum-prone, a bowl of rice pudding, swimming in cream and dotted with raisins, is the best medicine. This fact comes on the authority of A. A. Milne, who knew the ins and outs of nursery life better than anyone else:

What's the matter with Mary Jane?
It's lovely rice pudding for dinner again!

The answer is that Mary Jane was too young to appreciate her meal. Wait until she grows up and gets a notice from the IRS to appear for a tax audit. She'll head right to the stove and start stirring:

1 cup long-grain rice
2 cups water
1 teaspoon salt
¾ cup sugar
3 cups milk
½ cup raisins
3 egg yolks

1 cup cream, light or heavy
depending on how rich you
want pudding
2 teaspoons vanilla extract
Nutmeg or cinnamon
1 cup heavy cream

• Combine rice, water, and salt in saucepan and simmer 3 minutes. Add sugar and milk and bring to slow simmer over low heat, stirring occasionally. Cook, uncovered, 30 minutes, or until milk is absorbed. Cool.

Soak raisins in water until they plump.

Preheat oven to 300°. Butter a 1½-quart baking dish.

Whisk egg yolks with cream and vanilla. Combine with cooled rice and mix well. Drain raisins, and mix with rice. Turn into baking dish and sprinkle with nutmeg or cinnamon. Bake, uncovered, until set at edges, but still creamy inside (about 25 minutes).

Gently heat 1 cup heavy cream until lukewarm, and pour on top.

Serves 4 to 6.

CAMBRIC TEA

"Neither tea nor coffee is food," advised *Lessons in Cookery—Diet for Children* in 1919. "Both take away appetite and hinder growth." Yet, the *frisson* of nursery supper comes largely from the knowledge that you are mimicking the meals adults eat. And so our meal concludes with cambric tea, a childish beverage that is warming and cozy, with all the reassuring, soporific qualities of warm milk plus the thrill of knowing it is spiked with grown-up tea.

When supper's through, take your cup of cambric tea to bed, climb between freshly ironed white sheets, pull up a pile of mismatched quilts, and drift off to an untroubled sleep that few people past the age of ten ever know.

1 cup milk   *1 tablespoon sugar*
1 tablespoon brewed tea

• Scald milk, add tea and sugar. Pour into small mug that has been prewarmed with a splash of hot water.

For Cinnamon Cambric Tea, sprinkle a generous shower of cinnamon atop the warm milk.

Gentle Noodles

Noodles are soul food for sensitives, tranquillity in a bowl. We are not—let us make this clear—talking about *pasta,* with odoriferous garlic or weird green olive oil or sneezy clouds of pepper or even acidy tomato sauce. We are talking *noodles,* egg noodles, little velvet ribbonlets of sunny yellow, glistening with butter. Seminal nursery food.

All you have to do is cook the noodles until they are soft, drain them, and add plenty of sweet butter. Delicious . . . and good for you, according to Mrs. C. F. Leyel, who, in her 1936 book *Diet for Children,* informed her readers that "a good deal of butter is necessary for children with tendencies to colds and complaints."

For extra luxury, mix the just-cooked, buttered noodles with pot cheese or cottage cheese. You may want to use other cheeses, and that's fine; but remember, as you veer away from cottage and Velveeta toward gamy goat or stinging Cheddar: smelly, rank cheese, however delicious it may be at other times and for other purposes, hardly qualifies as nursery pap.

On a cold day, stir a dollop of sweet butter into the noodles, add pot or ricotta cheese, then top the bowl with a shower of cinnamon-sugar and poppy seeds. "Cinnamon and sugar are always wholesome accompaniments to butter," Mrs. Leyel advised.

There is no easier dish to cook than noodles and cheese, and if that is your idea of heaven, allow us to suggest a luscious extension of the theme:

MRS. STERN'S NOODLE KUGEL

On those occasions when we are arguing, all Jane needs to do to win the fight is bake a batch of Michael's mother's noodle pudding. As it comes out of the oven, Michael loses all interest in whatever trivial point he was asserting and focuses exclusively on the browned and sometimes blackened bits of noodle all across the top of the pudding, on the amber raisins peeping up through the crust, on the soft, creamy underside, visible through the Pyrex glass. The important issue of the day, the crucial matter to resolve, becomes *Is there sour cream?*

Florence Stern's version of the classic Jewish specialty is dense and rich. It can accompany a main course, it can be dessert, or it can be everything—all of childhood's happy moments pressed into a block of noodles, with plenty of sour cream on the side.

1 pound cottage cheese

3 ounces cream
    cheese, softened

2 cups milk

3 eggs

Juice of one lemon

¾ cup sugar

1 teaspoon vanilla extract

½ pint sour cream

1 cup yellow muscat raisins

8 ounces medium egg noodles

Cinnamon

Sour cream as garnish

• Preheat oven to 325°.

Mix all ingredients except noodles, cinnamon, and garnish. Add noodles, *uncooked,* and pour into well-buttered 9-by-13-by-2-inch baking dish. Sprinkle top with cinnamon.

Bake 1 hour, or until top is light brown. Cut into squares and serve with sour cream.

Serves 8 to 10. (Leftover kugel is excellent cold.)

KRAFT DINNER

Kraft Dinner is one of our all-time favorite comfort foods; so much so that several years ago, when a rumor circulated that Kraft was about to discontinue its manufacture and make only "Deluxe Kraft Dinner" (with fancy orange cheese sauce in a can inside the box—a sorry substitute for the plain original), we panicked. The thought of life without macaroni and cheese à la Kraft was so intolerable that we became nursery survivalists. We raided every supermarket in town, buying case lots to hoard in our basement.

The rumor was false. Over the years, we slowly ate our way through the hundreds of dinners, and now our cupboard is never without a couple, ready to go. Understand that we seldom eat it, being *très* sophisticated and preferring, for everyday use, fine imported Italian pastas. But it's good to know the Kraft is there; and there are times—an occasional dreary March afternoon or the evening of a day when everything's gone wrong—when nothing else will satisfy.

Complete cooking instructions are on the Kraft Macaroni & Cheese Dinner box, but if you are an aficionado of the tall blue-and-white cardboard container with the itty-bitty macaroni and dried Cheese Sauce mix inside, you know that Kraft's directions merely hint at the possibilities. They say:

> Add macaroni and 1 teaspoon salt to 6 cups boiling water. Stir. Boil rapidly, stirring occasionally, 7 to 10 minutes or to desired tenderness. Drain. Add ¼ cup Parkay margarine, ¼ cup milk, and Cheese Sauce mix. Mix well. Makes 3 cups.

On the side of the box, among the nutritional information, you find that 3 cups is supposed to be 4 servings. Fat chance.

To begin with, the connoisseur uses butter, not margarine. A quarter cup is hardly enough. Up the butter to a third of a cup, minimum. And unless you want macaroni soup, you will reduce the milk to a few tablespoons—just enough to give the Cheese Sauce mix sufficient liquid to blend with.

Now, here comes the really good twist: *Double* Kraft Dinner. Buy two boxes; steal the Cheese Sauce mix from one box; go back to ¼ cup milk (keeping the butter up at ⅓ cup), then mix the cooked and buttered macaroni with *two full packets of Cheese Sauce mix.* The results are stupendous . . . but perhaps too heady for beginners. If you choose to go this route, start with a package and a half. Two big ones, and you are toying with noodle dynamite!

Finally, you might eke two *nouvelle cuisine*-size servings from a single box, but we always plan on one box per person per meal. That will always leave some noodles for the next day. Straight from the refrigerator, cold and hardened, leftover Kraft Dinner is the nursery epicure's choice for a difficult morning after.

CHICKEN NOODLE SOUP

Chicken soup is magic; but its miracle powers have no more to do with ingredients than a witch doctor's cure depends on the wing of a bat or the eye of a toad. The strength is all in what you *believe* the chicken soup can do.

To illustrate, we offer the true story of a girl who was comforted many times as a child by her grandmother's wonderful chicken soup. Grandma passed away, leaving no recipe behind. The girl assumed she would never again know the comfort of that golden broth with little chunks of chicken and fine, slivery noodles. One gloomy winter afternoon, the girl went visiting. "Would you like some chicken soup?" asked her friend. "Yes," said the girl, sadly remembering Grandmother, walking slowly from the kitchen with a big steamy bowl of soup, perfuming the air with its goodness.

The girl's friend brought out the chicken soup . . . and there was something unmistakably familiar about the smell! And the warm, sunny broth; and the bits of chicken; and the silky inch-long noodles. No doubt about it—it was Grandma's soup!

"But where did you get the recipe?" asked the astonished girl, dipping in for a full, happy spoonful.

And the friend took the girl back to the kitchen to show her that there was no recipe at all. The soup, the wonderful, warming magic potion that Grandma made, was Lipton's Chicken Noodle.

Here is *our* family recipe for plain and warming Chicken Noodle Soup:

2 pounds chicken parts (breasts, back, legs, wings)

1 large onion, chopped

3 large carrots, peeled and cut into 2-inch segments, then halved

3 stalks celery, without leaves, cut into 2-inch segments

1 bay leaf

1 teaspoon pepper

1 teaspoon thyme

¼ teaspoon nutmeg

3 chicken bouillon cubes

½ cup chopped parsley

Salt to taste

2 cups egg noodles (fine or medium)

• Rinse chicken parts; quarter breasts. Place in large, uncovered stockpot with 12 cups cold water. Bring to rolling boil, reduce heat, and allow to simmer for 30 minutes, skimming off scum that rises to the surface. Add all other ingredients except noodles. Place lid on pot and cook over low heat 3 to 4 hours.

Remove from heat, and when cool enough to handle, remove chicken parts. Pick all meat from bones, discard skin, and return only meat to pot.

Refrigerate overnight.

Next day, carefully skim off all fat that has congealed on surface of soup. Bring to a boil and add noodles. Boil 10 minutes, or until noodles are tender. Discard bay leaf. Serve at once.

Serves 6 to 8.

Toast and Cereal

Bread is the staff of life, but that isn't why toast is primary nursery food. Children—and adults in need of comfort—enjoy toast because it is easy to make and easy to eat. And it's fun: cinnamon toast, toast with jelly, even deluxe recipes like French or milk toast are more like playing with food than serious cooking. And as for eating, there's no need for utensils, except with milk toast; but milk toast is extra fun, because you can pretend you are ill.

The one very adult obstacle to toast revelry is getting the right bread. Soft, spongy loaves of white bread tear under the jelly knife and fall to pieces if soaked too long in warm cream. Of course, tough hard-crusted French bread is utterly unacceptable, not to mention barbarian dark breads.

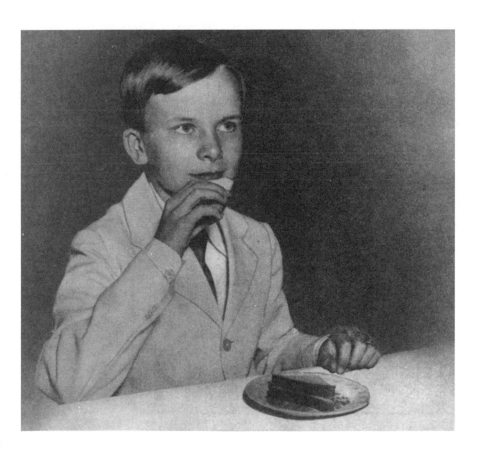

We have found that of all the brands available in the market, Pepperidge Farm Toasting White is best. It's dense and sturdy, and it tastes good. Better than that, though, is to bake your own. We don't pretend otherwise: bread baking is adult cooking, not in the essential repertoire of the nursery chef; but if you want to do some serious toasting, there is no substitute for homemade.

WHITE BREAD FOR TOASTING

When baked in a lidded pullman loaf pan, this milk-and-butter white bread recipe produces a dense, fragrant bread perfect for toasting. (You can easily improvise a pullman loaf pan by covering an ordinary bread pan with a cookie sheet and weighing the sheet down.)

1 package dry yeast dissolved in
¼ cup tepid water (about
110°) with 1 tablespoon sugar
5 to 5½ cups all-purpose flour
2 teaspoons salt

1½ cups milk, at
room temperature
5 tablespoons butter, melted and
cooled to lukewarm

• Measure 5 cups flour into a large mixing bowl. Add salt, milk, melted butter, and yeast mixture (which has stood long enough to be foamy), stirring to create a sticky dough.

Turn dough out onto a floured board, and let it rest while you clean and butter the mixing bowl. Knead dough vigorously for at least 10 minutes, adding flour as needed to create a smooth, stiff dough. Return to buttered bowl, cover with plastic wrap, and set in a warm place for 1 to 2 hours, or until dough doubles in bulk.

Punch down dough, turn it out, knead it a few more minutes, then return it to bowl and let it double in size again.

Turn out dough again, punch it down, and let it rest while you thoroughly butter either a pullman loaf form or two normal-size bread pans. (If using a cover on the pan, *don't forget to butter it, too.*) Knead dough a few minutes more, then shape it to fit pan (or pans). Cover with a cloth and let it rise again for 30 minutes.

Preheat oven to 400°.

Remove cloth, put pans in oven, and immediately reduce heat to 375°. If using uncovered bread pans, bake about 45 minutes, or until top is golden brown, then remove bread from pans and bake a few minutes longer directly in the oven, until loaves sound hollow when tapped.

If using pullman loaf pan, after 30 minutes, turn tin on one side for 5 minutes, then other side for 5 minutes. Set it upright and remove lid. Continue baking 10 minutes. Remove from pan, and bake a few minutes longer directly in oven, until loaf sounds hollow when tapped.

Cool on rack 1 full hour before serving or toasting.

HOW TO BUTTER TOAST

It is absolutely necessary to plan ahead when preparing buttered toast. So that it will be perfectly spreadable, butter must be out of the refrigerator at least an hour before the bread is toasted. For spur-of-the-moment toast, it will be necessary to use a sharp knife to "peel" thin leaves of butter off the top of a stick (or, better yet, a one-pound block), and place these leaves on the hot toast to melt. Trying to *spread* a cold pat of butter on warm toast is a nightmare. If the toast doesn't tear altogether, the press of the butter knife will bruise and batter the surface beyond the bounds of acceptable comfort food.

And while on the subject of disasters, if toast burns, *throw it out!* Don't let any home ec type tell you that it is possible to scrape the black stuff off that dry, overdone tile and get a normal, moist, chewy piece of toast. *It cannot be done!*

Sweet or lightly salted butter is a matter of choice . . . except with raisin bread toast, where sweet butter is definitely better.

How To Make Good Bread

1. Preparing sponge

2. Rising of sponge

3. Making dough

4. First kneading of dough

5. First rising of dough

6. Kneading dough down

7. Second rising of dough

8. Molding loaves

SEE NEXT PAGE

9. Rising of loaves

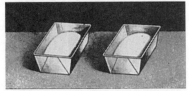

10. Baking

11. Cooling bread

Molding Loaves

Punch down risen dough

Divide into 2 even portions

Round each portion into a ball

Cover and rest 10 to 15 minutes

Flatten each piece into a sheet

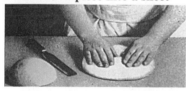

Double over and seal edges

Stretch into long sheet

Overlap to center and seal edges

Fold end over ⅓ and seal edges

Fold opposit end over and seal

Utensils and Ingredients

CINNAMON TOAST

A soigné delicacy to accompany warm milk before bedtime. An even more sophisticated presentation is at breakfast, with *lait au* café—milk that has been colored with a dash of coffee.

There are as many ways to make cinnamon toast as there are chefs. You can toast the bread on both sides, or toast only the bottom, then put the buttered and cinnamoned untoasted side under a broiler; you can mix the cinnamon and sugar with the butter and spread them on all at once, or you can butter the toast, then sprinkle on the cinnamon-sugar. After sugaring the toast, you must choose whether you want to bake it a few minutes, to bind the topping with the bread. Or did you put on so much butter that all the cinnamon oozes into the bread along with it?

We prefer instant cinnamon toast, no baking or broiling after it's sugared:

4 slices dense, thickly sliced	*2 tablespoons sugar*
white bread	*2 tablespoons butter, softened to*
1 teaspoon cinnamon	*spreading consistency*

• Toast bread until crisp outside, but still moist in center. As bread toasts, mix cinnamon and sugar. Butter toast and *immediately* shower each slice with cinnamon-sugar. Slice diagonally and serve.

Serves 2.

BROWN SUGAR OR MAPLE SUGAR TOAST

No cinnamon in the house? Try this nice twist on the cinnamon toast formula from *It's Fun to Cook,* a young people's cookbook published by the Junior Literary Guild in 1938. For an extra soupçon of elegance, it is suggested that the toast be trimmed of crusts and cut into fingers.

4 slices dense, thickly sliced white bread
2 tablespoons butter, softened to spreading consistency

2 tablespoons brown sugar or maple sugar

• Toast bread only on one side. Butter untoasted side, spread with sugar, and put under broiler until sugar melts.
Serves 2.

TOAST TOPPERS

"Everybody loves crisp, hot buttered toast," rhapsodized *Betty Crocker's Cook Book for Boys and Girls* in the 1950s, "even more when it's topped with something sweet or spicy."

CINNAMON HONEY
• For each slice of toast, mix ¼ teaspoon cinnamon with 1 tablespoon honey. Butter toast and spread with Cinnamon Honey.

ORANGE SUGAR
2 tablespoons butter, softened
3 tablespoons sifted confectioners' sugar

1 teaspoon grated orange rind
1 teaspoon orange juice

• Blend butter and sugar; stir in orange rind and juice. Spread on toast.
Serves 2.

RAISIN PEANUT BUTTER

¼ cup chunky peanut butter

2 tablespoons chopped
seedless raisins

2 tablespoons orange juice

• Mix peanut butter, raisins, and orange juice. Spread on toast.
Serves 2.

CINNAMON MARSHMALLOW

• For each slice of toast, mix 1½ teaspoons sugar and ⅛ teaspoon cinnamon. Butter toast, sprinkle cinnamon-sugar on butter, then top each slice with 1 marshmallow. Set under broiler until marshmallow is puffy and golden and has oozed over the toast.

CARAMEL COCONUT

1 tablespoon butter, softened

2 tablespoons brown sugar

2 tablespoons flaked coconut

• Blend butter, sugar, and coconut. Spread on light toast and toast under broiler until topping bubbles. Watch carefully.
Serves 2.

MILK TOAST

We used to make fun of milk toast. Baby food. Gruel for the toothless. Graveyard stew. We learned to love it at a fancy Boston hotel into which we dragged ourselves one evening after an exhausting day. We were beat, nerves frazzled, stomachs tense. Definitely time for a little room service pampering. Milk toast was the order of the day.

Up came a table set with two bowls of toast, a scoop of sweet butter, a dish of brown sugar, and in two tall, silver pitchers, warm milk and warm cream. "May I?" asked The Man from Room Service, and we weakly gestured him to proceed. With knife and fork he cut the toast into bite-sized pieces. A pitcher in each hand, he poured equal amounts of cream and milk onto the toast. With generous spoon, he dabbed on sweet butter. "Sugar?" Of course; and he showered the bowls with a sprinkling of brown sugar that melted with the butter into amber pools atop the toast and cream.

Never in our lives have we slept so well or dreamed so sweetly or awoke so refreshed.

4 slices toast

1 pint milk, or 1 cup milk and
  1 cup cream

3 tablespoons sweet butter

Salt or sugar to taste

• Slice 2 thick pieces of pullman loaf and toast until well browned, but not dark or crumbly. Break or cut into bite-sized pieces and lay on the bottom of a wide soup bowl.

Gently heat milk (and cream) until warm (do not boil). Pour over warm toast, and quickly dot with butter. Sprinkle lightly with salt—or sugar, or brown sugar, or cinnamon-sugar—and eat right away.

Serves 2.

MILK TOAST VARIATIONS
• *Lessons in Cookery—Diet for Children, written* in 1919 by Frances Elizabeth Stewart, Instructor in Home Economics at the Robert Lindblom Technical High School of Chicago, suggests adding chopped figs, raisins, and

prunes along with cream on the toast "for children over 8 years of age." A fabulous idea—just make sure there are no pits.

Ms. Stewart also suggests Cream of Peanut Butter Toast, the toast spread thickly with peanut butter, then topped with a thin stream of warm cream. This is for good children whose ribs are showing a bit too much.

Conversely, for little fatties, *Diet for Children* advises breakfast of "Water Toast"—toast soaked in boiling water, with a dash of salt. Ugh.

FRENCH TOAST

As the name suggests, this is the most chic of nursery toasts; so much so that you will see dolled-up versions on brunch menus of stylish restaurants. But let's not get carried away. French toast, nursery-style, is never Orange French Toast or Vanilla Toast, or—heaven forbid—*Pain Perdu*. It is good old white bread dipped in eggs and cream and fried in butter and served with either maple syrup or, maybe, jelly or, if you are quite worldly-wise, confectioners' sugar.

2 eggs	*Dash salt*
½ cup milk	*8 slices dense white bread*
¼ cup cream	*Butter for frying*

• Mix eggs, milk, cream, and salt in a bowl wide enough to hold bread slices. Dip bread into egg mixture. For heavy, eggy French toast, let each slice soak a while, both sides. For lighter toast, moisten both sides, but don't let egg mixture thoroughly soak bread.

Heat plenty of butter in a frying pan over medium-high heat. Add soaked bread. Cook until light brown, flip, and cook other side, adding butter. Serve warm, with bacon or sausage, and syrup (or jelly or confectioners' sugar).

Serves 3 to 4.

PRUNE FRENCH TOAST
• Instead of ½ cup milk and ¼ cup cream, use ⅓ cup milk and ⅓ cup prune juice. Proceed as above. Serve topped with quartered prunes, confectioners' sugar, and a squeeze of lemon.

CHOCOLATE BREAD WITH VANILLA BUTTER

If you have been especially good, or if life has been especially bad, you need an exceptional treat. Here is just the ticket: the comfort of bread and the hedonism of chocolate, all in one. Chocolate bread is truly one of our most beloved things to eat, but only on occasions—to compliment a dear guest, or for those days when we want to be extra nice to ourselves.

This doubly good loaf is a yeast bread, demanding punchdowns and risings, but it is worth the effort, a *trompe l'oeil* that masquerades as something much more serious that it really is. It is delicious both hot out of the oven, slathered with vanilla butter, and the next day, popped in your toaster. You won't believe the wonderful aroma!

CHOCOLATE BREAD

1 cup milk	*2 eggs, beaten*
2 tablespoons butter	*3½ cups all-purpose flour*
½ cup sugar	*⅔ cup sifted cocoa*
1 teaspoon vanilla extract	*1 cup chopped*
1 package dry yeast dissolved in	*walnuts (optional)*
¼ cup tepid water (110°) with	*1 heaping cup raisins (optional)*
1 tablespoon sugar	*Coarse sugar*

• Scald milk, remove from heat, and add butter, stirring until it melts. Add sugar and vanilla. When mixture is lukewarm (no more than 115°), add yeast mixture, which should be good and frothy by this point. Add beaten eggs and stir.

Measure flour and cocoa into a large bowl. (Add nuts and raisins.) Add yeast mixture and stir vigorously. Turn out onto a floured board and, as dough rests, clean and butter bowl.

Knead dough gently 3 to 5 minutes, adding flour if necessary to yield a smooth dough. Put into buttered bowl, cover with damp towel, and put in a draft-free warm place until doubled in size—about 2 hours. (Now is the time to make Vanilla Butter.)

Punch down and knead again 8 to 10 times. Pat into loaf shape and place in a well-buttered 9-by-5-inch loaf pan, or into 2 7-by-3-inch pans. Cover and let rise again, but not so much that it doubles—45 minutes is plenty.

Preheat oven to 350°.

Gently pat top of loaf with coarse sugar and bake for 1 hour on middle rack of oven. If making 2 smaller loaves, cut baking time down to 40 to 45 minutes.

Let cool 10 minutes in pan, then remove and cool on wire cake rack.

Serve with Vanilla Butter.

VANILLA BUTTER

12 tablespoons high-quality	*¾ cup confectioners' sugar*
sweet butter	*2 tablespoons vanilla extract*

• Cream butter and sugar. Slowly beat in vanilla. (If you are using a mixer, stop a few times to scrape vanilla butter from sides of bowl.) Transfer to serving bowl, cover, and chill.

Remove from refrigerator at least 30 minutes before serving.

AFTER SCHOOL GINGERBREAD

Nothing makes one feel more like a child waiting for something to come out of the oven than the smell of baking gingerbread. It is more festive than bread, yet when eaten in abundance, less likely than cake to make the nursery glutton feel queasy. This, our all-time favorite gingerbread, comes from *The Household Searchlight Recipe Book,* 1941. Serve it warm, with a glass of milk on the side.

2 eggs, well beaten	*1 teaspoon baking soda*
1 cup dark brown sugar	*¼ teaspoon salt*
12 tablespoons butter, melted	*1 teaspoon ground ginger*
¾ cup molasses	*1 teaspoon cinnamon*
3 cups all-purpose flour	*1 cup buttermilk*

• Preheat oven to 375°.

Combine eggs, sugar, butter, and molasses. Sift flour, measure, and sift with baking soda, salt, and spices. Add alternately with buttermilk to egg mixture. Beat until well blended. Pour into buttered 9-by-9-by-2-inch pan.

Bake 30 to 40 minutes.

Cool. Cut in squares.

Makes 25 squares.

NOTES ON CEREAL

Everyone eats cereal for breakfast; but only nursery food aficionados know the joy of cereal after noon, the happy-baby feeling of buttered farina with raisins and cream at midnight. The very fact that you are scooping your food with a large spoon from a bowl, rather than performing the complex choreography of knife and fork, celebrates the happy regression to uncaring, primitive life.

Of course, we are referring to hot cereal—oatmeal, Cream of Wheat, Maltex, farina, Wheatena, even Maypo. Cold cereal, especially weird brands (in the world of nursery food, anything other than Wheaties and Cheerios is weird), is simply not comforting food. Cold cereal is for grown-ups obsessed with regularity, a problem no prune-fed nursery gourmet ever has to face.

Think of cereal as moist toast, and you will know all you need to know to make it nursery-perfect. Just as with toast, the pleasure of cereal eating comes from being able to make something warm and friendly with so little effort. In fact, all the good things for topping toast are perfect also for cereal—plenty of butter, jam or jelly, cinnamon-sugar, brown sugar, warm cream, plus lots of raisins.

Cereal is security, as close to baby food as adults can get without stepping over the psychopathological line and actually eating strained peas or drinking formula.

Nursery Snacks: Bananas and Prunes

Just as eating caviar or sniffing brandy makes one feel wise and cosmopolitan, there are certain snacks that induce insouciance. It is impossible to be solemn about bananas and prunes. They are foods of childhood, good cheer for grown-ups who know the pleasures of culinary reversion. Soft, calorific, and fun, they are everything the nursery gourmet longs for when needing a jolly break from the rigors of the workaday world.

BANANAS AND SOUR CREAM

There is hardly anything easier to make or more thoroughly pleasurable than a large bowl of cut-up bananas heaped with fresh sour cream. If you want to get fancy, top the bowl with a sprinkle of sugar, cinnamon, or nutmeg; but don't let anyone tell you that it's all right to substitute yogurt for the sour cream. You *can* do it, but be advised that there is no room for smelly old yogurt in the nursery kitchen.

1 ripe banana   *¼ to ½ cup sour cream*

• Slice banana into cereal bowl. Top with sour cream.
   Serves 1

BROILED BANANAS WITH APPLESAUCE
AND SOUR CREAM

Bananas—How to Serve Them notes that bananas were "one of the earliest solid foods fed the Dionne Quintuplets." This dish requires no teeth for full enjoyment.

4 firm bananas	*1 cup applesauce*
Melted butter	*1 cup sour cream*
Salt	

• Peel bananas. Place on broiler rack, brush well with butter, and sprinkle lightly with salt.

Broil 3 to 4 inches from heat about 5 minutes on each side, or until bananas are browned, tender, and easily pierced with a fork.

Top each banana with ¼ cup applesauce and ¼ cup sour cream.

Serves 4.

BANANA RICE WITH
SAVORY CHEESE SAUCE

The nursery epicure doesn't limit banana eating to snacks and desserts. *Bananas—How to Serve Them* suggests fifty horrifying things to do with them which definitely don't belong in the nursery, from Banana Sardine Boats (hollow them out like gondolas, and stuff the hollow with a whole sardine) to Banana Meat Loaf. This dish, however, is a triumvirate of palliative ingredients—mushy bananas, pillowy rice, and a gooey, golden blanket of cheese.

SAVORY CHEESE SAUCE

2 tablespoons butter	*½ teaspoon*
3 tablespoons all-purpose flour	*Worcestershire sauce*
1 teaspoon salt	*2 cups milk*
Dash pepper	*1 cup grated American cheese*
1 teaspoon prepared mustard	

• Melt butter, add flour and seasonings, and stir until smooth. Stir in milk slowly. Add cheese and cook 5 to 10 minutes, stirring constantly, until sauce is smooth and thick.

Makes 2 cups.

BANANA RICE

3 cups boiled rice *3 tablespoons butter, melted*

2 cups hot Savory Cheese Sauce *Salt*

2 firm bananas *Paprika*

• Preheat oven to 375°.

Mix together rice and ½ cup cheese sauce. Spread over bottom of 10-by-6-by-2-inch baking dish. Peel bananas; cut crosswise into halves, and then cut halves lengthwise. Arrange pieces, cut side down, on top of rice. Drizzle bananas with butter and sprinkle with salt.

Bake 15 to 20 minutes, or until bananas are tender. Pour remaining cheese sauce over bananas and sprinkle with paprika.

Serves 6 to 8.

BANANA BACON WAFFLES
WITH GRAPE SYRUP

Elvis Presley was not merely the King of Rock 'n' Roll. He was unprecedentedly self-indulgent, and therefore it was natural that he also wore the crown of the King of Nursery Food. Elvis loved bowls full of mashed potatoes and plates piled high with mush; and he liked nothing better than buying a hundred Nutty Buddy ice cream cones and placing them, ice cream side down, in a big bowl, then eating as many as he could before they melted.

The King also had a favorite sandwich: bananas, sautéed in bacon fat, with plenty of peanut butter. We have yet to summon the courage to test that recipe, but we did find this nice, homey variation of the banana-bacon theme (*sans* peanut butter) in *The Wonderful World of Welch's*. It makes a dandy nursery breakfast.

BANANA BACON WAFFLES

¾ pound bacon

2 cups sifted all-purpose flour

3 teaspoons baking powder

¼ teaspoon salt

3 eggs, separated

1½ cups milk

6 tablespoons butter, melted

1 tablespoon sugar

1 cup mashed ripe bananas

(2 to 3)

• Fry bacon thoroughly, but not too crisp.

Sift flour, baking powder, and salt together. Beat egg yolks, combine with milk and butter. Add to sifted ingredients; beat until smooth. Beat egg whites stiff; gradually beat in sugar and fold into egg yolk mixture with bananas.

Pour batter into hot waffle iron and bake until brown. Sandwich bacon between waffles and top with Grape Syrup.

Serves 4.

GRAPE SYRUP

½ cup plus 2 tablespoons Welch's grape juice

½ cup Welch's grape preserves

1 teaspoon cornstarch

• Blend together ½ cup grape juice and preserves. Bring to a boil. Mix cornstarch with 2 tablespoons grape juice and stir gradually into boiling liquid. Cook until slightly thickened.

Makes 1 cup.

BANANA BUTTERSCOTCH PIE

Here is a nursery food that makes us happy we are grown-ups, because when we were children, Banana Butterscotch Pie was one of the Unattainables, a too-good-to-be-believed food that children in movies and TV ate, or maybe the rich kid in town ate, but our moms never made. We suppose it was considered too candylike for a healthy, growing youngster. But adults are free to make—and eat—all they want!

*¾ cup firmly packed dark brown
    sugar
5 tablespoons all-purpose flour
½ teaspoon salt
2 cups milk
2 egg yolks, slightly beaten*

*3 tablespoons butter
½ teaspoon vanilla extract
2 ripe bananas, plus 1 ripe
    banana for garnish
1 baked 9-inch pie shell*

• Combine sugar, flour, and salt in top of double boiler. Add milk slowly, mixing thoroughly. Cook over rapidly boiling water until well thickened, stirring constantly. Lower heat, cook 10 minutes longer, stirring occasionally. Stir small amount of hot mixture into egg yolks; then pour back into remaining hot mixture while beating vigorously. Cook 1 minute longer.

Remove mixture from heat. Add butter and vanilla; stir until butter melts. Cool to room temperature. Peel and slice 2 bananas into pie shell and cover immediately with filling.

Chill pie. When ready to serve, flute remaining banana by running prongs of a fork lengthwise along banana, then slice on a diagonal. Arrange crinkle-edged slices on top of pie and serve.

Serves 6 to 8.

BANANA PUDDING

In the South, where banana pudding is a favorite specialty, even the most sophisticated adults know to call it by its true name, 'Nanner Pudding, acknowledgment of its purely infantile goodness. This recipe is a variation of one from Buster Holmes' restaurant in New Orleans.

3 tablespoons all-purpose flour

3 cups milk

1 cup sugar

Dash salt

3 eggs, beaten

1 teaspoon vanilla extract

1 tablespoon butter

Vanilla wafers

2 ripe bananas, sliced

• Mix flour with ½ cup milk. Combine remaining milk, floured milk, sugar, salt, and eggs in top of double boiler. Cook over boiling water until mixture thickens. Remove from heat; add vanilla and butter; stir until butter melts,

Line bottom and sides of a 10-by-6-by-2-inch baking pan with vanilla wafers; add layer of bananas. Pour pudding over bananas. Top with vanilla wafer crumbs.

Refrigerate. Serve cold.

Serves 6.

PRUNE NOG

"When children tire of milk, this drink stimulates the appetite while giving them the milk they ought to have," says *The Pet Milk Cookbook*. Milk and prunes—two old friends who never let you down.

½ cup prune juice

1 teaspoon lemon juice

Sugar to taste

½ cup Pet milk, diluted
with ¼ cup water

• Mix prune juice, lemon juice, and sugar. Slowly add diluted milk. Shake thoroughly or mix in a blender; pour over ice to serve.

Serves 1.

BAKED PRUNE WHIP

An old-fashioned American dessert that appears in every pre-1950s cookbook, but has nearly vanished since then. It is soufflé-light, and as James Beard says in *American Cookery,* "nostalgic to a point."

1⅓ cups pitted prunes
⅓ cup water
⅓ cup sugar
1 teaspoon lemon juice

1 teaspoon vanilla extract
6 egg whites
¼ teaspoon cream of tartar

• Simmer prunes in water for 10 minutes, stirring constantly, until prunes are soft. Drain, chop prunes very fine, and combine in saucepan with sugar. Heat until sugar dissolves. Add lemon juice and vanilla.

Preheat oven to 300°.

Beat egg whites until frothy, add cream of tartar, and beat until stiff. Fold prunes as gently and quickly as possible into egg whites. Pour into buttered and sugared 2-quart baking dish.

Bake 30 minutes, or until golden brown. Serve immediately with heavy cream, or let prune whip deflate, refrigerate, and serve cold with whipped cream.

Serves 4.

ESCALLOPED NOODLES AND PRUNES

From Ida Bailey Allen's 1935 book, *Cooking, Menus, Service,* where it is listed as a dessert; but at nursery supper, this prune-noodle double whammy makes a nummy entrée, especially when buried under a mini-mound of sour cream.

3 cups cooked egg
noodles, buttered
½ cup sugar mixed with ½
teaspoon cinnamon

6 tablespoons butter
3 cups stewed pitted prunes
½ cup buttered bread crumbs or
crushed corn flakes

• Preheat oven to 350°.

Turn 1 cup noodles into buttered baking dish, sprinkle with sugar and cinnamon, and dot with 2 tablespoons butter. Top with 1 cup prunes. Proceed in layers until all ingredients are used. Cover with buttered crumbs or corn flakes.

Bake 20 minutes. Serve with sour cream.

Serves 4 to 6.

WAFFLE-IZED PRUNE SANDWICH

While not exclusively nursery fare, waffles are reassuring food, seldom pretentious or exotic. The checkerboard waffle pattern is a cheerful one, suggesting if not waffles, then the surface of an ice cream cone or a crisp little sugar wafer. That is why waffle-ized foods make for such a festive treat, You can use the waffle-izing technique on almost any sandwich, but we especially like to do it with these prune sandwiches, discovered in the 1933 pamphlet *Prunes for Epicures.*

Vitamin-packed, fattening, a natural laxative, gooey and sweet, prunes are nursery food supreme.

2 cups cooked prunes	*6 slices American cheese*
½ teaspoon	*3 eggs*
Worcestershire sauce	*¼ cup milk*
12 slices bread	*½ teaspoon salt*
Butter	*2 tablespoons butter, melted*

• Remove prune pits and mash prunes to pulp. Add Worcestershire and blend thoroughly. Spread 6 bread slices with butter, then with prune mixture. Top with cheese, cover with second slice of bread. Cut sandwiches corner to corner, forming triangles.

Beat eggs, add milk, salt, and melted butter, and mix thoroughly. Dip each sandwich in this mixture and fry on hot waffle iron until golden brown, two triangles at a time. Press upper part of waffle iron down slightly when closing in order to waffle-ize. Sandwiches require 2 to 4 minutes to cook, depending on temperature of iron.

Makes 12 small sandwiches, enough to serve 4.

PRUNE DUFF

Here is the ultimate prune foodstuff, the richest dessert in the history of the world. As "Bettina" says in *A Thousand Ways to Please a Family,* "the best and fluffiest dessert that ever melted in our mouths! Little Robin is sure to pound on the table and call so loudly for a second helping that all of the neighbors will wonder what in the world we have done to him!"

This recipe is adapted from Stella Standard's *Complete American Cookbook,* published in 1957.

4 tablespoons butter	1½ cups pitted and
½ cup brown sugar	mashed prunes
1 egg, beaten	½ teaspoon baking soda
½ cup all-purpose flour	½ tablespoon milk
Dash salt	

SAUCE

3 tablespoons butter	1½ cups confectioners' sugar
1 egg, beaten	½ cup heavy cream, whipped

• Preheat oven to 350°.

Cream butter, mix with brown sugar until fluffy. Add egg. Sift flour and salt and mix with mashed prunes. Combine mixtures and add soda dissolved in milk. Pour into a buttered casserole. Set casserole in a larger dish of hot water.

Bake 45 to 60 minutes, or until firm.

Make sauce by creaming butter, adding egg and sugar, and folding together with whipped cream.

Serves 4.

Primary Puddings

It isn't easy to be a pudding person in a world where mousse is king. Only in roadside diners and a few doddering old restaurants will you find pudding for dessert. And at a couth dinner party, no modern hostess would dare!

But in the privacy of one's own home, for moments of solitary reflection, when solace and peace are absolutely top priority, can a tarted-up rinky-dink mousse offer the honest satisfaction of a nice dish of tapioca? Of course not.

Real homemade pudding is neighborly, reassuring, old-fashioned pleasure, guaranteed to lull the most fragile neurotic into unflappable contentment. Yet puddings are so passé that few modern cookbooks offer recipes. Never afraid to be behind the times, *Square Meals* bravely presents this roster of fuddy-duddy puddings to all who crave to savor the pleasures of culinary atavism.

CHOCOLATE PUDDING

Smooth, dark, and utterly simple, chocolate pudding is a basic staple of nursery cuisine. Its goodness depends on just one thing: high-quality cocoa. Use Droste's or an equally good Dutch brand.

We are almost afraid to bring up the subject, because it is a source of terrible anxiety to some timid pudding eaters, but an important decision must be made concerning chocolate pudding. You must choose what you want to do about the thin leathery coating that forms across the surface of the pudding as it cools.

There, we've said it. Now, what are you going to do about it? The chewy skin—or, as one pudding aficionado we know swears it is called, the "skim"—is considered by some a delicacy, while others abhor the mere mention of it.

If you are one who likes a thick, chewy skin, chill the pudding uncovered. You can further encourage the growth of skin by constantly opening and closing the refrigerator, playing havoc with the humidity. The longer pudding chills, the thicker the skin. For a smooth, skinless top, tightly seal the top of pudding dishes with plastic wrap.

Since whipped cream is for rich adults, you may top this pudding with a splash of cold milk. Watch it crack the skin, creating milky fissures in the chocolate.

4 tablespoons cocoa	*¼ teaspoon salt*
4 tablespoons cornstarch	*2 cups light cream*
⅔ cup sugar	*1 teaspoon vanilla extract*

• In top of double boiler combine cocoa, cornstarch, sugar, and salt. Add ½ cup cream and stir to a smooth paste. Scald remaining cream and stir slowly into cocoa mixture. Cook over hot but not boiling water, stirring constantly, until thick and smooth. Stir in vanilla extract. Pour into individual serving dishes and chill.

Serves 4.

BUTTERSCOTCH PUDDING

Long ago, before nursery cuisine made a full retreat to the safety and privacy of home, there were restaurants that specialized in soft comfort food: friendly meals of boneless turkey and popovers, cheese soup and chiffon pie. Meals for old aunts and young children. The sweetest and kindest of them was the White Turkey Inn of Danbury, Connecticut (and subsequently New York City, too). This recipe for rich and luscious butterscotch pudding was inspired by *Let's Talk Turkey,* the recipe book of the White Turkey Inn, with a little help from James Beard's *American Cookery.*

4 tablespoons butter	*2 eggs*
1¼ cups light brown sugar	*7 tablespoons all-purpose flour*
1 cup heavy cream	*½ teaspoon salt*
2 cups milk	*1 teaspoon vanilla extract*

• In a heavy 2-quart saucepan, melt butter, add brown sugar, and stir over low heat until sugar and butter melt together and bubble up. Add cream and 1 cup milk; stir until smooth. Remove from heat.

In a small bowl, beat together eggs, flour, and 1 cup milk. Add to sugar mixture, add salt, and return to stove. Over medium heat, stir constantly until thickened. While still over medium heat, beat with rotary hand mixer at medium speed for 3 minutes.

Remove from heat, stir in vanilla, and pour into 2-quart casserole dish or 6 to 8 individual pudding cups. Chill.

Serves 6 to 8.

BREAD AND BUTTER PUDDING

"All children like sugar," said Mrs. C. F. Leyel in *Diet for Children* in 1936. "And sugar on their bread and butter is good for them." The only thing that makes sugared bread and butter better is baking it with eggs and cream. This medley of dairy riches is an elegant, yet utterly familiar custard, to be served plain or dolloped with raspberry jam.

10 slices day-old white bread	*2 cups milk*
8 tablespoons butter	*1 cup cream*
4 eggs	*1 teaspoon vanilla extract*
2 egg yolks	*⅓ cup sifted*
⅔ cup granulated sugar	*confectioners' sugar*
⅛ teaspoon salt	

• Heavily butter the inside of a 2-quart baking dish. Butter each slice of bread. Arrange bread in several layers, butter side up, across bottom of pan, cutting slices to fill in any large gaps.

Beat together eggs, yolks, sugar, and salt. Scald milk and cream together, add to egg mixture, and add vanilla. Pour over bread in baking dish. Let sit 15 to 20 minutes.

Preheat oven to 325°.

Set baking dish in a large pan in about 1 inch of hot water. Bake 1 to 1½ hours.

Sift confectioners' sugar atop pudding and put under hot broiler for a few minutes to glaze. Watch carefully to make sure it doesn't bum.

Serves 6 to 8.

CINNAMON SWIRL RAISIN BREAD PUDDING

1 16-ounce loaf cinnamon raisin
bread (we like Sun-Maid
brand)
1 quart milk

3 eggs
2 cups sugar
2 tablespoons vanilla extract
1 tablespoon butter

• Preheat oven to 350°.

Tear bread into 2-inch pieces, drop in a large mixing bowl, and pour milk over. Toss gently until bread is coated. Let bread soak about 15 minutes.

In a small bowl, beat eggs together with sugar until mixture is light yellow, smooth, and thick. Add vanilla. Pour mixture over milk-soaked bread and gently but thoroughly mix together until bread is evenly coated with egg mixture.

Transfer to a buttered 9-by-13-by-2-inch baking dish and place dish (uncovered) in another pan containing 1 to 2 inches of water. Place these dishes in oven and bake until set, when a knife inserted in center comes out clean—about 1 hour.

If you like a less crusty pudding, dot top with butter before baking. Serve with heavy cream.

Serves about 12.

CHOCOLATE BREAD PUDDING

Chocolate gilt for the lily, from an old Carnation milk brochure entitled *100 Glorified Recipes*. It is basically a chocolate pudding, but the torn bread slices add a soft textural cushion of which Granny would approve.

Stale bread, torn into small	*¾ cup sugar*
chunks to make 4 cups	*2 eggs, slightly beaten*
2 cups Carnation milk	*¼ teaspoon salt*
2 cups hot water	*1 teaspoon vanilla extract*
2 ounces unsweetened chocolate	

• Soak bread chunks 20 minutes in 1 cup Carnation milk diluted with 1 cup hot water. Melt chocolate in double boiler, add sugar and 1 cup Carnation milk diluted with 1 cup hot water. Cook until smooth.

Preheat oven to 300°.

Combine soaked bread with chocolate mixture. Add eggs, salt, and vanilla. Pour into a greased 10-inch-square baking dish and set in a pan of hot water.

Bake 1 hour, or until knife inserted in center comes out clean.

Serves 8 to 10.

GENTLE PERSON'S GRAPE-NUT PUDDING

Grape-Nuts cereal is scary. What are those little rough nubs anyway? And what are you supposed to do with them? If you pour them in a bowl with milk, they soak it all up and seem to grow twice their size. They are a fascinating dilemma; despite their abnormal behavior, they taste good. And they can be tamed . . . by incorporating them into this traditional New England nursery pudding. Without a grain of sugar, it is a dowdy dish indeed, but dates, raisins, and spices give it powerful aromatic allure on a winter afternoon.

3¼ cups boiling water	*1 teaspoon nutmeg*
2 cups Grape-Nuts	*2 cups chopped walnuts*
2 eggs, separated	*½ cup raisins*
1 tablespoon cinnamon	*½ cup chopped dates*
1 teaspoon ground cloves	*Pinch salt*

• Pour boiling water over Grape-Nuts and set aside to cool.

Preheat oven to 350°.

Beat whites stiff and set aside. Beat yolks with spices; add nutmeats, raisins, dates, and salt. Mix with Grape-Nuts and fold in stiffly beaten egg whites. Pour into buttered 10-cup soufflé dish.

Bake 45 to 60 minutes.

Serves 6 to 8.

TAPIOCA PUDDING

Tapioca is the teddy bear of desserts, an edible security blanket, especially when served with an Arrowroot cookie on the side. We admit that not everyone loves the funny little pellets of cassava plant starch, known in diner lingo as "fisheyes," but no nursery chef can allow personal prejudice to limit his or her repertoire. Love it or leave it, tapioca is a nursery staple. Besides, if you use Minute Tapioca instead of the all-day large pearl variety, you minimize the fisheye effect.

3 tablespoons Minute Tapioca	*2 cups milk*
Dash salt	*2 eggs, separated*
5 tablespoons sugar	*1 tablespoon vanilla extract*

• Mix tapioca, salt, 3 tablespoons sugar, milk, and egg yolks in heavy saucepan. Let stand 5 minutes. Bring to full boil, stirring constantly, over medium heat (this will take 8 to 10 minutes). Remove from heat.

Beat egg whites until foamy; gradually beat in 2 tablespoons sugar until whites stand in soft peaks. Fold egg whites into warm tapioca. Add vanilla. Stir and serve warm; or chill and serve cold.

Serves 4 to 6.

PETER PAN PUDDING

It would seem that of all peanut butters, Peter Pan would be the least suited to the nursery, since the joy of eating peanut butter lies in its thick, gummy texture, like infantile denture adhesive or edible Play-Doh, and Peter Pan is "the peanut butter that does not stick to the roof of your mouth." That's no fun at all! And yet, it was in our *Peter Pan in Your Daily Diet* brochure that we discovered this undeniably juvenile confection.

3 cups light cream	*¾ cup sugar*
¼ cup cornstarch	*½ cup cold water*
⅛ teaspoon salt	*½ cup Peter Pan peanut butter*

• Scald cream in heavy saucepan. In small bowl, blend cornstarch, salt, sugar, and water. Stir slowly into hot cream. Stir over low heat until thickened. Stir in peanut butter and cook until well blended (about 2 minutes). Turn into 6 cup molds or a large bowl. Chill.

Serves 6.

BAKED CARAMEL CUSTARD

Quivering custard is no more than eggs and sugar and milk: pure, elementary luxury; the balmiest sweet. For an even richer custard, substitute evaporated milk for 1 cup of the milk.

6 egg yolks	*Dash salt*
½ cup plus ⅔ cup sugar	*2 cups milk*
1 teaspoon vanilla extract	

• Preheat oven to 350°.

Thoroughly beat yolks, ½ cup sugar, vanilla, and salt. Scald milk, and add very slowly to egg mixture, beating as you add.

Cook ⅔ cup sugar in a cast-iron skillet over low heat until sugar caramelizes (at 325° to 350°). Pour caramel into 6 custard cups and let cool 2 to 3 minutes.

Carefully pour custard mixture into cups on top of caramel pool. Set cups in a baking pan and pour 1 inch hot water into pan around cups.

Bake 1 hour, or until a knife inserted in custard comes out clean.

Serve in custard cups, or remove from cups by running a thin, sharp knife around sides of cup, and in a swift move, unmold onto a saucer, allowing caramel to drip over sides.

Serves 6.

FAIRYLAND FRIED JUNKET EGGS

Junket is the meekest of foods, beloved by infants, invalids, and Jane and Michael Stern. Made of rennet, its magic is that it congeals milk into soft, custard of the loveliest pastel hues. But our favorite Junket is pure-white vanilla, especially when it masquerades as the albumen of a sunny-side-up egg. Oh, Junket, you naughty scamp!

1 package vanilla Junket mix or 1 Junket rennet tablet (available in most supermarkets)
1 tablespoon cold water

3 tablespoons sugar
1 teaspoon vanilla extract
1 pint milk
4 canned apricot halves

• If using boxed Junket, follow directions on box to prepare.

If using tablet, crush in cold water, dissolving thoroughly. Add sugar and vanilla to milk; warm slowly to lukewarm, stirring constantly. Test milk on wrist to determine proper temperature. It should feel barely warm. Remove from stove.

Add dissolved rennet tablet to lukewarm milk and stir quickly for a few seconds only. Pour at once into 4 dessert glasses and let stand undisturbed until firm—about 10 minutes. When set, place in refrigerator to chill.

Just before serving, top each serving with 1 canned apricot half, round side up. Serve with sliced, toasted pound cake.

Serves 4.

STEAMED MARMALADE PUDDING

There are two schools of steamed food—Oriental things steamed in woks with all their vitamins sealed inside . . . and glorious wads of sugar and spice, steamed for hours in a pudding mold designed to forge their ingredients into a solid high-calorie mass: steamed puddings.

Called "boiled babies" because of the cheesecloth swaddling traditionally used to bind the pudding before it was lowered into its steam bath, "puds" are from an age before health food existed, perfect for keeping the frail youngster from blowing away in an ill wind.

This hearty marmalade and suet pudding is from *The Household Searchlight Recipe Book.* If you have never had a boiled baby, it is a revelation—the ultimate in languorous cuisine, requiring so little effort to eat. In fact, it is less a dessert than it is invalid dinner—plenty of soft cushy nutrition. Serve it warm, with zwieback on the side.

1 cup flour
3 teaspoons baking powder
¾ teaspoon salt
1 cup soft bread crumbs
    (we made ours in a food
    processor using 3 slices of
    Wonder Bread)

⅓ cup sugar
3 eggs, well beaten
1 cup finely ground suet
1 cup orange marmalade
1 cup milk

• Grease an 8-cup pudding mold and coat with sugar. Sift flour, measure, and sift again with baking powder and salt. Combine crumbs, sugar, eggs, suet, marmalade, and milk. Add dry ingredients. Mix thoroughly. Fill pudding mold two-thirds full. Cover.

In kettle with cover, large enough to hold pudding mold, place a metal trivet or mason jar ring. Put pudding mold on trivet. Add 3 inches of water and bring to boil.

Steam 3 hours, adding water to keep level up.

When cooked, remove pudding from steamer and let stand 10 minutes before unmolding. Serve hot, topped with cream.

Serves 6.

GUMDROP PUDDING

The nursery dietician knows that the more fattening a food is, the better it is. That's the whole point of a "pud"—to pack it in, rich and sweet. What, then, could be more appropriate—or more fun—than this pudding of sugar and spice and pretty-colored gumdrops, all steamed together.

2 cups flour	*1 cup brown sugar*
2 teaspoons baking powder	*2 cups milk*
½ teaspoon cinnamon	*1 cup seedless raisins*
½ teaspoon allspice	*1 cup walnuts*
½ teaspoon nutmeg	*2 dozen small gumdrops*
2 tablespoons butter	*(assorted colors)*

• Grease an 8-cup pudding mold and coat with sugar. Sift together flour, baking powder, cinnamon, allspice, and nutmeg. Cream butter, adding brown sugar. To butter-sugar mixture, alternately add sifted dry ingredients and milk. Beat thoroughly. Add raisins, nuts, and gumdrops. Pour into pudding mold.

In kettle with cover, large enough to hold pudding mold, place a metal trivet or mason jar ring. Put pudding mold on trivet. Add 3 inches of water and bring to boil.

Steam 1½ hours, adding water to keep level up.

When cooked, remove from steamer and let stand 10 minutes before unmolding. Serve hot, topped with cream.

Serves 8 to 10.

What Nice Children Drink

When the going gets tough, the nursery gastronome craves to suckle. What could possibly be more comforting than our first food? With the exceptions of grape juice and gruel, nearly all nursery drinks are made of milk.

The fun of milk is that you can do so many things to it: hot or cold, chocolate or—as it is known at school—"white." Many a youngster's early lessons in discrimination among foods come from the decisions that must be made concerning the powders, granules, and syrups available for turning white milk chocolate.

Indeed, we learned to judge our playmates' taste and social status based on which chocolate milk their mothers served: exotic Ovaltine mix; solidly middle-class Hershey's syrup; chintzy Quik powder (unless two spoonfuls are used, or unless—wonder of wonders—chocolate Quik and strawberry Quik are blended); and that fascinating but forbidden low-class syrup duo, Fox's U-Bet and Bosco.

Then, in our early teens, coinciding exactly with puberty and the discovery of sex, we discovered Horlick's malted milk powder. A new world of culinary pleasure had dawned. No food supplement on earth so intensified milk's blissful luxury.

Even today, as mature and measured adults, it is torture to keep a jar of Horlick's chocolate malted milk in the house. It is too tempting, too good, even if there is no milk in the refrigerator. Simply take a soupspoonful, straight, in your mouth. It is dry, and only slowly does the grainy chocolate powder moisten on the tongue, first into a paste, then a thick syrup. It clings to teeth and gums; it's an awful, uncouth mess. But does that stop the connoisseur of nursery pleasures? Hah! It's Horlick's by the bowl for us.

MILK AND HONEY

A sugar teat in a cup, the most soporific of drinks, milk and honey should be reserved for episodes of profoundly regressive behavior.

One note of caution: when heating milk and honey, or any warm milk drink, stir it constantly over very low heat. If you let it cook unattended, you run the risk of confronting the dreaded "skin" that grows across the surface of the liquid and clings unpleasantly to lips and teeth.

1 cup milk   *1 tablespoon honey*

• Scald milk. Stir in honey. Pour into cup. Assume fetal position. Drink.

HOT COCOA

The nursery drink that even food snobs like. For superior cocoa, we recommend using Droste's, High-quality cocoa powder makes all the difference,

2 cups milk (2 tablespoons   *½ teaspoon vanilla extract*
  reserved)   *Whipped cream or marshmallows*
1½ tablespoons cocoa   *as garnish*
2 tablespoons sugar

• Heat milk, but do not boil. Mix cocoa and sugar, dry, in bowl. Add reserved 2 tablespoons milk to form syrup. Add vanilla. Add cocoa mixture to warm milk; warm again.

Pour into warm cups. Garnish each with 1 large marshmallow or a few miniatures, or whipped cream.

Serves 2.

COCOA VARIATIONS

If you are blasé about pure cocoa, it is possible to doctor it up in many ways. Add these enhancers after the cocoa is brewed:

CANADIAN COCOA

• Stir in ½ tablespoon maple syrup.

VIENNESE COCOA

• Once cocoa is in cup, sprinkle top with a dash of cinnamon and a dash of nutmeg. Serve with a cinnamon stick.

COCOA JULEP

• Stir in ⅛ teaspoon mint extract or 3 to 4 fresh mint leaves.

RICH HOT CHOCOLATE

Cocoa is by nature mild; if you crave the stronger kick of bittersweet chocolate, you've got to move on to the hard stuff—melted chocolate bars or Nestle's semisweet morsels. Less calming than cocoa, hot chocolate is a vivid cold-weather pick-me-up.

3 ounces semisweet chocolate   *½ cup milk*
½ cup water   *1 cup heavy cream*
Dash salt

• Put water in bottom of double boiler; bring to boil. On another burner, in top of double boiler, melt chocolate, ½ cup water, and salt directly over low heat. Stir until well blended. Bring to boil, then immediately remove from flame and put over boiling water. Add milk and cream; heat to scalding. Beat with rotary beater until very fluffy. Serve immediately.

Makes 2 large mugfuls.

CHOCOLATE SOUP

An egg-enriched cocoa inspired by Iris lhde Frey's *Crumpets and Scones,* chocolate soup is properly served in a cup on a saucer with a soup spoon, with animal crackers on the side. Animals that swim, such as hippopotami, may be dunked in the soup.

¾ cup half-and-half
1 tablespoon sugar
½ teaspoon vanilla extract

2 teaspoons cocoa
1 egg yolk

• Heat half-and-half. Pour into cup, leaving about ¼ cup in pan. Add sugar, vanilla, and cocoa to half-and-half in pan and mix to syrup. Add egg yolk and stir over low to medium heat. Gradually stir in preheated half-and-half. Stir until blended and thick. Pour back into cup.

Serves 1.

CHOCOLATE PEANUT CREAM

The point of most nursery beverages is to maximize one's caloric intake, and sometimes milk and chocolate are not enough. That's when you need to supplement the robust duo with a corpulent dollop of peanut butter. Save this drink for the coldest winter day, when you come in from a sleigh ride or building a snowman.

1½ cups milk
¼ cup chocolate syrup
1 tablespoon creamy
peanut butter

1 tablespoon sugar
Whipped cream

• Combine all ingredients except whipped cream in saucepan. Stirring constantly, bring to boil over moderate heat. Remove from heat immediately. Beat well. Pour in cups. Top with whipped cream.

Serves 2.

HOT CHOCOLATE NOG

A creamy cup of chocolate foam. Enriched with eggs, nogs are the most robust beverages of all.

1 egg	*¼ cup chocolate syrup*
3 tablespoons sugar	*Cinnamon*
1 cup milk	

• Beat egg with sugar until thick. Bring milk and chocolate syrup to boil, remove from heat, and slowly add to egg mixture, stirring constantly. Cook (but do not boil) over medium heat 2 to 3 minutes, stirring constantly. Serve, garnished with cinnamon.

Serves 2.

BEEF TEA

Feeling cranky? How about a cup of pure, homemade bouillon? Suitable for a cozy night in bed, or to accompany hot cross buns on an autumn afternoon, this humble-hearted tea is a recipe from the Fannie Merritt Fanner *Boston Cooking-School Cook Book* (1924 edition).

2 pounds lean beef, cubed	*1 teaspoon salt*
1½ quarts cold water	*1 tablespoon diced carrot*
Marrow from 2 marrow bones	*1 tablespoon diced onion*
¼ teaspoon peppercorns	*1 tablespoon diced celery*

• Put 1½ pounds meat in soup kettle to soak in water for 30 minutes. Brown remaining ½ pound meat and marrow in hot frying pan. Put browned meat and marrow bones in kettle. Heat to boiling point. Skim thoroughly. Cook at temperature just below boiling 5 full hours. Add seasonings and vegetables. Cook, below boiling, 1 hour. Strain thoroughly. Cool. Remove fat. Clear broth will remain.

May be stored in refrigerator and heated as desired.

Makes about 6 cups.

CRUST COFFEE

Nursery gruel, suitable for invalid and child alike. Unlike other nursery drinks, crust coffee is no fun at all. Yet, aren't there times when you are feeling sorry for yourself, and rather than striving to get happy, want to feel worse? Chocolate is too cheerful; nogs are festive party drinks. Even bouillon is clear and bracing. A cup of crust coffee will fix you up just right; on the sunniest of days, it can turn the sky gray. This recipe is from *Lessons in Cookery—Diet for Children,* which suggested it "for school children, as a desirable warm liquid at noon if the child is to return soon to work."

1 cup bread crumbs   *½ cup hot milk*
4 cups boiling water   *Salt to taste*

• Add bread crumbs to boiling water. Simmer 10 minutes, then strain. Add milk and salt. Serve.

Makes 3 to 4 cups.

VICTORY DINNER

"Wars may come and wars may go," Prudence Penny wrote in her 1943 book of *Coupon Cookery,* "but real, red-blooded American Homemakers will put up a struggle to preserve the cherished custom of good eating."

During World War II, square meals were patriotic. They provided strength and morale for the men and women behind the men behind the guns. All of America—not just the army—was marshaled to fight on its stomach.

But it wasn't going to be easy. Lurking in the corners of wartime cookbooks were nasty little caricatures of Hitler and Hirohito, encouraging Americans to waste, or worse, to hoard food, coaxing housewives to overcook vegetables and pack family lunch pails with nothing but doughnuts. These cunning enemies knew that unbalanced meals were the best way to sap our stamina. They wanted to see the American spirit darkened as black as the coarse bread that Russians were reduced to eating, "smeared with lard."

Here was the problem: our armed forces were gobbling up forty million pounds of chow per day, and the lend-lease countries took more; supply lines from South America were choked with vital war minerals, leaving little room for importation of coffee, sugar, and fruit; oil was diverted into the manufacture of synthetic rubber and explosives.

Was Mrs. American Housewife going to sink to the dehumanizing expediency of Germany, where, according to one wartime magazine, "neutral-tasting protein powder" was replacing meat? Could John and Jane Q. Citizen wind up like the miserable lard-eating Russians?

Of course not, not if Yankee ingenuity was applied to the situation; and not if people cheerfully accepted their rationed lot. Nearly every major food company pitched in, printing wartime pamphlets suggesting how *their* product could help

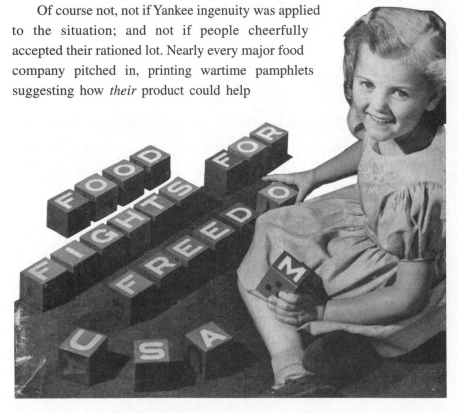

the homemaker skimp on precious foods like meat, sugar, fat, cheese, and coffee.

(In fact, it seems that there was hardly a man or woman who didn't have some way around the shortages—a friendly butcher, access to the commissary, or a shadowy acquaintance known as "Mr. Black." It is estimated that one-fifth of the nation's meat supply was sold on Mr. Black's market. "In New York, you could always wangle more," James Beard told us. "It was considered chic to circumvent rationing. The attitude was like that towards prohibition.")

Some of the emergency food measures designed to keep prices low were nothing more than silly inconveniences—such as the Agriculture Department's temporary ban on the sale of sliced bread (bakery slicing being considered a luxury), which led not only to a shortage of bread knives, but to the still-popular hyperbole "the greatest thing since sliced bread." On the other hand, meat rationing, instituted in early 1943, came in response to a winter in which beef had all but disappeared from butchers' shelves.

However mismanaged federal rationing programs, the ideal of a new, belt-tightened cuisine was disseminated during the war with utmost urgency by both government and industry. The American housewife was told that she had been drafted—as a soldier on the home front. "Hail to the women of America!" declared General Mills's Betty Crocker, in a foreword to a ration cookbook called *Your Share*. "You have been strengthening your country's defenses as plane watchers, as flyers, as members of the armed forces, as producers in war plants and homes, and in Red Cross and Civilian Defense activities. But whatever else you do, you are, first and foremost, homemakers— women with the welfare of your families deepest in your hearts. You must heed the government request to increase the use of available foods, and save those that are scarce—and at the same time, safeguard your family's nutrition."

No hoarding, no complaining, no wasting of food allowed. S-t-r-e-t-c-h those scarce supplies . . . but don't let on that anything is wanting. *That* was the trick of Victory dining, to make ration-shrunk meals seem bountiful and appetizing. *Health for Victory Meal Planning Guides* were abuzz with articles suggesting how to gussy up abundant but unpopular foods: "And My Family Swore They Didn't Like Liver!" . . . "Fish Today—But Oh So Different! . . . "Braised Oxtail for Dinner? Boy, Does That Smell Good!"

There would be no protein powder or lard sandwiches for the U.S.A. After all, the more appetizing the dinner, the happier a family would feel. And the happier they felt, the more eagerly they could tackle the task of building war machines. "Sound nerves, good appetite, the ability to thrive on hard physical work are the result of wholesome, nutritious meals," wrote Phillip W. Pillsbury in a brochure called *Fightin' Food.* War Manpower commissioner Paul V. McNutt said bluntly, "Better food for workers can increase production 14,000 bombers, 33,000 tanks a year."

Fightin' food is foremost an economical cuisine. However unchic the chow, wartime expediencies were—and still are—great ways to get maximum nutrition for the least money. But what we like best about Victory Dinner is how unabashedly clunky it is, as full of purpose and determination as a "Why We Fight" war movie. To us, it is the essence of the 1940s—the forthright taste of an idealized America.

Ration Point Cookery

LOW-POINT DINNER
Civilian Defense Cocktail • 207
Chicken in the Garden with Parsley Biscuits • 207
Cabbage, Apple, and Pickle Salad
 with Evaporated Milk Dressing • 209
Yankee Doodle Prune Pie in Victory Pie Crust • 210

The Heroic Hamburger

**STAND UP AND CHEER
HAMBURGER DINNER**
Boot Camp Spud Soup • 213
V-for-Victory Hamburgers • 214
Kitchen Patrol Carrots • 214
Gold Star Mom's Jelly Roll • 215

Burgers Again!

Military Meatballs • 216
Smack • 217
Hamburg Deep Dish Pie • 217

Victory Garden Dining

VICTORY GARDEN SUPPER
Home Front Vegetable Plate with Hot Cheese Sauce • 221
Tomato Cottage Cheese Salad with Garden Herbs • 222
Patriotic Applesauce • 223

Molasses Johnnycake • 223
Butterless Butter Spread • 224
Mock Whipped Cream (for Fresh Fruit) • 225
Soya Cocoa • 225

Health for Victory Bread

Tomato Juice Bread • 227
Sharpshooter Carrot Rolls • 228
Salute to Soya Corn Bread • 228
Boston Brown Bread • 229

Rosie the Riveter's Lunch Pail

Swing Shift Sandwich Filling • 231
Stretch-Your-Wiener Sandwich Filling • 231
Peanut Butter "Pep-Up" Sandwich Filling • 231
Carrot Sandwiches with Raisins and Peanuts • 232
Depth-Charged Prune Sandwich Filling • 232
Assembly Line Carrot-Meat Sandwiches • 232
Interlinked Doughnuts, U.S.N. • 233

Low-Point Budget Desserts

Wartime Cake • 234
E-Z Fluffy Frosting • 235
Eggless Chocolate Cake • 235
Cocoa Mile-a-Minute Frosting • 236
Hurry-Up Cake • 236
Flattop Orange Frosting • 237

Ice Cream and the War

Rookie Cookies

The War's Aftertaste

Ration Point Cookery

"Shortages will appear suddenly," *American Cookery* magazine wrote in 1942. "New foods will come to the fore; less-known foods will rise in popularity. Be prepared—the months that lie ahead of us will bring the greatest changes in our eating habits of any months in our lives."

In May 1942, sugar was rationed, then coffee, processed food, meat, and dairy products. Every civilian man, woman, and child got a ration book at the local elementary school. The book contained coupons with "point values" for different types of food—48 blue points per month for canned foods, 64 red points for meat, cheese, and oil. The tricky part of this system was that each week the point value of a particular food was liable to change, depending on its scarcity. But even if you had a purseful of red coupons, that was no guarantee you would find the cut of meat you wanted in the butcher's case.

Americans were suddenly called on to produce food (in Victory gardens), conserve food (by canning and preserving, and using every crumb and drop), share food (with the armed forces, with our allies, and with hardluck neighbors), and play square with food. It was nothing less than a vital war material. "Pledge yourself to accept no rationed food without giving up ration

IS THE MIGHTIEST WEAPON

stamps," beseeched one *Health for Victory Meal Planning Guide,* ". . . and to pay no more than top legal prices."

It was the American homemaker's duty to be flexible and clever, to plan menus that spread rationed food thin, and most important of all, to serve meals that would make the men and children in her charge healthy and strong . . . meals like this hale Victory Dinner. Its name comes from the fact that it uses up so few ration points.

Low-Point Dinner

Civilian Defense Cocktail ◆ *Chicken in the Garden with Parsley Biscuits* ◆ *Cabbage, Apple, and Pickle Salad with Evaporated Milk Dressing* ◆ *Yankee Doodle Prune Pie in Victory Pie Crust*

CIVILIAN DEFENSE COCKTAIL

Developed by Bridgeport, Connecticut's Civilian Defense Health and Nutrition Council, this working man's beverage required no rationed milk, and was extra healthy because of the vitamins in the tomato juice.

1 cup cold evaporated milk	*1 cup cold tomato juice*
1 cup cold water	*⅛ teaspoon salt*

• Mix milk and water. Stir in tomato juice and salt. Serve chilled.
  Makes 3 cups.

CHICKEN IN THE GARDEN
WITH PARSLEY BISCUITS

If you had no meat points left at all, or if your butcher's shelves were bare, ration cookbooks suggested chicken, which was unrationed, pointing out that it didn't have to be fried in scarce oil. It wasn't even necessary to pay top dollar for a young pullet.

If you've spent all your meat stamps
And haven't any more
Eating chicken is a pleasant way
To help to win the war.

—"Be Fair to the Fowl," Prudence Penny

This recipe comes from "Meeting the Meat Problem" in Ms. Penny's *Coupon Cookery*. We were dubious about using a stringy old stewing hen, but discovered that if slowly simmered till tender, it is far more flavorful than a callow spring chicken. With snapping fresh produce from the Victory garden, this is an eminently healthful stew, its biscuit top and cream gravy filling seductively nostalgic.

CHICKEN

1 3- to 4-pound stewing fowl
Salt and pepper
1 cup fresh green peas
1 cup sliced fresh carrots (3 to 4
*   medium carrots)*
2 cups diced celery
6 tablespoons chopped onion

8 tiny new potatoes
4 tablespoons enriched
*   all-purpose flour*
2 cups cooled broth, reserved
*   from chicken and*
*   cooked vegetables*
1 cup evaporated milk or cream

• Cut up fowl and cover with hot water. Add salt and pepper to season, cover, and simmer gently until tender (about 3 hours). Cool and remove from bones. Remove skin.

Place vegetables in saucepan with close-fitting lid. Add ½ teaspoon salt and 1 cup water, or enough to cover. Cover and place over full heat until water boils; reduce heat to simmer and continue cooking for 25 minutes, or until vegetables are just tender. The liquids should cook down to just a few table-spoons, which can be used in the gravy.

Make gravy by blending flour with a few tablespoons of cooled chicken broth, then adding the remainder of the 2 cups and stirring until smooth. Return to saucepan and continue cooking until thick, then add salt and pepper to taste, and evaporated milk or cream.

Preheat oven to 425°.

Alternate chicken and vegetables in large (3-quart) casserole, and mix ingredients with gravy. Top with Parsley Biscuits.

Bake 25 minutes, or until biscuits are golden brown.

Serves 6.

PARSLEY BISCUITS

2 cups enriched all-purpose flour   *4 tablespoons shortening*

2 teaspoons baking powder   *⅔ to ¾ cup milk*

½ teaspoon salt   *½ cup finely chopped parsley*

1 teaspoon sugar

• Mix and sift dry ingredients; cut in shortening finely (a food processor is perfect for this), then add milk and parsley, mixing very lightly until you have a stiff dough.

Pat out to ¼-inch thickness and cut in rounds with a drinking glass or biscuit cutter, or in squares or doughnut shapes. Proceed as in recipe for chicken, above.

"PENNY TIP: *Little things bring big results! Here the parsley pays flavor dividends.*"

CABBAGE, APPLE, AND PICKLE SALAD
WITH EVAPORATED MILK DRESSING

From the *Health for Victory Meal Planning Guide of* "point-thrifty menus," a pamphlet of recipes, nutrition guidance, and moral support published monthly by the Home Economics Institute of Westinghouse Electric Company. "Who'd ever have believed so few points could do so much?"

SALAD

2 cups shredded cabbage	¼ cup chopped sweet pickle
⅛ teaspoon salt	3 tablespoons pickle juice
1 cup diced, unpeeled apple	

• Combine all ingredients. Add Evaporated Milk Dressing.
Serves 4 to 6.

DRESSING

"Milk is our most nearly perfect food," said the *Health for Victory Meal Planning Guide.* "All of us should have as much milk as possible." And yet fresh milk was scarce. This tangy white froth requires no fresh milk, and is excellent for any cole slaw or cabbage salad.

½ cup sugar	½ teaspoon salt
⅓ cup vinegar	
½ cup well-chilled evaporated milk	

• Add sugar to vinegar, and stir until sugar is dissolved. In a separate bowl, beat chilled milk with rotary mixer until it thickens. Continue beating; add sugar-vinegar mixture and salt. Pour over salad. Mix lightly with fork.

YANKEE DOODLE PRUNE PIE
IN VICTORY PIE CRUST

Sugar was rationed and in short supply, yet it was among the most wasted foods. According to Margot Murphy's *Wartime Meals,* published in 1942, "One of the most obvious leaks is the undissolved sugar in the bottom of a cup of tea or coffee—in New York City alone it reaches the amazing total of 3½ tons a day!"

The dearth of sugar made dessert a special problem of wartime dining. This powerfully satisfying pie, listed as a "Wartime Dessert" in the May 1942 issue of *American Cookery,* substitutes unrationed honey.

PIE FILLING

2½ cups uncooked prunes	*2 tablespoons butter*
1 lemon, unpeeled	*½ teaspoon salt*
1 cup water, reserved from	*1 tablespoon cornstarch*
cooking prunes	*1 tablespoon cold water*
½ cup honey	

• Preheat oven to 450°.

Cover prunes with water, bring to a boil and cook 10 minutes. Reserve 1 cup "prune water." Drain, pit, and coarsely chop prunes. Slice lemon, remove seeds, chop into small bits; return prunes, chopped lemon, "prune water," honey, and butter to saucepan. Stir over low heat until butter melts. Add salt. Add cornstarch that has been moistened with 1 tablespoon cold water, and stir until mixture thickens. Pour filling into a 9-inch pastry-lined pie plate. Cover with strips of pastry.

Bake 30 to 40 minutes.

VICTORY PIE CRUST

"You can be patriotic and yet have grand pies by adopting this prize, low-shortening pie crust for the duration," proclaimed *How to Bake by the Ration Book,* a General Foods publication of 1943. Because of its low ratio of shortening to flour, Victory Crust is an indelicate affair, thick and sturdy, for heavy fruit pies.

2½ cups cake flour	*6 tablespoons cold shortening*
½ teaspoon baking powder	*8 tablespoons ice water*
1 teaspoon salt	

• Sift flour once, measure, add baking powder and salt, and sift again. Cut shortening into small pieces; add to flour and cut in until mixture is almost as fine as cornmeal. In food processor or by hand, add ice water tablespoon by tablespoon to dough until dough forms ball. Divide into 2 parts, and dust lightly with flour. Wrap in wax paper and chill 1 hour.

Roll each part out on floured pastry board. Makes top and bottom crust.

The Heroic Hamburger

Fowls be damned! To Americans *meat* meant *red meat,* hunks of cow. And yet, in the East especially, beef was among the scarcest wartime foods. The solution suggested by most cookbooks was hamburger, a wartime staple—inexpensive, stretchable, quick to cook, and usually available; but best of all, it was *meat.*

Or was it something more than meat? To poet Hazel Sage, writing for a wartime issue of *American Cookery,* it was "a sizzling success story . . . a great institution with a heroic history. Who could imagine America without it?"

The Heavenly Hamburger

Now come, all you lovers of dining,
Who tackle the menu with zest,
Come join in a toast to our national boast—
The viand that vies with the best,
That singular succulent spheroid
Of strictly American make,
The meaty but natty symmetrical patty:
The hamburger steak!

Stand Up and Cheer Hamburger Dinner

Boot Camp Spud Soup ◆ V-for-Victory Hamburgers ◆ Kitchen Patrol Carrots ◆ Victory Garden Salad (recipe not included) ◆ Gold Star Mom's Jelly Roll

BOOT CAMP SPUD SOUP

New York Times food editor Margot Murphy, also known as Jane Holt, suggested that men who wanted to keep their budget low and nutritional intake high ought to eat 7½ pounds of potatoes per week; a moderately active woman required 4 pounds; for a growing teenager, 7 pounds was enough.

And if, somehow, the family couldn't finish all their mashed potatoes at dinner one night, the conscientious housewife would never throw the leftovers away. She brought them back to the table the next day, made into this potato soup, a surprisingly delicate bowl of economical *richesse,* from a 1943 *Meal Planning Guide.*

4 cups milk
2 tablespoons grated onion
2 cups mashed potatoes, buttered
* and seasoned*
3 tablespoons butter or
* fortified margarine*

1 tablespoon enriched all-purpose
* flour*
1½ teaspoons salt
⅛ teaspoon pepper
1 tablespoon chopped parsley

• Scald milk with onion, mix slowly with potatoes. Melt half the butter or margarine, add dry ingredients, mix well. Add to hot soup. Stir well. Boil 1 minute. Add rest of butter or margarine and sprinkle with chopped parsley.

  Serves 4 to 6.

V-FOR-VICTORY HAMBURGERS

A simple way to stretch a pound to feed four to six people, from a 1944 Westinghouse *Meal Planning Guide.*

1 teaspoon salt	*1 pound ground beef*
⅛ teaspoon pepper	*6 slices onion, browned in 2*
¼ cup water	*tablespoons shortening*
⅓ cup soya meal	*6 slices bacon*

• Add salt, pepper, and water to soya meal and mix thoroughly with meat. Pat mixture into 12 thin cakes. Spread browned onion slices on half the meat cakes. Put remaining cakes on top as a sandwich. Press edges together. Wrap each with a strip of bacon and fasten with a toothpick.

Broil on each side about 5 minutes or until brown.

Serves 4 to 6.

KITCHEN PATROL CARROTS

To cook the carrots properly, abide by this poem, from "Vegetables on the Home-Front" in *Coupon Cookery:*

A vegetable correctly cooked
Has color, health and taste!
A vegetable that's murdered
In the pot is so much waste.
Use just a little water
And not too long a time—
Make your vegetables a perfect dish
And not a perfect crime!

6 carrots, cut in half	*⅛ teaspoon salt*
2 tablespoons butter, melted	*Dash pepper*
¾ cup corn flakes, crushed	*Dash paprika*

• Cook carrots in boiling water until just barely tender.

Preheat oven to 400°.

Lay carrots in heatproof dish. Add butter; turn carrots gently to coat. Sprinkle with corn flakes and seasoning, turning carrots gently.

Bake, uncovered, 10 minutes.

Serves 4 to 6.

GOLD STAR MOM'S JELLY ROLL

"Running low on shortening? This is the day for a jelly roll—no shortening and no frosting, either." (From *How to Bake by the Ration Book.*)

¾ cup cake flour	*¾ cup granulated sugar*
¾ teaspoon baking powder	*1 teaspoon vanilla extract*
¼ teaspoon salt	*Confectioners' sugar*
4 eggs	*1 cup raspberry jelly*

• Preheat oven to 400°.

Grease a 10-by-15-by-1-inch jelly-roll pan. Line with parchment paper or aluminum foil and grease top of lining.

Sift flour once, measure. Combine baking powder, salt, and eggs in the top of a double boiler over hot water. Beat with electric hand mixer on high for 3 minutes, adding granulated sugar gradually. Remove from heat and beat 2 more minutes, adding flour and vanilla. Pour batter into pan.

Bake 13 minutes.

Turn out on a clean dishtowel dusted with confectioners' sugar. Remove paper. Spread with jelly and roll up. Wrap with dishtowel to cool.

Burgers Again!

Suppose the family's sick of hamburgers, but there's still a pound of ground round in the icebox? The smart wartime homemaker figured out a way to get her burger meat to look like something else. "Thou shalt get out of thy food rut!" Prudence Penny commanded, suggesting these all-American ways to glorify chopped meat for a family dinner.

MILITARY MEATBALLS

"Not all ground meat ends up between buns," noted *American Cookery* in 1942. "A deft cook can dazzle at dinner with a pound of ground meat and an uninhibited flair for what goes into it."

1 pound ground beef	*4 slices bread*
3 tablespoons grated onion	*2 tablespoons flour, plus flour for*
1 teaspoon salt	*dredging*
¼ teaspoon pepper	*2 tablespoons bacon drippings*
1 egg	*1 cup milk*

• Combine meat, onion, seasonings, and egg.

Toast bread slowly until dry and brown. Cover with water and allow to soak thoroughly. Squeeze water from toast and combine toast with meat mixture.

Shape into small balls, dredge with flour, and brown in drippings. Remove meat from pan. Add flour to fat, stir until smooth, then gradually add milk, stirring constantly until smooth and thickened.

Place meatballs in gravy, cover, and simmer about 45 minutes or until tender.

Serves 4.

SMACK

A grand anything-goes casserole that just may be the inspiration for Hamburger Helper. How this dish got its name, Prudence Penny doesn't say, but she does proclaim, *"Experiment with this recipe! You won't go far wrong."*

*1 pound round steak or
  lean beef
½ pound salt pork or
  slab bacon
1 large onion, chopped
2 tablespoons bacon fat
  or butter
1 clove garlic, minced
1 teaspoon salt
½ teaspoon pepper
8 ounces uncooked spaghetti,
  broken in small pieces*

*2 to 3 cups cooked
  tomatoes, crushed
1 cup cooked peas or corn or
  ½ cup each
1 4-ounce can pimiento,
  chopped fine
½ pound American cheese,
  grated coarse
½ cup ripe black olives, sliced*

• Grind meats together. In a very large skillet, cook onion in shortening until soft; add meat and garlic, salt and pepper, cook until dark brownish red, stirring frequently.

Preheat oven to 350°.

Cook spaghetti in boiling salted water, drain, and add to meat with tomatoes, vegetables, half the pimiento, half the grated cheese, and half the olives. Mix ingredients well, then pour into oiled 3-quart casserole, put balance of pimiento, olives, and cheese over top, and cover.

Bake 30 to 45 minutes.

Serves 6 to 8.

HAMBURG DEEP DISH PIE

Hamburg Pie, taken from the February 1942 issue of *American Cookery*, is a meat-stretcher recipe that serves four, although if you're feeling flush, you might want to up the meat to a full pound. The filling will accommodate near-ly any kind of leftover vegetables ("Waste during war is sabotage!").

MEAT PIE FILLING

¾ pound hamburg steak

3 teaspoons salt

Few grains pepper

¾ cup tomato puree

6 small young carrots,
   sliced lengthwise

½ cup peas

2 large potatoes, diced

5 small onions

• Grease a casserole. Add a layer of meat, flaked with a fork. Sprinkle with part of salt and pepper, add some tomato puree and vegetables, and continue to layer within an inch of top of casserole. Use enough vegetables to fill space; distribute meat and seasonings well. Pack lightly so there will be room for them to expand as they cook. The tomato puree and the natural meat and vegetable juices will provide sufficient moisture.

BISCUIT CRUST

2 cups enriched all-purpose flour

¾ teaspoon salt

3 tablespoons shortening
   (margarine, butter, lard)

5 teaspoons sifted baking
   powder

¾ cup milk

• Preheat oven to 400°.

Sift flour and salt, cut in shortening (a food processor is perfect for this); add baking powder and mix lightly. Add milk all at once and mix to form a ball.

Turn out dough on a floured board and knead lightly about ½ minute, then flatten ball. Place it over Meat Pie Filling and score with a knife dipped in milk.

Bake 25 minutes, then reduce temperature to 300° and bake 35 minutes longer. Serve as soon as baked.

Serves 4.

Victory Garden Dining

Although it isn't
Our usual habit,
This year we're eating
The Easter Rabbit.
—*Gourmet* magazine, 1943

What if all your meat points were used up, there was none to stretch, and the grocer had neither fowl nor pigs' tails? That was a day to take a deep breath, roll up your sleeves, and go meatless! "No Meat Today . . . but Plenty of Protein!" heralds a headline in the February 1944 *Meal Planning Guide*, assuring readers that it was actually possible to live an entire day without eating beef. In fact, it was a great patriotic sacrifice to set aside one day each week as your family's meatless day. Even Dad could be fooled into enjoying a meatless dinner. "Not a speck of meat on this menu!" boasted one wartime cookbook, adding in smaller, timid type, "But who cares?"

The problem was compounded by a severe shortage of tin, which made canned vegetables a convenience of the past for most households during the war. In early 1942, to help remedy the situation, Secretary of Agriculture Claude R. Wickard conceived the idea of Victory gardens. Civilians were encouraged to grow their own produce, in backyards or in patches of land

near their factory, thereby lessening the burden on Uncle Sam, who had all those soldiers to feed.

Of all home front emergency measures, the Victory garden movement was by far the most successful and popular. It provided good, cheap food; it was an activity that whole families or groups of workers could do together in a spirit of patriotic comradeship; and unlike rationing and price control, where there was so much bureaucratic mismanagement and cheating, it was back-to-the-land wholesome. By 1943, nearly half the vegetables eaten in America were picked from Victory gardens—one million tons a year.

Kitchens grown accustomed to the ease of supermarket shopping were forced back to a rediscovery of fresh, homegrown food—an unexpected (but temporary) fringe benefit of patriotism.

With its emphasis on vegetables from the Victory garden and its substitution of soybeans and fish (both abundant) for red meat, wartime cooking was surprisingly like the health food of modern times.

Of course, health in the 1940s did not mean, as it does today, trim and slim. Nineteen forties health signified *might*. Children, women, and men were supposed to be as sturdy as tanks, and the way to get that way was to consume vast amounts of protein—the "first class protein" of meat, eggs, and cheese, plus the "second class protein" provided by cereals, nuts, and beans.

Given those standards of healthy eating, even a meatless Victory garden meal could be astoundingly robust. "Serve this vegetable dinner with pride! Eat it with gusto!" said the August 1944 *Meal Planning Guide*.

Victory Garden Supper

Home Front Vegetable Plate with Hot Cheese Sauce ◆ *Tomato Cottage Cheese Salad with Garden Herbs* ◆ *Patriotic Applesauce* ◆ *Molasses Johnnycake with Butterless Butter Spread* ◆ *Fresh Fruit with Mock Whipped Cream* ◆ *Soya Cocoa*

HOME FRONT VEGETABLE PLATE
WITH HOT CHEESE SAUCE

The discomforting thing about a Victory garden meal was that it lacked the reassuring anchor provided by a large hunk of meat. In this recipe, a whole head of cauliflower substitutes as a formidable visual cue.

1 head cauliflower
4 large carrots, cut in strips
2 medium summer squash, sliced
  in disks
2 bunches beets, sliced
2½ cups cleaned
  Brussels sprouts

2½ cups snap beans, cut through
  lengthwise
Salt
Butter, fortified margarine,
  or drippings

• Steam cauliflower in deep pot with salted water. Cook all other vegetables in separate pots with salted water until tender. Add salt and butter (or margarine or drippings) to taste.

Put cauliflower in center of a large plate and arrange other vegetables around cauliflower. Pour Hot Cheese Sauce over cauliflower and let it flow onto other vegetables.

Serves 4.

HOT CHEESE SAUCE

"Cheese is an economical protein food," said Kraft in a 1943 brochure called *Cheese Recipes for Wartime Meals*. "And it is all food . . . there is no waste. An entire meal can be planned around a splendid cheese main dish."

3 tablespoons butter or fortified margarine	*¼ teaspoon salt*
	Dash pepper
2 tablespoons enriched all-purpose flour	*2 teaspoons prepared mustard*
	1 cup grated Cheddar cheese
1 cup milk	

• Melt butter or margarine in heavy saucepan. Blend in flour. Add milk slowly. Cook until thickened, stirring constantly.

Remove from heat. Add seasonings and cheese. Stir until cheese is melted.

TOMATO COTTAGE CHEESE SALAD WITH GARDEN HERBS

"Most spices come from parts of the world now lost to us," lamented *Wartime Meals*. "The time is here to learn how to get along without them. Herbs are the answer, and a most agreeable one at that. We forgot all about herbs, until interest was revived a few years ago by a handful of enthusiasts. As a result of their activities, herbs became 'smart.' Now they have a job to do in our war effort. You may grow them in your own garden, even right at hand in your kitchen if you have a sunny window."

5 medium tomatoes	*Fresh herbs—basil, bay,*
1¼ cups creamed cottage cheese	*chervil, marjoram, or tarragon*
	Lettuce or other salad greens

• Scald tomatoes in boiling water and peel. Chill.

Cut tomatoes into wedges, being careful not to cut all the way through. Spread gently and fill centers with ¼ cup cottage cheese. Sprinkle with herbs. Serve on lettuce or salad greens.

Serves 5.

PATRIOTIC APPLESAUCE

No sugar needed!

2 pounds summer apples
¾ to 1 cup water

⅓ cup honey
¼ teaspoon cinnamon

• Wash apples, remove blossom and stem ends, also any bad spots. Cut into quarters. Trim away core, but do not peel.

Put apples into a saucepan; add water. Cover and bring to a boil. Simmer until apples are soft. Drain.

Put apples through a ricer, blender, or food processor. Add honey and cinnamon. Heat thoroughly so honey dissolves.

Serves 4 to 6.

MOLASSES JOHNNYCAKE

This cakelike bread, named to honor Rhode Island's favorite little cornmeal pancake, is moist and sweet, thanks to ration-free molasses. It is a good companion to dinner, or as a savory snack by itself, with a schmear of room temperature butter.

1 cup cornmeal
¾ cup sifted enriched all-purpose
  flour
4 teaspoons baking powder
¾ teaspoon salt

1 egg, well beaten
¾ cup milk
½ cup molasses
1 tablespoon shortening, melted
  and cooled

• Preheat oven to 425°.

Sift dry ingredients together. Combine egg, milk, molasses, and melted shortening. Combine liquid and dry ingredients and pour into greased cast-iron skillet about 8 inches in diameter.

Bake 25 minutes.

Cut into wedges and serve.

Serves 8.

BUTTERLESS BUTTER SPREAD

"Your butter points don't go far enough?" Don't complain. "We folks at home are pretty lucky after all," said the March 1944 *Meal Planning Guide*. "Be glad you're not in China, where butter costs $500 a pound in Chinese money . . . if by hook or crook, one can find any at all." This inexpensive butter substitute tastes like a cross between butter and mayo. From *Coupon Cookery's* chapter on "Lunch That Packs a Punch."

1 tablespoon	*½ cup fresh or evaporated milk*
unflavored gelatin	*½ cup mayonnaise*
1 tablespoon cold water	*½ pound margarine*
3 tablespoons boiling water	*½ teaspoon salt*

• Soften gelatin in cold water, then add boiling water and stir until gelatin is completely dissolved. Add milk, then gelatin mixture, gradually to mayonnaise, stirring until smooth. Cool until thickened.

Soften but do not melt margarine. Add mayonnaise mixture, one-quarter at a time, and add salt, beating with rotary egg beater after each addition. Store in covered dish in refrigerator.

Makes about 2½ cups, or enough for 20 sandwiches, 2 tablespoons each.

MOCK WHIPPED CREAM (for Fresh Fruit)

A milkless topping from *Coupon Cookery*.

2 egg whites	*1 cup grated apple*
½ cup confectioners' sugar	*1 teaspoon fresh lemon juice*

• Beat egg whites until stiff. Add ¼ cup confectioners' sugar while beating. Then add grated apple and ¼ cup confectioners' sugar alternately as beating continues. Flavor with fresh lemon juice.

Dollop on fresh berries.

SOYA COCOA

"Soya flour is so rich in protein that one pound gives you as much as two pounds of lean beef," said the February 1944 *Meal Planning Guide*. "Use it to enrich meat loaves, patties, stews, meat pies, gravies, biscuits, griddle cakes, bread, pastry, candy, ice cream, and cocoa!"

1 tablespoon soya flour	*⅛ teaspoon salt*
3 tablespoons cocoa	*3 cups milk, scalding hot*
3 tablespoons sugar	*½ teaspoon vanilla extract*
½ cup water	

• Mix soya flour, cocoa, sugar, water, and salt to a paste. Bring to a boil and cook until smooth (1 or 2 minutes). Add to hot milk, then add vanilla.

Serves 6.

Health for Victory Bread

S hocked by the many rejections of draftees for disabilities due to poor nutrition, a pamphlet called *Fightin' Food* scolded its readers in 1942: "We Americans have always eaten just the way we like to eat, whether or not we got the food elements we needed."

Housewives were encouraged to skimp but admonished to *get the vitamins into their food!* One shining patriotic example was Miss E. Thompson Wylie, who opened a small shop in New York specializing in bread. "As bread is the one food eaten by practically every member of the family," she said, "I decided that it was the best form in which to give them their vitamins. Grass bread seems so sensible, since grass is what the cow eats to produce the milk we lay such store by." Her repertoire included not only grass bread, but watercress bread, carrot bread, even—look out, kids!—spinach bread ("a wonderful way of feeding children the spinach which is so good for them but which they refuse to eat in its natural form").

Equally all-American was the army's attempt to squeeze the vitamins from tomatoes into loaves of bread:

Enriched White flour now contains important nutrients natural to the whole wheat berry.

TOMATO JUICE BREAD

Notorious "Red Bread," developed by the Army Subsistence Research Laboratory as a means of upping bread's nutritional value, was made by the army with powdered tomato juice . . . and was a complete failure among G.I.'s—"jarringly unappetizing," according to *Chow: A Cook's Tour of Military Food.*

But we sampled this tomato bread recipe from Pillsbury's 1942 *Fightin' Food* pamphlet and thought it swell—pretty pink, hearty, with just the faintest tomato tang. (Try it toasted, for a BLT sandwich!)

1 cup hot tomato juice	*1 package dry yeast dissolved in*
4 tablespoons sugar	*1¼ cups tepid water (110°) with*
1 tablespoon salt	*1 tablespoon sugar*
1½ tablespoons melted	*6 cups enriched all-purpose*
* shortening*	* white flour*

• Combine tomato juice, sugar, salt, and shortening, stirring until dissolved. Cool to lukewarm.

Add yeast mixture to lukewarm tomato mixture.

Sift flour once, measure; add to yeast mixture, blending thoroughly.

Turn onto floured board and knead. If dough sticks, add a little flour. To obtain a fine grain, kneading should be continued for a full 10 minutes.

Place dough in greased bowl; cover and allow to rise in warm place (80° to 85°) about 2 hours, or until dough will retain impression of a finger.

Punch gas from dough by plunging fist into center. Fold over edges; turn upside down. Cover and allow to rise in a warm place until dough is half as large as its original size (about 30 minutes).

Remove dough to floured board and flatten out. Divide into 2 pieces; mold into balls; allow to stand, closely covered, for 15 minutes. Shape into loaves.

Place in 2 greased 9-by-4-by-3-inch bread pans and cover. Allow to stand in warm place until dough fills pan and center is well above top of pan (1 to 2 hours).

Preheat oven to 400°.

Bake about 40 minutes. Remove from pan to cool.

Makes 2 1-pound loaves.

SHARPSHOOTER CARROT ROLLS

From Prudence Penny's *Coupon Cookery,* these old-fashioned rolls are delightfully dopey looking—great with stew or soup, or nearly any square meal. The grated carrots give them a faintly sweet taste, and they can be enjoyed with minimal amounts of butter.

"PENNY TIP: *Golden color, rich flavor, and high food value!*"

3 to 3½ cups enriched all-purpose flour	*1 package granular yeast dissolved in ¼ cup tepid water (110°)*
1 cup soya flour	
4 tablespoons sugar	*4 tablespoons melted shortening*
1 teaspoon salt	*1 cup finely grated carrots*
1 cup warm water	*1 egg, beaten*

• Sift dry ingredients and add water, yeast, and melted shortening.

Add grated carrots and well-beaten egg. Mix thoroughly; knead lightly a few minutes, adding flour as necessary until dough is smooth and elastic.

Place in well-greased bowl, cover, and allow to rise until double in bulk.

Knead lightly, then roll out to ½-inch thickness. Cut with floured 2½-inch glass. Place on greased baking sheet, cover with cloth, and allow to rise again (about 1 hour).

Preheat oven to 425°.

Bake until golden brown—about 20 minutes.

Makes 18 rolls.

SALUTE TO SOYA CORN BREAD

Of all the vegetable sources for supercharged nutrition, it was soybeans that became, as *American Cookery* effervesced, the "Star on the Food-for-Defense Stage." Superabundant during the war, the humble legume was touted as a meat extender or all by itself as a main dish, a soya loaf, or cream of soya soup. You could grind the beans in salad, mash them for sandwiches or casseroles. You could roast them and serve instead of nuts. "They are a friend in need when ration points run low."

½ cup soya flour	1 teaspoon salt
¾ cup cornmeal	2 tablespoons sugar
1 cup sifted enriched	2 eggs, beaten
all-purpose flour	1½ cups milk
4 teaspoons baking powder	4 tablespoons butter, melted

• Preheat oven to 375°.

Sift dry ingredients together. Add beaten eggs to milk, and add to dry ingredients. Add melted butter last, Pour batter into a greased 8- or 10-inch cast-iron skillet or pan.

Bake 30 to 40 minutes, or until brown.

Cool and serve directly from cast-iron pan.

BOSTON BROWN BREAD

"In many countries of the world, milk isn't considered ready to drink until it sours. But in America, we're apt to throw away that last cup or two when it turns. That's wasteful and unpatriotic." This recipe from *Fightin' Food* is doubly right-minded—it uses up leftover sour milk, and it requires no sugar.

1 cup enriched all-purpose flour	1 cup whole wheat or graham
2 teaspoons baking soda	flour
1½ teaspoons salt	¾ cup molasses or strained honey
1 cup cornmeal (yellow or white)	2 cups sour milk or buttermilk

• Sift all-purpose flour once, measure; add soda and salt; sift together. Add cornmeal and whole wheat flour; mix well.

Combine molasses and sour milk; add to dry ingredients; mix thoroughly.

Fill greased 8-cup pudding mold two-thirds full. Cover. In kettle with cover, large enough to hold pudding mold, place a metal trivet or mason jar ring. Put pudding mold on trivet. Add 3 inches of water and bring to boil.

Steam 2½ to 3 hours, adding water to keep level up. When cooked, remove from steamer and let stand 10 minutes before unmolding.

Note: Leftover Boston Brown Bread may be reheated in the top part of a double boiler.

Rosie the Riveter's Lunch Pail

If Uncle Sam can carry food
To all our fighting men—
It's not too much for us to pack
A lunchbox now and then.
The mid-day meal must fight fatigue
That's always somewhere lurkin'—
It takes a tasty, hearty lunch
To keep our workers workin'.

—Prudence Penny, *Coupon Cookery*

A child who skipped his noonday meal would likely grow up weak and fail his army physical; workers, both men and women, who missed lunch were liable to suffer "midafternoon slump"—the cause of many a careless accident and lost hours in defense plants. No question about it—to go without a square meal in the middle of the day was treason.

When Nell Giles, known to readers as Smooth Susan, author of a syndicated column on charm and poise, toured America's defense plants in 1942, the girls on the assembly line told her, "We want lunches we can work on . . . it takes stamina to turn out bomber parts!"

Nell found sandwiches "the most monotonous part of factory life" until she met a worker named Margaret, with a repertoire so varied that "she can go for a solid month and not have the same sandwich twice." Margaret suggested varying the bread (try Tomato Juice Bread), substituting curry for salt and pepper, and mixing mayonnaise with hot Mexican relish; but her one unshakable rule was to make the sandwich thick, "hearty enough to be held firmly between two hands."

For two-handed Victory lunch sandwiches, try these bomber maker's favorites from the November 1943 *Meal Planning Guide*.

SWING SHIFT SANDWICH FILLING

2 cups baked beans	*½ teaspoon salt*
¾ cup peanut butter	*⅛ teaspoon pepper*
½ cup evaporated milk	
¾ cup finely chopped	
sweet pickle	

• Drain beans and mash with a fork. Blend in peanut butter and milk. Add pickle, salt, and pepper and mix thoroughly.

Makes 3 cups sandwich filling.

STRETCH-YOUR-WIENER SANDWICH FILLING

1 pound cooked wieners	*Dash Tabasco*
½ cup pickle relish	*¼ cup sweet pickle juice*
1 cup mayonnaise	*3 hard-boiled eggs*
1 tablespoon minced onion	*½ teaspoon salt*

• Chop wieners and mix well with other ingredients.

Makes 15 to 20 sandwiches.

PEANUT BUTTER "PEP-UP" SANDWICH FILLING

• To sufficient peanut butter for 4 or 5 sandwiches (about 1 cup) add ¼ cup honey and 1 cake compressed yeast. This makes an excellent sandwich, because yeast is rich in vitamins.

CARROT SANDWICHES
WITH RAISINS AND PEANUTS

1 cup raw carrots	*½ teaspoon salt*
1 cup salted peanuts	*2 teaspoons lemon juice*
1 cup seedless raisins	*2 tablespoons mayonnaise*

• Chop carrots, peanuts, and raisins; mix together. Add remaining ingredients. Mix well and store in refrigerator. Use on whole wheat or rye bread.

Makes 10 sandwiches.

DEPTH-CHARGED PRUNE
SANDWICH FILLING

½ cup peanut butter	*6 pitted prunes, cut into*
⅓ teaspoon salt	*small pieces*
½ cup evaporated milk	*1 cup seedless raisins, chopped*
1 tablespoon lemon juice	

• Put peanut butter and salt in a bowl and blend with milk and lemon juice. Add fruit and mix well.

Makes 6 large sandwiches.

ASSEMBLY LINE CARROT-MEAT SANDWICHES

"They'll eat leftovers and love 'em!"

½ cup mayonnaise	*1 cup ground cooked meat*
1 teaspoon grated onion	*(leftover beef, veal, chicken,*
¾ teaspoon salt	*or ham)*
⅛ teaspoon pepper	*½ cup chopped raw carrot*

• Mix all ingredients together.

Makes enough for 6 sandwiches.

For dessert on the assembly line, rookie cookies, fruit, or candy bars were fine to pack, but in March 1942, *American Cookery* suggested this hommage to the boys at sea as a way to deal with lunch pail monotony: doughnuts that resemble the anchor chain on a ship.

INTERLINKED DOUGHNUTS, U.S.N.

4 tablespoons butter	**2 tablespoons baking powder**
1½ cups sugar	**⅛ teaspoon nutmeg**
3 eggs, well beaten	**¼ teaspoon cinnamon**
1 teaspoon salt	**1 cup milk**
3 cups fine whole wheat flour	**Fat for frying (48 to 64 ounces,**
3 cups enriched all-purpose flour	**depending on size of fryer)**

• Cream butter and sugar; add eggs. Sift dry ingredients together and add to mixture, alternating with milk. Mix well.

Sift a little all-purpose flour on a breadboard. Turn dough onto board; knead lightly (about 10 strokes), roll to about ¾ inch thick, and cut out doughnuts with standard cutter. Let them stand on board a few minutes.

Make diagonal slits with knife in half the doughnuts. Slip a cut doughnut through a whole one; moisten ends and press together.

Fry doughnuts until golden brown a few pairs at a time, about 2½ minutes in deep fat at 375°. As soon as they rise to top of fat, pull them apart lightly with 2 forks, so that 2 interlinked doughnuts will not stick together.

Makes 20 pairs and an extra single doughnut.

Low-Point Budget Desserts

E ven if you completely ran out of eggs, milk, and butter, there was no need
to end a meal feeling gloomy. "Who said 'no cake'?" asked *How to Bake
by the Ration Book*. "Of *course* you can have cake,
as delicious as in the good old unrationed days."

WARTIME CAKE

Eggless, milkless, butterless! A classic
cake going back to World War I (when
it was called Canadian War Cake), so
delicious that many homemakers kept it
in their repertoire long after rationing
ended. An easy recipe from a wartime Betty
Crocker booklet called *Your Share*. The moist, spicy
cake is swell for dessert or snacking.

1 cup dark brown sugar	*½ teaspoon ground cloves*
1¼ cups plus 2 teaspoons water	*1 teaspoon salt*
⅓ cup vegetable shortening	*1 teaspoon baking soda*
2 cups raisins	*2 cups sifted enriched*
½ teaspoon nutmeg	*all-purpose flour*
2 teaspoons cinnamon	*1 teaspoon baking powder*

• In saucepan, mix sugar, 1¼ cups water, shortening, raisins, nutmeg, cinnamon, and cloves. Boil 3 minutes. Cool.

Preheat oven to 325°.

Dissolve salt and soda in 2 teaspoons water. Add to mixture. Blend in
flour mixed with baking powder. Pour into greased and floured 8-inch-square
pan.

Bake 50 minutes.

Top with E-Z Fluffy Frosting; or this cake is delicious un-iced.

E-Z FLUFFY FROSTING

1 egg white　　　　　　　　　　*½ cup light corn syrup or honey*
Dash salt　　　　　　　　　　　*1 teaspoon vanilla extract*

• Beat egg white with salt until stiff enough to hold up in peaks, but not dry. Pour syrup in fine stream over egg white, beating constantly 4 or 5 minutes, or until of right consistency to spread. Add vanilla.

Makes enough frosting to cover top of 10-by-10-by-12-inch cake, or tops and sides of 2 8-inch layers.

EGGLESS CHOCOLATE CAKE

"They won't believe you, but it's true. No eggs at all and only ⅓ cup shortening in this tender, delicious, quick chocolate cake that took you only 1 minute to beat." An easy and surprisingly luscious pastry from *How to Bake by the Ration Book*.

2 ounces unsweetened chocolate　　*1 cup sugar*
1 cup milk　　　　　　　　　　　*⅓ cup shortening (we*
1¾ cups cake flour　　　　　　　　*recommend butter)*
¾ teaspoon baking soda　　　　　*1 teaspoon vanilla extract*
¾ teaspoon salt

• Preheat oven to 375°.

Combine chocolate and milk in top of double boiler and cook over rapidly boiling water 5 minutes, stirring occasionally. Blend with rotary egg beater; cool.

Sift flour once, measure, add soda, salt, and sugar, and sift together three times. Cream shortening; add flour, vanilla, and chocolate mixture and stir until all flour is dampened. Then beat vigorously 1 minute.

Bake in 2 buttered and lightly floured 8-inch layer pans 20 to 25 minutes, or until sharp knife inserted in cake comes out clean.

Cool in pans 5 minutes, then on rack; but be careful handling the layers—they are fragile! Spread with Cocoa Mile-a-Minute Frosting.

COCOA MILE-A-MINUTE FROSTING

To give the patriotic look to your wartime cake, spread this low-shortening frosting thin—between the layers and on top, but leave the sides as bare as a boot camp haircut.

> *1 tablespoon butter*
>   *or shortening*
> *3 tablespoons milk*
> *1½ cups sifted*
>   *confectioners' sugar*
>
> *4 tablespoons cocoa*
> *Dash salt*
> *½ teaspoon vanilla extract*

• Heat shortening with milk until melted.

Mix together sugar, cocoa, and salt. Add hot milk, stirring to blend; then add vanilla and beat 1 minute. If too thick, a little more milk may be added.

HURRY-UP CAKE

It wasn't only sugar and shortening that were in short supply. Many women, caught between home and the new demands of a wartime job, found that *time* was suddenly just as scarce. Wartime cookbooks are filled with suggestions for cutting corners in the kitchen.

"What? No time to make a cake? Nonsense!" scolds one *Meat Planning Guide,* suggesting the one-bowl miracle of Hurry-Up Cake. It is ready in a jiffy, and although it is as plain as crockery, we like this pure-white fluffy legacy of home front cookery.

> *2 cups sifted cake flour*
> *1¼ cups sugar*
> *3½ teaspoons baking powder*
> *1 teaspoon salt*
> *½ cup vegetable shortening*
>
> *1 cup milk*
> *1 teaspoon vanilla extract*
> *¼ teaspoon lemon extract*
> *3 egg whites, unbeaten*

• Preheat oven to 350°.

Sift flour, sugar, baking powder, and salt into mixing bowl. Add shortening. Add ⅔ cup milk and flavorings. Beat until perfectly smooth—about 2 minutes with an electric mixer set at medium, or about 100 strokes with a hand beater.

Add egg whites and remaining milk, and beat until well blended for 2 minutes longer, or for 100 more strokes if you are using a hand beater. Pour into 2 greased and floured 8-inch pans.

Bake 30 minutes.

Turn out of pans onto cooling rack. When cool, frost with Flattop Orange Frosting.

FLATTOP ORANGE FROSTING

From *How to Bake by the Ration Book*. This recipe makes just enough to thinly frost the tops of 2 8-inch layers, leaving the sides nude. That was the patriotic, sugar-stretching look of wartime cakes. To splurge, double the recipe, and slather this sweet citrus frosting thickly on tops *and* sides.

*1½ cups sifted
  confectioners' sugar
1½ teaspoons grated
  orange rind*

*2 tablespoons lemon juice
Dash salt
2 tablespoons hot melted butter
  or margarine*

• Combine sugar, orange rind, lemon juice, and salt. Add hot butter and beat vigorously 1 minute, adding more lemon juice if too thick.

Makes enough frosting to cover tops of 2 8-inch layers.

Ice Cream and the War

Pile on the protein, fill the Victory garden salad bowl, stretch the red and blue points, enrich your bread with vegetables, and sift in the soya flour . . . a homemaker's duties were still only half done. Because all the soybeans in Kansas were no substitute for the one vitamin that Americans needed most—Vitamin Z . . . for Zest. While the other food groups were repairing, regulating, and energizing the body, Vitamin Z built morale.

Where was Vitamin Z to be found? In the flavor and appearance of a meal. In laughter and pleasant conversation at the table. In, according to Westinghouse's Home Economics Institute, "a couple of lettuce leaves, a sprig of parsley, a few strips of green pepper garnishing the platter of a meat loaf—the difference between 'let's get this over with' and 'what a grand dinner!'" . . . or in a July Fourth breakfast of red raspberries, white cream of wheat, and blueberry muffins.

But there was one food that was uncut Vitamin Z. The men aboard the aircraft carrier *Lexington* could tell you that. You see, during the battle of the Coral Sea, they were hit hard. The ship was sinking. No hope. What did the sailors do in those precious moments before they went overboard?

American housewives from coast to coast knew the answer to that question. The men *ate up the ship's ice cream supply!* And what they couldn't eat, they stuffed into their helmets to carry into the lifeboats. "Why does ice cream mean so much to our fighting men?" asked the October 1943 *Meal Planning Guide,* "Because it spells 'home.' Because all that is dear and familiar is summed up in something as simple and commonplace as a dish of ice cream!"

It was the most flag-waving, patriotic food of all, the best source of Vitamin Z on earth. Fighting men insisted on it. The navy perfected a "mechanical cow" to produce milk (from powder) to be made into ice cream for the boys on submarines. Even in below-zero Alaska, soldiers made it in ammo cans and froze it in the snow. And yet, on the home front, ice cream was scarce, limited by government decree to eight flavors for the duration of the war; and even if you were willing to make it yourself, you couldn't count on getting heavy cream. Wartime cookbooks to the rescue!

ABANDON SHIP ICE CREAM

From the *Health for Victory Meal Planning Guide,* March 1943, this rich custard reminds us of good vanilla soft-serve. It can be flavored by adding bits of chocolate, canned fruit, or cookie crumbs when it is partially frozen.

1 package unflavored gelatin	*6 tablespoons sugar*
2 cups cream	*4 tablespoons light corn syrup*
2 eggs, separated	*1 teaspoon vanilla extract*

• Soak gelatin in 2 tablespoons cream. Melt over hot water in top of double boiler. Cool.

Beat egg yolks, sugar, and corn syrup until thick and lemon colored. Add remaining cream, dissolved gelatin, and vanilla. Place in freezer set to coldest setting.

Freeze until firm.

Put frozen mixture in chilled bowl add unbeaten egg whites, and beat until fluffy. Return to freezing compartment and continue freezing until firm.

Serves 5.

TRAY SMOOTH CHOCOLATE ICE CREAM

From *Coupon Cookery.*

1 13-ounce can evaporated milk	*1 egg*
3 ounces unsweetened chocolate	*1 cup confectioners' sugar*
1 tablespoon butter	*1½ teaspoons vanilla extract*

• Chill evaporated milk 6 to 8 hours.

Melt chocolate with butter in top of double boiler. Cool but do not chill.

Combine egg, sugar, vanilla extract, and chocolate mixture in a bowl and beat until thick. Beat chilled evaporated milk until thick as whipped cream.

Fold mixtures together in shallow trays and place in freezer set to coldest setting, Stir every 20 minutes until set.

Serves 4.

VICTORY AT SEA MARBLE CREAM

From Frigidaire's book of *Wartime Suggestions to Help You Get the Most out of Your Refrigerator.*

> *2 cups evaporated milk*
> *1 13-ounce can sweetened*
>   *condensed milk*
> *1 cup cold coffee*
>   *(or coffee beverage)*

> *1 teaspoon vanilla extract*
> *⅛ teaspoon salt*
> *6 ounces semisweet chocolate bar*
>   *or chips*
> *4 tablespoons milk*

• Chill evaporated milk in freezing tray about 1 hour, when fine ice crystals will begin to form around the edges. Turn into bowl, and whip until milk peaks.

Combine sweetened condensed milk with coffee, vanilla, and salt. Fold chilled evaporated milk into this liquid, and pour into *shallow* metal freezing trays.

Freeze at lowest possible temperature until quite firm, stirring every 30 minutes. This will take about 3 hours.

Meanwhile, melt chocolate in saucepan over boiling water. Add milk, and stir until smooth, Cool, but do not chill. Pour in thin layer over top of "quite firm" cream, or stir chocolate into "quite firm" cream in streaks for marbled effect. Return to refrigerator, and freeze until firm.

Makes approximately 3 quarts.

Rookie Cookies

It was the boys in service who needed Vitamin Z the most; and packages from home were the best way to supply it. "You know a serviceman somewhere," hinted a 1943 advertisement for Burnett's Flavoring Extracts. "One who sure does love to get mail—especially the mail he can eat!"

What could raise the spirits at boot camp higher than a batch of "Rookie Cookies" from home? Made with dried sweet fruits and molasses, they were easy on the sugar rations. So, Mrs. American Housewife, why not make big batches— some for that special serviceman, some for the family's lunch boxes, and some for dessert—to accompany economy ice cream!

These recipes, from the Rolling Kitchen Unit of the "Cookies for Rookies Brigade," were published by the Home Service Division of the Hartford Electric Light Company.

RISE AND SHINE!
(oatmeal-apple cookies)

Soft, plump cookie-pillows that, thanks to the dates, stay moist for days—perfect for shipping overseas.

8 tablespoons butter or margarine
1 cup packed brown sugar
2 eggs
½ teaspoon vanilla extract
½ cup nuts
1 small apple
¾ cup pitted dates (about 18)

½ cup quick oatmeal
½ teaspoon baking soda
½ teaspoon baking powder
½ teaspoon cinnamon
1¾ cups enriched
    all-purpose flour

- Preheat oven to 425°.

Cream butter; add sugar. Add eggs and vanilla and beat well.

Grind nuts, apple, and dates in food chopper (or chop with 6 to 10 short pulses in a food processor), and add to first mixture.

Mix oatmeal, soda, baking powder, and cinnamon with flour. Add to fruit and butter mixture; beat well. Drop on oiled cookie sheet by heaping teaspoon.

Bake 10 to 12 minutes.

Makes about 3 dozen.

'TENSHUN! (chocolate drop cookies)

A vanished species of cookie—plain everyday chocolate. If too stark for your taste, these smooth, dark domes may be iced.

2 ounces unsweetened chocolate	*½ cup milk*
8 tablespoons butter or	*½ teaspoon soda*
margarine, melted	*2 cups enriched*
1 cup brown sugar	*all-purpose flour*
1 egg	

- Preheat oven to 375°.

Melt chocolate on top of double boiler and add to the melted butter. Add sugar, egg, and milk. Sift together soda and flour, and add to mixture. Drop by tablespoonfuls on greased pans.

Bake 15 minutes.

Makes about 3 dozen.

HALT! (corn flake macaroons)

3 tablespoons butter or	*¼ cup chopped nutmeats*
margarine, melted	*¼ cup shredded*
¼ cup brown sugar	*coconut (optional)*
¼ cup granulated sugar	*2½ cups slightly*
1 egg	*crushed corn flakes*

• Preheat oven to 350°.

Blend butter and sugars thoroughly. Add egg and beat well. Add nutmeats, coconut, and corn flakes. Mix well.

Shape cookies, using a tablespoon and pressing filled spoon against side of bowl. Then drop lightly on a greased cookie sheet.

Bake 10 minutes.

Makes 2 dozen.

WHO GOES THERE? (fruit cookies)

½ pound butter
  or margarine
2 cups brown sugar
2 eggs, well beaten
3½ cups flour
1 teaspoon salt
1 teaspoon baking soda

1 teaspoon nutmeg
1 teaspoon cinnamon
½ cup cold coffee
¾ cup seeded raisins
¾ cup chopped dates
1 cup broken nutmeats

• Preheat oven to 400°.

Thoroughly cream butter and sugar; add eggs and beat well. Sift flour with salt, soda, and spices, and add alternately with coffee. Stir in fruits and nutmeats. Drop from teaspoon onto greased cookie sheet.

Bake 15 minutes.

Makes about 3 dozen.

LIGHTS OUT (ginger drop cookies)

8 tablespoons butter or margarine	*¼ teaspoon baking soda*
¼ cup brown sugar	*1 teaspoon baking powder*
1 egg	*¼ cup milk*
⅜ cup dark corn syrup	*½ teaspoon vanilla extract*
1 cup soya flour	*1¼ cups quick oatmeal*
½ teaspoon salt	*2¼ teaspoons grated lemon rind*
1 teaspoon ground ginger	

• Preheat oven to 400°.

Cream butter and sugar with mixer. Add egg and beat well. Add corn syrup and beat thoroughly.

Sift all dry ingredients except oats, and add alternately with milk and vanilla to shortening mixture. Add oatmeal and lemon rind; mix well. Drop by teaspoonfuls onto a greased cookie sheet.

Bake 10 to 12 minutes.

Makes about 3 dozen.

G.I. FRUIT BARS

"Chewy cookies ship best," advised the July 1944 *Meal Planning Guide.* "It's pretty disappointing to open a box and find a mess of crumbs." In these packed squares of pure energy, moist centers of chopped dried fruit, lemon rind, and sugar keep that chewy quality the boys like.

1 cup dried pitted fruit, cut fine

⅓ cup granulated sugar

½ cup water

1 tablespoon lemon juice

1 tablespoon grated lemon rind

1 cup sifted enriched
   all-purpose flour

1 cup brown sugar,
   lightly packed

½ teaspoon salt

8 tablespoons butter or margarine

1½ cups quick oatmeal

3 tablespoons milk

• Preheat oven to 350°.

Cook fruit, sugar, and water until thick. Add lemon juice and rind. Cool.

Mix flour, brown sugar, and salt. Cut in shortening until mixture resembles meal (at least 1 full minute in food processor). Add oatmeal and mix well. Add milk and blend.

Pack half of dough into greased 8-inch-square pan. Spread fruit mixture on top. Spread remaining flour mixture over fruit.

Bake 40 minutes. Cool. Cut in bars.

Makes about 2 dozen 1-by-2-inch bars.

The War's Aftertaste

By August 1944, the *Meal Planning Guide* ran an article about "The Man Who Will Come Back to Dinner," in the form of a memo from Mess Sergeant Bob McDevitt to "Mrs. Jones, regarding her Star Boarder, temporarily eating at Uncle Sam's." The point of the article was that Johnny will soon come marching home, hungry, but with a whole new outlook on chow, having been made into a square-shouldered, hard-muscled fighting man by army food. "Johnny has come to thoroughly enjoy three squares a day at Uncle Sam's table," the sarge assures Mrs. Jones. "He's learned to eat what he's served. Yes, ma'am, and he likes it."

It is certainly true that many men entered the armed forces with poor eating habits and came out healthier thanks to the government's scientific nutrition programs. In fact, many boys in the navy (where the large ships were well equipped for storage and cooking) ate steak and ice cream nearly every day. But as to G.I.'s *liking* army chow, yes, ma'am . . . perhaps Sergeant McDevitt overstated things a wee bit. One foodstuff he neglects to mention in his article is Spam—known to soldiers as "ham that didn't pass its physical."

M-M-M! HAM BAKED IN MILK, BAKED SWEET POTATOES AND BRAN BREAD . . . WON'T THEY TASTE GOOD?

Spam was one food few soldiers learned to like. In fact, a popular joke of the time tells about the downed pilot who, having spent weeks in the jungle eating only roots and berries, is rescued by a team that has only Spam to feed him. The pilot runs back into the jungle.

Hormel's loaf of pork parts was, in fact, introduced before the war, in 1936. But it was G.I.'s, sometimes finding it dished out at mess three times a day, who made Spam notorious. And yet, as much as they joked about it and swore they'd sooner starve than face another slab, Spam left its mark on returning soldiers' taste buds. Despite its seeming ignominy, it became the most popular canned meat on the shelf in the years following World War II.

BASIC BAKED SPAM

1 loaf Spam luncheon meat, any size	*1 teaspoon vinegar*
Whole cloves	*2 teaspoons yellow mustard*
⅔ cup brown sugar	*2 teaspoons water*
	1 teaspoon Worcestershire sauce

• Preheat oven to 375°.

Score Spam loaf in diamond pattern and dot with cloves. Mix sugar, vinegar, mustard, water, and Worcestershire. (These measurements are enough for a large loaf.) Brush mixture on Spam.

Bake 25 to 30 minutes, basting three or four times.

The apocryphal notion that Spam was simply K-rations adapted for civilian use is based on the fact that Spam was quick and easy, just as battlefront rations had to be.

But it wasn't only the soldiers who had to eat fast and on the go. On the home front, too, time traditionally spent cooking was turned topsy-turvy by night and swing shifts. The patriotic housewife who might ordinarily take all afternoon to prepare old-fashioned recipes for a swell family supper was called away from her kitchen to serve double duty. Baking powder sales plummeted during World War II—who had the energy to bake after a day at the defense plant? "Our hats are off to the woman who must dash home from her job or the Red Cross, and tired as she is, get a good dinner on the table in little more than half an hour," said the February 1944 *Meal Planning Guide*.

Nearly four decades after the war, in the 1982 Centennial Cookbook of the small town of Oakland, Iowa, we found these recipes for Spam, wartime legacies ideally suited to the homemaker with little time to spend in the kitchen, and sure to bring back memories of army chow to the taste buds of veterans:

BACK TO BATAAN SPAM

½ cup vegetable shortening

1 large bell pepper, sliced

1 onion, sliced

1 large can Spam luncheon meat, cut into bite-sized cubes

4 tablespoons applesauce

Salt and pepper

1 teaspoon sugar

1 16-ounce can whole potatoes

Dash oregano

• Put shortening in large skillet, add bell pepper and onion, and cook until partly done. Add rest of ingredients.

Cover and cook on medium heat 18 minutes.

Serves 4 to 6.

DRILL INSTRUCTOR'S DELIGHT

1 can condensed chicken noodle soup

1 large can Spam luncheon meat, chopped

¼ green pepper, chopped

1 egg, beaten

1 cup quick oatmeal

1 13-ounce can evaporated milk

Pepper

Crushed potato chips

• Preheat oven to 350°.

Mix all ingredients except potato chips and pour in baking dish. Add crushed potato chips on top.

Bake 30 to 45 minutes.

Serves 6.

Even more than Spam, dehydrated food—the quickest and most convenient of all—was a staple for our men in service and the lend-lease countries. It seemed logical and good that when the war was over, the new technology that turned food into shavings and chips and nuggets and crystals would prevail. After all, it was cheap, and it was *modern*.

Manufacturers' advertisements teased homemakers with an imminent end to drudgery, a future composed of products designed to make life miraculously easy. General Mills's promises included "new foods rich in flavor, wonderfully nutritious, easy to prepare and keep"—all thanks to the discoveries of wartime research.

As for taste, Eleanor Early visited the Department of Agriculture in 1942 and reported in *American Cookery*, "They gave me golden powder as yellow as turnips and little envelopes of macerated stuff dry as hay. You could never tell to look at them what they were—dried onions and dried cabbage. I cooked them ten minutes . . . and when they were drained and seasoned, you'd think they had just come out of the garden.

"The day is coming," Ms. Early enthused, "when a woman can buy a boiled dinner, and carry it home in her purse . . . when a well-stocked pantry will be reduced to a few boxes . . . when dinner will be cooked in ten minutes . . . when you'll serve the girls luncheon bridge of dehydrated meat with powdered potatoes and powdered onions, a dehydrated cabbage salad, and custard made with powdered eggs and powdered milk for dessert. . . . When the war is over, dried foods will be for sale in every corner store."

In fact, dried food composed what was probably the best known of a wartime dishes. Soldiers called it S.O.S., but it was more politely known as creamed chipped beef. The army's version, *to serve 100,* went like this:

BEEF, DRIED, CHIPPED ON TOAST

From *The Army Cook*, TM 10-405, GPO, 1942.

2 pounds fat, butter preferred	2 bunches parsley, chopped fine
1 pound flour	½ ounce pepper
4 13-ounce cans evaporated milk	130 slices bread, toasted
4 gallons beef stock	
7 pounds chipped or sliced dried beef	

• Melt fat in pan and add flour. Cook a few minutes to brown flour. Add milk and beef stock, stirring constantly to prevent lumping. Add dried beef and cook 5 minutes. Add parsley and pepper.

Serve hot on toast.

A more manageable, home front version of the same dish was offered in the April 1942 issue of *American Cookery:*

WELCOME HOME CREAMED DRIED BEEF

This recipe appears in an article titled "Madam, Dehydrated Dinner Is Served," the point being that dehydrated food, as smart as it is convenient, will soon be an everyday miracle available to housewives. (Dried eggs, milk, and beef can be found in most stores that specialize in camping supplies.)

½ pound dried beef	6 tablespoons butter
½ cup dried milk	6 tablespoons flour
2 cups, plus 2 tablespoons cold water	⅛ teaspoon pepper
	2 tablespoons dried whole egg

• Shred dried beef, removing any stringy portions; freshen if necessary by covering with hot water; drain.

Combine dried milk with 2 cups cold water placed in a mixing bowl; beat with a rotary beater until smooth.

Melt butter in upper part of double boiler over direct heat. Blend in flour and pepper. Add milk gradually; when mixture thickens, place over hot water and cook 15 minutes.

Meanwhile, place dried egg and 2 tablespoons water in a bowl and allow to stand about 5 minutes. Beat with rotary beater.

Remove sauce from heat; stir in egg quickly. Add dried beef.

Serve on noodles or toast.

Serves 4.

When the war was over, most Victory gardens went to seed, and soya flour was forgotten (until more than two decades later, when both were rediscovered as sources of good health).

In the meantime, although ration book cooking quickly became nothing more than a memory of inconveniences, there was one enduring legacy of Victory dining. The American homemaker had discovered, for better and worse, the lure of convenience cookery.

THE CUISINE OF SUBURBIA

As suburbs set the pace of modern life in the 1950s, TV trays, coffee tables, and buffets superseded the dinner table. "Modern" cookbooks suggested progressive house-to-house dinners, patio picnics, rec room pizza parties, and theme meals . . . but contained little advice about ordinary dinner in a dining room.

That immovable kitchen stove began looking awfully clunky compared to portable roasters, electric frying pans, chafing dishes, and—most suburban of all—the rotisserie on wheels. These new appliances, according to the *Complete Small Appliance Cookbook,* written in 1953 by John and Marie Roberson, were "the *social* way of preparing meals."

What a reversal from the image of an ideal family meal cultivated by cookbooks prior to World War II: everyone seated around one table in the dining room, partaking of a meal that was Mom's moment of glory. Dinner was supposed to be a communing time for the close-knit family, not a social event.

Triumphantly convenient, modern life had little use for the old-fashioned skills of a housewife. "You only need to spend an average of 90 minutes a day in the kitchen as compared with the 5 hours your mother used," advised Campbell's in a book called *Easy Ways to Delicious Meals* aimed at "modern young-thinking cooks who enjoy using convenience foods."

The cuisine of suburbia is a battery of snacks, one-dish meals, and jiffy recipes. It is Dad putting on an apron with a wiener design that says "Dog Catcher" and cooking on the patio. It is stylized "exotic" party meals of sukiyaki or Polynesian ham bake. It is, in contrast to the Sunday family dinner table, the flowering of culinary mannerism.

And while we are classicists at heart, this problematic cuisine is IRRESISTIBLE. Encouraged, indeed *created,* as it was by big food companies, it is far from innocence. But there is a compelling charm about the housewife who "goes gourmet" by serving Meat Loaf Wellington, or who strives to achieve, as one brochure suggests, "glamour with a can opener." Only a snob could find no joy in the igniting of a cabbage head appetizer flamed in Sterno, or the serving of Hobo Dinner in a Can by an executive's wife.

No one can deny its cultural significance and the radical departure suburban-style cookery marks from traditional home cooking. But it is not as cultural archeologists that we embrace the likes of Impossible Cheeseburger Pie. The famous dishes that epitomize suburbia—tuna noodle casserole, corn flake oven-fried chicken, chocolate ice box cookie cake, and S'mores—are delicious by any measure. And the more "difficult" ones—such as Pepsi-Cola Cake and Eight Can Casserole—are so audacious that they are positively subversive.

A little treason in the form of culinary silliness is good for the soul. In the face of so much solemnity about modern cooking, it is exhilarating to reach back to Jell-O Cut Glass Dessert and Chow Mein Candy Clusters.

We dare you to make your next party menu Queen for a Day Noodleburger Casserole and Gauguin Aesthetic Cake. You may find, as we who grew up during the 1950s have found time and again while testing these recipes, that the cuisine of suburbia is a trove of forgotten flavors, and a rumpus room full of fun.

TV Snacks, Dips, and Dunks

The Miracle of Dry Onion Soup

Casseroles—
Glamour with a Can Opener

Luau in Your Living Room

TROPICAL DRINKS

Blue Hawaii • 285

Trader Vic's Babalu • 285

Hawaiian Punch • 286

Leilani Grass Hut • 286

Purple Poodle • 286

Claire's Apricot Slush • 287

SOUTH SEAS ADVENTURE

Flaming Cabbage Head Weenies with Pu Pu Sauce • 288

Polynesian Tiki Sweet and Sour Chicken • 289

Kilauea Purple Passion Rice • 289

Gauguin Aesthetic Cake • 290

Patio Parties

Hobo Dinner in a Can • 293

KABOB COMBINATIONS

Bali Hai Vegetables • 295

Maui Laulau • 295

Wikiwiki Tidbits • 295

BARBECUED BREAD

Beatnik Buns • 296

Most Happy Fella Bread • 296

BARBECUED DESSERT

Cape Canaveral Bananas • 297

Ginger-Mint Pears • 297

Honey-Rum Grapefruit • 297

Camp Caramel Apples • 298

Teen Food

English Muffin Pizzas • 300
Merry Pizza Rounds • 301
Sloppy Joes • 302
Downbeat Dogs on a Stick • 302
Impossible Cheeseburger Pie • 303
Peachy Peach Sundae • 303
Famous Chocolate Wafer Roll • 304
Cookies à la Kookie • 305

Corn Flake Cookery

Oven-Fried Corn Flake Chicken • 307
Baked Corn Chex 'n' Cheese Custard • 307
Checkerboard Square Clam Crunch • 308
Chow Mein Candy Clusters • 308
Rice Krispie Cookies • 309
Choco-Scotch Clusters • 310
John Beresford Tipton Bars • 310
Teenage Rocky Road • 311
Chocolate Chip Torte • 311

Look What You Can Do with Dr. Pepper

Duckling L'Vernors • 313
Dr. Pepper Baked Beans • 315
Lemonade Fried Chicken • 315
Cherry Coke Salad • 316
Pepsi-Cola Cake with Broiled Peanut Butter Frosting • 317
Fresca Cake with Maraschino Frosting • 318
Mr. Pibb Pralines • 319
Sputnik Tea • 320

Dessert ex Machina

Jell-O—the Chef's Magic Powder

TV Snacks, Dips, and Dunks

As the dining table faded away as the focal point of the family at home, dinner splintered into nibbles, appetizers, and tidbits. For parties, cocktail hour, midnight suppers, and TV watching, it was so much more convenient to set out a buffet, or a tray, or bowls of easy-to-eat finger food.

The venerable chafing dish, which had been enormously popular *before* gas stoves, was reborn as the suburban chef's flashy friend. "Use it in your dining room, on porches, terraces, in game rooms and small quarters everywhere," advised the *Complete Small Appliance Cookbook.* "It's versatile. It's glamorous. It will make a big hit at all your parties." And best of all, the chafing dish keeps food warm while you watch TV.

The important things about TV food are that it must be something that you can eat without utensils, and without taking your eyes away from the screen. And it has to be prepared either very quickly between programs, or in advance, before the show goes on.

TV PARTY MIX

TV Party Mix is the archetypal snack food. It can be stored forever; and it goes great not only with TV, but at cocktail hour or any time neighbors pop in unexpectedly. Teens gobble it up, too.

This recipe comes from the Checkerboard Kitchens of Ralston Purina, but, for variety's sake, we occasionally substitute other cereals, like Cheerios or Kix for one of the Chex. Or use Spanish peanuts or pecans, straight, instead of mixed nuts. At our house, no Party Mix is complete without a generous handful of Veri-Thin pretzel sticks tossed in. For what might be called Nouvelle Party Mix, modern nibbles such as sesame sticks and corn Bugles would be appropriate. If you do add other ingredients, increase the butter and seasonings accordingly.

8 tablespoons butter	*2 cups Rice Chex*
1 teaspoon seasoned salt	*2 cups Wheat Chex*
4 teaspoons Worcestershire sauce	*¾ cup salted mixed nuts (not*
2 cups Corn Chex	*dry-roasted)*

• Preheat oven to 250°.

Melt butter in a 13-by-9-by-2-inch baking pan. Remove pan from oven, stir in seasoned salt and Worcestershire sauce. Add cereal and nuts. Mix until all pieces are coated. Return pan to oven and heat 45 minutes, stirring occasionally.

Spread on paper towels to cool.

Makes 1½ quarts.

KRAFT TELEVISION THEATER
CLAM APPETIZER DIP

Easy to prepare and always in the best of taste, clam dip adds an elegant flair to snack time (especially elegant if the potato chips are rippled). This recipe comes from a 1951 booklet called *Food Favorites from the KRAFT Television Theater . . . Selected by Popular Request.* Needless to say, the substitution of fresh clams for canned is out of the question. On the other hand, if no fresh garlic is handy, a healthy dose of garlic powder will do just fine.

1 7-ounce can minced clams

1 clove garlic (or ½ teaspoon
  garlic powder)

1 8-ounce package
  cream cheese, softened

2 teaspoons lemon juice

1½ teaspoons
  Worcestershire sauce

½ teaspoon salt

Dash pepper

• Drain clams, reserving broth.

Rub a mixing bowl with halved garlic clove, then stir in cream cheese until smooth. Blend in lemon juice, Worcestershire, salt, pepper, and clams. Gradually add 4 tablespoons clam broth—or a bit more if a thinner dip is desired.

Serve with chips, raw vegetables, or crackers.

Serves 4 to 6.

CHEESE BALL

"The cheese ball is a necessity for modern entertaining," advised *Mary Meade's Magic Recipes for the Electric Blender* in 1956.

We're not sure who invented it, but the cheese ball's phenomenal popularity during the 1950s corresponded to the success of that indispensable suburban appliance, the kitchen blender. Originally invented as a bartender's tool, the blender stood side by side with the chafing dish as a totem of cooking ease and sociability. "The blender is your servant," said *Magic Recipes.* "It will swallow up the garlic and the parsley, making them one with the cheese."

Without blenders, there would be no cheese balls.

The joy of cheese ball cookery is that you can be as creative as you like, using almost any varieties of cheese, herbs, and seasonings to your heart's content, and your cheese balls will always come out pretty much the same. Have the cheese at room temperature when you begin, and make the ball a day ahead to let the flavors blend. Serve with novelty cheese knives stuck into the ball at the angle of rabbit-ear TV antennas.

This recipe was suggested by *Super Deluxe Osterizer Recipes*.

¼ cup milk	*½ teaspoon*
4 ounces blue cheese, crumbled	*Worcestershire sauce*
4 ounces Cheddar	*8 ounces cream cheese*
cheese, cubed	*½ cup pecans*
1 small wedge onion	*4 sprigs parsley*

• Blend milk and blue cheese in food processor or blender at high speed. Add Cheddar cheese, onion, Worcestershire, and cream cheese. Blend until smooth. Refrigerate at least 3 hours or overnight.

Next day, shape cheese into a ball. Coarsely chop pecans and parsley in blender. Roll cheese ball in nut-and-parsley mixture.

To serve, place in center of a plate, surrounded by crackers.

Serves 8.

BRAUNSCHWEIGER EN GELÉE

A worthy supplement (or substitute) for your cheese ball, Braunschweiger en Gelée goes well with beer, hence, while watching sports on TV. Eating it requires a bit more concentration than a cheese ball, since one must attempt to get a proper proportion of braunschweiger and aspic. Serve with cocktail rye bread.

1 package unflavored gelatin	*3 tablespoons mayonnaise*
1 10-ounce can condensed	*1 tablespoon prepared mustard*
beef consommé	*1 tablespoon white vinegar*
½ cup cold water	*1 tablespoon minced onion*
8 ounces braunschweiger	

• Soften gelatin in consommé and water. Heat to boil, stirring to dissolve. Pour into oiled 2-cup mold. Chill until set.

Mix braunschweiger, mayonnaise, mustard, vinegar, and onion. Scoop out center of jellied consommé, leaving ½-inch shell. Fill with braunschweiger mixture. Melt spooned-out consommé over low heat; pour over meat.

Chill until set. Unmold to serve.

Serves 6 to 8.

HOT CRAB DUNK

When it's time to soak up culture on educational TV, cheese balls and clam dip hardly seem smart enough. For deep dish programs, or for fancy dinner guests, you want an appetizer that trumpets "class." Enter Hot Crab Dunk— the high tone hors d'oeuvre. This version is from *Southern Living* magazine.

8 ounces cream cheese, softened	*1 teaspoon prepared mustard*
⅓ cup mayonnaise	*½ teaspoon garlic salt*
1 tablespoon	*¼ teaspoon salt*
confectioners' sugar	*1 6-ounce can crabmeat*
1 tablespoon dry white wine	*Chopped parsley*
½ teaspoon onion juice	*Paprika*

• Preheat oven to 375°.

Mix cheese, mayonnaise, sugar, wine, onion juice, mustard, garlic salt, and salt. Drain and flake crabmeat; stir into cheese. Pour into buttered 1-quart baking dish. Sprinkle with parsley and paprika.

Bake 15 minutes.

Serve warm with thin melba toast or Ritz crackers.

Serves 6 to 8.

EXOTIC EGG DUNK

Italian seasonings give this dunk its gay flavor. It's one of the dishes guaranteed to "add living color to your gourmet repertoire" from the vintage *TV Guide Cookbook*.

4 hard-boiled eggs	*2 teaspoons grated onion*
2 teaspoons dry Good Seasons	*¼ teaspoon Worcestershire sauce*
Italian dressing	*½ cup sour cream*

• Reserve 1 egg yolk for garnish. Chop remaining eggs finely. Combine all ingredients, blending well. Spoon into bowl. Sieve reserved egg yolk over top.

Serve with potato chips.

Serves 4.

BACON HORSERADISH DUNK

"A real flavor tease," says Lila Pearl in *What Cooks in Suburbia*. "Wonderful but mysterious."

⅓ cup mayonnaise	*8 ounces cream*
2 tablespoons horseradish	*cheese, softened*
1 teaspoon salt	*8 strips bacon, fried, drained, and*
¼ teaspoon white pepper	*crumbled*

• Beat mayonnaise, horseradish, salt, and pepper with cream cheese until smooth. Stir in bacon.

Serve cool but not cold with chips or crackers.

Serves 4.

GAS COMPANY RUMAKI

There is no suburban snack more classy than these gourmet tidbits, with their touch of the Orient—curry powder and ginger. Rumaki are special occasion hors d'oeuvres—for Academy Awards night or televised coronations. This recipe is from *Festive Foods,* published by the Milwaukee Gas Light Company in 1961 to encourage the use of gas stoves.

4 scallions

1 8-ounce can water chestnuts

⅓ pound chicken livers, cut into thirds or halves

8 strips bacon, cut crosswise into halves

½ cup soy sauce

¼ teaspoon ground ginger

¼ teaspoon curry powder

• Cut scallions into 1-inch lengths. Wrap a water chestnut (or half a chestnut, if they are large), a piece of chicken liver, and a strip of scallion with ½ slice of bacon. Secure with a toothpick.

Marinate 1 hour in mixture of soy sauce, ginger, and curry powder.

Place broiler rack about 4 inches below burner. Turn burner on full and preheat broiler.

Broil rumaki about 7 minutes; turn, and broil 7 more minutes.

Makes 16.

PIGS IN BLANKETS

Pigs in blankets are a wonderful paradox—goony yet, in some mysterious way, elite. For us as kids they were, along with pecan "turtles," the last word in rich man's food, the royal hors d'oeuvre. Should you want to add a twist to the formula, substitute Smokies or eight halved Slim Jim sticks for the miniature frankfurters. (It is also possible, if you desire the more ascetic classical version, to eliminate the cheese and condiments inside the blanket, and serve the pigs in blankets plain, with only bright yellow mustard as an accompanying dip.)

6 ounces Cheddar cheese,
  shredded
1 tablespoon finely
  minced onion
2 tablespoons sweet pickle relish,
  drained

2 tablespoons ketchup
1 teaspoon dry mustard
1 8-ounce can refrigerated
  crescent dinner rolls
16 cocktail franks

• Preheat oven to 375°.

Mix cheese, onion, relish, ketchup, and mustard.

Unroll the refrigerated dough and separate into 8 triangles. Cut triangles in half. Pat them down and stretch them out a bit. Spread each piece of dough with cheese mixture, then wrap it around a frank.

Place on baking sheet, seam side down.

Bake 10 minutes or until golden brown. Serve immediately.

Makes 16.

PHYLLIS RICHMAN'S MOTHER'S PARTY BURGERS

Washington Post food editor Phyllis Richman told us that her mother, Helen Chasanow, used to serve these tasty mouthfuls in front of the TV. They were known as Grandma's Little Cheeseburgers, and the fun of them was to see who could eat the most. Phyllis claims that most adults consume four to six, but a healthy child can down a dozen.

> *1 package Pepperidge Farm Party Buns (tiny 1-inch-square rolls)*
> *¾ pound lean ground beef, formed into small balls*
>
> *Salt to taste*
> *Velveeta cheese—about 6 ounces*
> *40 slices cucumbers*
> *20 slices sour dill pickles*

• Remove buns from foil baking tin. Separate and slice into tops and bottoms, then repack bottoms in baking tin. Place a small ball of ground beef on each bottom, pressing to cover entire roll. Sprinkle with salt. Put under broiler 3 to 5 minutes, or until meat is cooked.

Remove tray full of burgers, place little squares of Velveeta on tops of patties, and return to broiler just long enough to melt cheese.

Put tops on buns, and press down. Return to broiler to warm.

Remove sandwiches from pan, inserting 2 cucumber slices and a pickle slice in each. It is important that no other condiments be used.

Phyllis also reports that party burgers are good the next day, cold . . . if you like cold cheeseburgers.

Makes 20.

HAWAIIAN MEATBALLS

The suburban gourmet will tell you that any food becomes Hawaiian by the simple addition of pineapple. These meatballs, from *Favorite Foods of St. Francis Families,* are a chafing dish specialty from a local cookbook published in Lake Geneva, Wisconsin. They make a good TV mini-meal, or, like pigs in blankets or Swedish meatballs, a sophisticated party appetizer.

1½ pounds ground beef	½ cup vinegar
1 teaspoon seasoned salt	3 tablespoons soy sauce
1 cup finely diced celery	½ cup sugar
2 medium carrots, grated	½ teaspoon salt
1 20-ounce can pineapple	¼ teaspoon pepper
chunks, drained	½ teaspoon ground ginger
(reserve juice)	2 tablespoons cornstarch
2 tablespoons salad oil	2 tablespoons water
½ cup pineapple juice	1 8-ounce jar stemless
(from can)	Maraschino cherries

• Mix beef and seasoned salt. Form into rounds ¾ to 1 inch in diameter. In a very large skillet, brown meatballs with vegetables and pineapple in oil.

Remove meatballs from pan. Add pineapple juice, vinegar, soy sauce, sugar, salt, pepper, and ginger. Bring to simmer.

Mix cornstarch and water; stir into pan. Return meatballs to pan, coating them with pineapple mixture. Add cherries with juice.

Simmer gently 15 to 20 minutes.

Serve in chafing dish to keep meatballs warm.

Makes 15 to 30 meatballs, depending on size.

The Miracle of Dry Onion Soup

The astute gastronome will note that our discussion of dips, dunks, and spreads was missing what may be the cornerstone of the cuisine of suburbia or, if not, is certainly its mortar. Of course, we mean California Dip, created in 1954 by Lipton as an ingenious transformation of dry onion soup mix into party dip by the addition of sour cream. Since then, inventive cooks have found dozens of ways to use their packet of dehydrated onions and flavor enhancer like a magic powder, turning the humblest ingredients into special fare.

No chef can seriously consider himself a master of suburban cookery unless he knows his way around dry onion soup.

CALIFORNIA DIP

There are two styles of preparing the classic dip. The safe way is to mix the soup and the sour cream an hour before serving, giving the onions time to soften and all the enhancers time to spread their savor evenly through the sour cream. A punkier approach is to mix the soup and sour cream immediately before serving—and don't even mix them extremely well! The onions will retain a dehydrated crunch for a good half hour, and the sour cream will be streaked with veins of zest, little nuggets radiating a raunchy salt sting.

We do not, however, recommend blending California dip so far in advance that it must be refrigerated for more than an hour or two. When chilled too long, it attains a gluey texture reminiscent of drywall.

1 package dry onion soup mix   *2 cups sour cream*

• Combine.

PRE-FAB ONION BREAD

"Want the wonderful yeasty aroma of bread baking in the oven . . . without the trouble of mixing, kneading and shaping, and without long waiting time?" So asked *Easy Ways to Delicious Meals,* suggesting a shortcut Souper Dooper Bread for "home-style eating." This recipe, which is like instant garlic bread, but onion-flavored, calls for ½ *can* of dry onion soup mix. If you can't find a can, the familiar Lipton packet will do—use ¼ cup (about one-third of the package), but mix it up well before dividing, and crush the ingredients fine.

¼ cup dry onion soup mix   *2 loaves French bread*
8 tablespoons butter, softened

• Preheat oven to 400°.
Combine soup mix and butter. Slice bread almost through. Spread seasoned butter on each slice. Wrap loaves in aluminum foil.
Heat 20 minutes.

SOUPER DOOPER BREAD

This is our version of a recipe found in community cookbooks around the country. It makes a savory snack all by itself, with sweet butter. Leftovers should be cut into small cubes and baked at 300° for about a half hour, to produce sensational croutons.

2 packages dry yeast dissolved in
  ½ cup tepid water (110°) with
  1 tablespoon sugar
1 package dry onion soup mix
1 cup warm water

8 tablespoons butter, melted and
  cooled to tepid
3½ to 4 cups sifted flour
1 cup grated Cheddar cheese

• When yeast mixture is dissolved, stir in soup mix, 1 cup water, butter, and 2 ½ cups flour. Beat until well blended. Add enough flour (about 1 cup) to produce a sticky but workable dough. Turn out onto floured board and let rest while you clean and butter bowl.

Knead 10 minutes, adding flour if needed, to produce a resilient but not too stiff dough. Return to bowl, cover, and let rise in warm place until double in bulk, about 1 hour.

Beat down dough, knead a few minutes, and form into buttered baking pan about 9 inches square. Cover and let rise in warm place until double in bulk again, about 30 to 45 minutes. Spread grated cheese over top.

Preheat oven to 400°.

Bake bread 30 to 35 minutes.

Remove from oven; cool a few minutes, then remove bread from pan. Serve warm.

ANN LANDERS' MEAT LOAF

We found this recipe in the 1971 Walnut, Iowa, Centennial Cookbook ("Firmly Rooted—Branching Out"). As far as we're concerned, there is none better. We are told that Ann Landers runs the recipe in her column every year, presumably because its very goodness can miraculously cure almost any sick marriage. We eat a lot of this loaf, and have yet to even contemplate divorce.

1 pound ground beef
½ pound ground veal
½ pound ground pork
1 teaspoon
 Worcestershire sauce
2 eggs

1½ cups cracker crumbs
¾ cup ketchup
½ cup warm water
1 package dry onion soup mix
4 strips bacon
1 8-ounce can tomato sauce

• Preheat oven to 350°.

Mix meats together by hand in large bowl. Add Worcestershire, eggs, cracker crumbs, ketchup, water, and soup mix. Mix. Shape into a loaf in a shallow baking dish. Drape loaf with bacon strips, then pour tomato sauce over loaf.

Bake 1½ to 2 hours, or until done to your liking.

Serves 6 to 8.

IGLOO MEAT LOAF

Igloo Meat Loaf was suggested to us by the mother of a friend of a friend. The mom's other claim to fame was Mystery Soup, which she made every Sunday by opening three to five mismatched cans, combining them in a pot, and stirring with glee.

Igloo Meat Loaf is made just like Ann Landers' Meat Loaf, but formed into an igloo-shaped mound on the baking dish. Bake as directed, without bacon, and when ready to serve, "frost" the loaf completely with mashed potatoes. You may mound the potatoes thick enough on top to form a large crater for holding gravy, although this dilutes the igloo effect.

MEAT LOAF WELLINGTON

Through the wonder of refrigerated crescent roll dough, a simple meat loaf becomes regal luxury, as solidly British as Sebastian Cabot. All you have to do is prepare Ann Landers' Meat Loaf, as directed above, eliminating the tomato sauce poured over the top. Bake until done. Cool 10 to 15 minutes.

Separate 2 packages of crescent roll dough into 6 rectangles (2 crescent forms make 1 rectangle). Reserve the remaining 2 for decorating, as below. Overlap the rectangles on a lightly floured pastry board to form 1 large rectangle. Place over meat loaf and mold to fit. Trim off excess dough and use remaining rectangles to make a fleur-de-lis or a similar heraldic design for the top. Brush dough with egg white. Return to oven and bake 15 to 20 minutes, or until golden.

COMPANY PERFECT CASSEROLE

From *You Asked for It Recipes,* published by the ladies of Portland's 11th Ward. The onion soup steps out of the spotlight to take a supporting role in this elaborate production, suitable for the fussiest gourmet guests—if, for instance, it is 1968 and Vincent Price is coming to dinner at your house.

2 pounds ground chuck
½ cup sour cream
3 tablespoons dry onion soup mix
(mix well before measuring)
1 egg, slightly beaten
1½ cups soft bread crumbs
⅓ cup flour

1 teaspoon paprika
4 tablespoons butter
1 8-ounce can sliced mushrooms,
with liquid
1 can condensed cream of
chicken soup
1⅔ cups water

• Form first 5 ingredients into 16 balls. Roll meatballs in flour blended with paprika until well coated. Brown slowly in butter. Mix and add last 3 ingredients. Simmer 20 minutes, adding more water if needed.

Place balls and gravy in 3-quart casserole and top with Butter Crumb Dumplings.

BUTTER CRUMB DUMPLINGS

2 cups sifted flour	*2 teaspoons dried onion flakes*
4 teaspoons baking powder	*¼ cup oil*
1 tablespoon poppy seeds	*¾ cup plus 2 tablespoons milk*
1 teaspoon celery salt	*4 tablespoons butter, melted*
1 teaspoon poultry seasoning	*2 cups soft bread crumbs*

• Preheat oven to 400°.

Mix first 6 ingredients together. Mix and blend in oil and milk. Stir melted butter into crumbs. Drop dough by tablespoon in 12 equal portions into buttered crumbs and roll to cover. Place on top of hot meat and gravy. Bake, uncovered, 20 to 25 minutes, until dumplings are golden.

If extra sauce is desired, simmer 1 can condensed cream of chicken soup, flavored with ¼ teaspoon poultry seasoning and 1 teaspoon onion flakes. Stir in ½ cup sour cream and reheat.

Serves 6 to 8.

Casseroles —
Glamour with a Can Opener

In the suburban chef's pantry, cans of Campbell's are a staple—not for soup, which is ordinary and old-fashioned, but for aspics and casseroles. With a couple of cans and a creative flair, the world is your oyster.

Dinner in a single dish is not unique to suburbia, but it was as suburban food that the casserole became a paradigm of convenience cooking.

"Every homemaker dreams of creating memorable main dishes," said the Culinary Arts Institute's *Casserole Cookbook* in 1956. "These dreams come true when she's cooking a casserole. Often, with minutes and hours so precious, she can fill her convenient casserole the day or night before—or even a month before, if she has a freezer—and it is ready for the oven except for quick finishing touches."

Perfect for the busy gourmet, casseroles are also the basis of a whole genre of party—the potluck or covered-dish supper, to which everybody brings a different casserole, from chafing dish hors d'oeuvres to cobblers or custards for dessert. The only rule about potluck is that everything has to be made ahead of time and reheated at the party. Also, in her 1952 book called *Pot Luck,* Barbara I. Gillard advised that "it is better to have too much than too little. Appetites increase under sociable conditions, and you will have little left over. In planning a party for 40, have six casseroles for 10. And there is always the man with the sweet tooth who will finish up the desserts."

All suburban cooks have their own favorite casserole recipes, perhaps originally clipped from a ladies' magazine, but then personalized—by crumbling potato chips or Ritz crackers on top, or blanketing it with melted cheese, or adding sour cream or mayonnaise to enrich it.

The repertoire is limitless, but we have selected those casseroles that are quintessentially suburban—the basic tuna variations, a noodleburger combo, a taste of the South Seas, and finally, one casserole that is, with the possible exception of eating raw cookie dough, the ultimate in no-fuss food.

THE PERFECT TUNA CASSEROLE

Simple, basic, and infinitely adjustable to one's own palate (by adding beans or asparagus instead of peas, or using, cream of potato or celery soup instead of mushroom), and yet just about impossible to improve upon, this Campbell's recipe is the classic tuna casserole. It is the dimly remembered taste that expatriate suburbanites are looking for when, as sophisticated adults, they secretly crave the tuna casserole of their youth.

Although either light or dark tuna works fine, we prefer the latter for its gamier flavor. Either way, oil-packed is essential.

1 can Campbell's condensed cream of mushroom soup	*2 hard-boiled eggs, sliced*
⅓ cup milk	*1 cup cooked peas*
1 6½-ounce can oil-packed tuna, drained and flaked	*1 cup slightly crumbled potato chips*

• Preheat oven to 350°.

Blend soup and milk in 1-quart casserole. Stir in tuna, eggs, and peas. Bake 20 minutes. Top with chips; bake 10 minutes longer.

Serves 3 to 4.

HE-MAN'S TUNA NOODLE CASSEROLE

We got this recipe by sending away a buck to a lady in Muskogee, Oklahoma, whose address we found in *Women's Household* magazine (where we also learned how to make pretty dolls out of old Lux detergent bottles).

Her casserole calls for cream of chicken soup and a topping of shredded American cheese. That's good, but we like it better when cream of mushroom soup is used, and Ritz crackers are sprinkled on top instead of cheese. We also like sour cream, whereas the Muskogee original calls for mayonnaise. However you do it, this one is, as the name suggests, a rib-sticker, and has become a wintertime favorite around our place.

6 ounces medium egg noodles	*1 cup chopped celery*
2 tablespoons butter	*1 6½-ounce can oil-packed tuna,*
1 can condensed cream of	* drained and flaked*
* mushroom soup*	* (an additional 3-ounce can*
1 cup milk	* is optional, for a*
½ cup sour cream	* meatier casserole)*
½ teaspoon salt	*15 Ritz crackers (half a stack),*
½ cup finely chopped onion	* broken but not crumbled*
¼ cup sliced pimiento	*Parsley for garnish*
½ cup finely chopped	
* green pepper*	

• Cook noodles in salted water; drain. Coat with butter. Preheat oven to 425°.

In a large saucepan, mix soup, milk, sour cream, salt, onion, pimiento, pepper, and celery. Cook over low heat, stirring frequently, for 15 minutes. Add tuna. Combine with noodles and pour into 2-quart casserole. Sprinkle top with Ritz crackers.

Bake 20 to 25 minutes. Garnish with parsley. Serves 6 large men.

TUNA CASSEROLE SUPREME

If Cole Porter had written songs about tuna casseroles, he would have swooned with inspiration over this supreme creation. It is the apex of couth, to be savored with chilled cold duck wine.

½ cup chopped onion
½ cup finely chopped green pepper
1 cup chopped celery
8 tablespoons butter
1 can condensed Cheddar cheese soup
½ cup milk
1 8-ounce can sliced mushrooms, drained

1 teaspoon salt
1 cup chopped green pimiento stuffed olives
1 6½-ounce can oil-packed tuna, drained and flaked (an additional 3-ounce can is optional)
1 cup crushed corn flakes
½ cup slivered almonds

• Preheat oven to 400°.

In a large saucepan, sauté onion, pepper, and celery in 4 tablespoons butter. Stir in soup and milk, and cook over low heat 10 to 12 minutes. Add mushrooms, salt, olives, and tuna. Pour into 2-quart casserole.

Melt 4 tablespoons butter; stir in corn flakes and almonds. Spread on top of casserole.

Bake, uncovered, 25 minutes.

Serves 6 to 8.

QUEEN FOR A DAY NOODLEBURGER CASSEROLE

"This is one of my very favorite recipes," wrote Jack Bailey, host of radio's (and subsequently TV's) *Queen for a Day* in his cookbook, *What's Cookin'*, published in 1949. Hamburger—cheeseburger—nutburger, all kinds of burgers. But friends, a noodleburger in this manner and baked in a casserole is a full-fledged filling feed, and a meal in itself. You try—you see."

We tried—we saw; and discovered Jack Bailey's concoction to be a *déjà vu* of fondly remembered school cafeteria casseroles—the quintessence of institutional lunch.

½ onion, chopped
Bacon drippings or butter
1 pound ground round steak
1 can condensed cream of tomato
   soup
1 cup water

2 cups uncooked
   elbow macaroni
1 17-ounce can creamed corn
Salt and pepper to taste
1 cup grated cheese

- Preheat oven to 375°.

In a large saucepan or skillet, sauté onion in bacon drippings or butter. When barely brown, mix in meat and continue cooking until meat is browned.

Stir in soup and water. Stir in macaroni and continue cooking until noodles are tender, adding up to a cup more water, as needed. Add corn, salt, and pepper to taste. Pour mixture into a buttered 2-quart casserole.

Bake, uncovered, 45 minutes, adding grated cheese after 25 minutes. Serves 4 to 6.

MING DYNASTY CASSEROLE

Casseroles suffer the reputation of being plain food. To prove otherwise, here's a dishful of exotic Orientalia, submitted by a viewer to Martha Dixon's *Copper Kettle* television cooking show in Lansing, Michigan. Have guests leave their shoes at the door when they come for this dinner, and serve it on a low coffee table, so everyone must sit cross-legged on toss pillows.

*1 3-ounce can chow
    mein noodles
1 8-ounce can water
    chestnuts, sliced
1 can condensed cream of
    mushroom soup
1 cup half-and-half*

*1 cup finely chopped celery
Dash pepper
1½ cups cooked chicken or tuna
¾ cup coarsely cut cashew
    nuts
¼ cup minced onion*

• Preheat oven to 350°.

Set aside ½ cup chow mein noodles. Combine all other ingredients in a 2-quart casserole.

Bake, uncovered, 30 minutes. Sprinkle remaining noodles on top of casserole. Bake 15 minutes longer.

Serves 4 to 6.

EIGHT CAN CASSEROLE

It came from Iowa, specifically from the Oakland Centennial Cookbook, a treasury of recipes that revel in all manner of canned soups, and brands such as Jell-O, Cool Whip, Kix, Trix, and Cremora. Eight Can Casserole is without doubt the end of that line, nothing but streamlined convenience, not even pretending to be real cookery.

We do not recommend preparing Eight Can Casserole when you are by yourself. It seems too naughty—even derelict, like drinking alone. Its creation ought to be a social event. When the guests arrive and ask what's for dinner, invite them into the kitchen, where you have eight cans lined up: ready, set, go! Open the cans and dump them into the casserole. Wham, into the oven; zip, zip; it's ready to eat. No mess, no fuss, no nothing. And yet, despite the lack of talent needed to prepare it, Eight Can Casserole is a darn good meal, every bit as delicious as it is convenient.

If you are feeling particularly numerative, or if a mathematician is coming to dinner, serve Eight Can Casserole with Five Cup Salad (page 17), accompanied by Double Chocolate Malts (page 96).

2 5-ounce cans boned chicken
1 can condensed cream of
mushroom soup
1 can condensed cream of
chicken soup

1 8-ounce can
mushrooms, drained
1 5-ounce can chow mein noodles
1 13-ounce can evaporated milk
1 can fried onion rings

• Preheat oven to 350°.

In a 3-quart casserole, mix everything except onion rings.

Bake 20 minutes. Sprinkle on onion rings. Bake 15 minutes longer.

Serves 6 to 8.

Luau in Your Living Room

To the suburban cook, food is never enough. Parties need themes; meals, accents. "Must we always have the inevitable meat loaf?" groaned the Foreword to *Pot Luck—Casserole Entertaining* in 1952, "Try something new, use more imagination, be different."

Why serve a pickle when you can offer your guests pickle-on-a-stick? Why make meat loaf when you can wow them with Meat Loaf Wellington? Convenience is often denigrated as the end of creativity in the kitchen. Just the opposite is true.

Before convenience cooking, most home cooks had a limited, parochial repertoire. But with mix-and-match ingredients, the potential for experimentation broadened beyond tradition to include imitation exotic fare from around the world.

There is no cuisine more adventurous, or more totally spurious, than that called Polynesian. We don't know what Polynesians eat, but that doesn't matter, because it has no bearing on Polynesian food, suburban style.

Polynesian dining is the ultimate in exotica. It is a cuisine that encourages you to flame foods, tint them unnatural shades of red and blue, and generally create a very sexy mood. It is the food of love, suggesting a Hawaiian honeymoon or a moonlight cruise.

Polynesian Night calls for a romantic setting, the dining area fit with pagoda lanterns, the table set with fragrant gardenias bobbing in glasses of tinted water, and centerpieces constructed from tropical fruits and nuts. The man of the house wears his most colorful aloha shirt, the woman her muumuu or grass skirt.

After dinner, in keeping with the romantic motif, plan a game of "Taro-San and Hanachan," in which all the guests gather in a circle around a blindfolded couple. Taro-San (the man) calls after Hanachan and tries to find her; but Hanachan tries to evade Taro-San. When Taro-San finally catches his mate, they are replaced by another couple.

Adventuring in Home Living, our textbook in beginning home ec, suggests that a good luau concludes with the singing of Hawaiian love chants such as "O Makala Pua," "Imi Ao Ia Oe," or "Lovely Hula Hands." What? You say Hawaii isn't Polynesia? Who cares? To the suburban gourmet, that is a petty distinction. All Pacific cuisines are one, their escutcheon a Maraschino-red banner bearing a parasol and scowling Tiki god engulfed in the Sterno-blue flame of the pu pu platter.

Tropical Drinks

No matter how elaborate the decor, or authentic the after-dinner love songs, nothing will put guests in a more romantic tropical mood than the right drink. In the South Pacific, beverages are a symbol of hospitality. Opening a bottle of soda or combining Kool-Aid powder with water or, for that matter, merely stirring any mixed drink at all seems so *Occidental* compared with the possibilities of blenderized fantasies of froth and fizz. When it comes to gourmet cooking and bartending, the electric blender is as important to the suburban chef as the can opener.

BLUE HAWAII

The ultimate tropical drink, tinted ocean blue with Curaçao liqueur, always decorated with pineapple slice, orange slice, and Maraschino cherries.

2 ounces pineapple juice

2 ounces rum

1 ounce Mi-Lem sweetened
   lemon juice

1 ounce blue Curaçao liqueur

• Combine all ingredients; stir. Serve in tall tulip glass.

TRADER VIC'S BABALU

1 scoop shaved ice

¾ ounce pineapple-
   grapefruit juice

½ ounce lemon juice

2 ounces gold rum

• Blend until frothy and serve (with straw) in tall glass with cracked ice, decorated with mint and a paper parasol.

HAWAIIAN PUNCH

3 ounces gin
3 ounces coconut milk
1½ ounces lemon juice
1 teaspoon Curaçao liqueur

2 teaspoons sugar
2 cups ice
2 coconuts

• Bore a large hole in each coconut; drain out milk. Blend all ingredients until thick and foamy. Use a small funnel to put drink back inside coconuts. Serve with straw.

Serves 2.

LEILANI GRASS HUT

2 ounces white rum
½ ounce lemon juice
½ ounce pineapple juice
½ ounce papaya juice

1 ounce orange juice
Dash grenadine
Club soda

• Pour all ingredients except soda over ice in a tall glass. Mix well. Fill glass with soda. Garnish with Maraschino cherry, pineapple slice, and wedge of orange on a long cocktail stick.

PURPLE POODLE

From *The Wonderful World of Welch's* cookbook.

3 ounces Welch's Concord grape juice
1 ounce brandy

1 teaspoon lime juice
Club soda

• Combine ingredients, stir well, and pour over cracked ice into 12-ounce glass. Fill glass with club soda.

CLAIRE'S APRICOT SLUSH

From Oakland, Iowa, Centennial Cookbook.

*6 ounces frozen orange
  juice concentrate*
*6 ounces frozen
  lemonade concentrate*

½ cup sugar
6 cups water
1 pint apricot brandy

• Blend and freeze.
   To serve, scoop about ½ cup into a glass and fill with 7-Up.
   Serves 8.

South Seas Adventure

A complete Polynesian menu for the serious culinary adventurer. Begin with
Blue Hawaiis or Hawaiian Punch in a coconut, then proceed to:

*Flaming Cabbage Head Weenies with Pu Pu Sauce ◆ Polynesian
Tiki Sweet and Sour Chicken ◆ Kilauea Purple Passion Rice ◆
Gauguin Aesthetic Cake*

A Luau

FLAMING CABBAGE HEAD WEENIES
WITH PU PU SAUCE

South Seas cooking is best enjoyed by moonlight. Even if the main meal is prepared in the oven, why not start the ball rolling with this festive appetizer, served on the patio. It gives each guest the opportunity to relish the pleasure of do-it-yourself cookery, by holding his own food to the flame.

PU PU SAUCE

½ cup sour cream	*1 tablespoon wine vinegar*
2 tablespoons yellow mustard	*1 small onion, minced fine*
1 tablespoon chili sauce	*1 teaspoon lemon juice*
1 tablespoon brown sugar	*Chili powder to taste*
½ tablespoon	*Salt to taste*
Worcestershire sauce	

• Combine all ingredients in a saucepan. Bring to boil, stirring occasionally. Remove from heat; let stand at least 1 hour before serving.

FLAMING CABBAGE HEAD WEENIES

1 large head cabbage,	*25 to 30 cocktail frankfurters*
red or green	
1 can Sterno	

• Rinse cabbage and trim base so it stands evenly. Form decorative petals by curling a few outer leaves down from top. Cut a space in top center of head deep enough to hold Sterno inside, with rim of can even with cabbage.

Light Sterno. Stick cocktail franks into flaming cabbage on toothpicks or, if you are worried about burned fingertips, provide long forks. Set warm Pu Pu Sauce nearby for dipping.

Serves 4 to 6.

POLYNESIAN TIKI
SWEET AND SOUR CHICKEN

Pineapple and soy sauce—you can practically smell the Pacific breezes as this dish cooks. Get out the Don Ho records and brace yourself for an evening of volcanic passion. (Inspired by Mrs. Anson Bob Chunn's recipe in *Southern Sideboards*, published by the Junior League of Jackson, Mississippi.)

6 chicken breasts, split	*2 tablespoons soy sauce*
½ cup flour	*1½ teaspoons ground ginger*
⅓ cup salad oil	*1 chicken bouillon cube*
1½ teaspoons salt	*2 tablespoons cornstarch*
½ teaspoon white pepper	*1 10-ounce can crushed*
1 cup sugar	*pineapple, drained*
1½ cups pineapple juice	*1 green pepper, cut in strips*
⅔ cup cider vinegar	

• Preheat oven to 350°.

Dust chicken with flour and brown in oil on both sides. Place on roasting pan, season with salt and pepper.

Combine sugar, pineapple juice, vinegar, soy sauce, ginger, and bouillon cube in medium saucepan. Before heating, dissolve cornstarch in 3 table-spoons mixture, then return dissolved cornstarch to pan and bring mixture to boil, stirring constantly. Lower heat; simmer 3 minutes, stirring occasionally. Pour mixture over chicken.

Bake, uncovered, 15 minutes. Add crushed pineapple and green pepper. Continue baking until chicken is tender, 15 to 20 minutes.

Serves 4 to 6.

KILAUEA PURPLE PASSION RICE

3 cups grape juice	*1 cup uncooked rice*
2 vegetable or chicken	*2 ounces slivered*
bouillon cubes	*toasted almonds*
4 tablespoons butter	

• Preheat oven to 350°.

Bring grape juice to boil. Dissolve bouillon cubes in juice.

Heat butter and brown rice until golden. Transfer rice to 1-quart casserole.

Pour boiling grape juice over rice. Sprinkle with almonds.

Bake, uncovered, 50 minutes, or until rice is tender,

Serves 4.

GAUGUIN AESTHETIC CAKE

The South Seas can be conjured up merely by combining prunes with the right paradisiacal spices, as Kate Smith does in this native-style layer cake, a "masterpiece in cake artistry" taken from her *Company's Coming Cookbook*. "A wonderful blend of flavors," Kate boasts, "and a cake that will keep well!"

CAKE

¾ teaspoon baking powder	*8 tablespoons butter*
Pinch salt	*1½ cups sugar*
1 teaspoon baking soda	*2 eggs, beaten*
1 teaspoon allspice	*1¼ cups pitted and coarsely cut*
1½ teaspoons cinnamon	*cooked prunes*
¼ teaspoon ground cloves	*1 cup buttermilk*
2½ cups cake flour	

• Preheat oven to 375°.

Sift baking powder, salt, soda, spices, and flour together three times.

Cream butter, add sugar gradually; cream until fluffy. Add eggs slowly, then prunes, and mix gently until blended. Add buttermilk alternately with flour mixture, a little at a time, beating each time. Pour into 2 well-buttered and floured 8-inch layer cake pans.

Bake 30 minutes. Remove layers from pans and cool on racks.

ICING

6 tablespoons butter	*⅓ cup lemon juice*
1 teaspoon grated lemon rind	*Pinch salt*
3 cups confectioners' sugar	*Food coloring, if desired*

• Mix butter and lemon rind well; when creamy, add part of sugar and blend. Add remaining sugar, alternating with lemon juice, until icing attains spreading consistency. Beat thoroughly; add salt and, if desired, a few drops of food coloring for an artistic effect.

When cake is cool, spread icing on layers, sides, and top.

Patio Parties

One day, a couple of million years ago, one of our ancestors was having a snack of saber-tooth tiger steak, when it accidentally fell into the fire. Before he could get it out, it was ruined—all horrible brown, instead of nice and bloody. Nevertheless, since the cave was running low on saber-tooth tiger that week, he decided to eat it anyway. And he liked it! . . .

Today, most of us have meals outdoors every chance we get—on porch, patio, or lawn.

—*General Foods Kitchens Cookbook*, 1959

The call for meals to have themes reaches a crescendo on the patio, where the theme is nature. In keeping with the caveman concept, patio cuisine is basically Neanderthal—hunks of meat cooked over fire. The point is to *go primitive,* to eat with your hands, to step away from the sophisticated cuisine of the suburban gourmet, stroll to the deck or patio, and rediscover the simplicity of the great outdoors.

The back-to-nature theme demands that the man of the house wear a flamboyant chef's hat and apron, while the woman play *sous chef.* That is the way it was in prehistoric times; and so, using the natural skills with fire and meat that they have inherited from their ancient ancestors, men do all barbecuing, "Outdoor cooking is a man's art," proclaimed *The Master Chef's Outdoor Grill Cookbook* in 1960.

But going back to nature isn't merely a matter of digging a pit and roasting a freshly killed squirrel on a stick over hot stones. Required paraphernalia for a proper patio party includes not only cooking apron and chef's hat, but asbestos mitts, basting tubes, skewers and long-handled forks, plus, of course, a grill—anything from a simple metal basin to a rolling, hooded, stainless-steel, gas-powered, electric-spit-equipped brazier wagon.

Games are crucial to the success of a patio party, lest guests spend the evening merely conversing or, even worse, coaching and teasing the harried chef. Before dinner, provide guests with the opportunity to play badminton, darts, Ping-Pong, or beanbags. Or do as the *Sunset Barbecue Book* of 1947 suggests: spend this time decorating paper plates. Set up a card table with poster paints, brushes, and white paper plates; then ask each guest to create an original design. The next day, shellac the masterpieces and thumbtack them up near the barbecue grill, so when you have another party, you will have instant, handmade decor.

When the dinner's over, play charades or plan a singalong, with a musical motif that fits the meal—cowboy ballads to follow steaks, Hawaiian love chants after a luau, protest songs if it's a hobo dinner. The *Sunset Barbecue Book* suggests that games of "Who Am I?" "Geography," or "Coffeepot" are "amazingly successful." "Who Am I?' and "Geography" sound great to us. But does anyone remember how to play "Coffeepot"?

As for what you cook outdoors, remember that anybody can slap beef, chicken, or ribs on the fire, but for pizazz on the patio, try some of these ideas for a really special outdoor party.

HOBO DINNER IN A CAN

Since bums do their eating around a campfire, the hobo motif is perfectly suited to the patio. What fun it is for suburbanites to gather around the barbecue wagon and mimic the carefree tramp by each cooking his or her own hobo hamburger on a stick (bind the ground meat with crushed corn flakes and eggs). Or for a more civilized hobo-style dinner, try this idea, suggested by *Festive Foods*.

FOR EACH SERVING

1 coffee can	*1 medium ripe tomato, sliced*
1 medium raw potato,	*1 thin slice onion*
sliced thin	*½ cup canned*
1 4-ounce ground-beef patty,	*whole-kernel corn, drained*
seasoned to taste	*Salt and pepper*
1 large carrot, cut into thin 2-inch	
strips	

• Butter inside of coffee can. Put some potato slices on bottom; add beef patty, then layers of carrot, tomato, onion, potato, corn, and a few generous sprinkles of salt and pepper. Cover can with heavy aluminum foil, but punch a couple of holes in foil for steam to escape.

Cook on hot grill 30 minutes, or until done.

Serve in can with long-handled forks and asbestos mitts, or empty can onto a plate.

Kabob Combinations

A kabob is the outdoor version of a casserole—an entire meal is cooked together on a stick. But it's even easier because you can lay out an assortment of ingredients near the fire, hand each guest a skewer, and tell everyone to create and grill their own. According to *The Master Chef's Outdoor Grill Cookbook,* here is what goes with what:

Lamb: bacon, mushroom, small cooked onions

Beef: small onions, small tomatoes, green peppers

Pork (must be precooked before grilling to avoid trichinosis): apples, pineapple chunks

Sausage, franks, Spam: sweet pickles, bacon, olives, green pepper slices, banana chunks

Shellfish: bacon, pineapple chunks

Charkets Outdoor Chef cookbook, published in 1961, suggests these Polynesian kabob combos to accompany steak or chicken, or as tidbits for nibbling:

BALI HAI VEGETABLES

• Skewer zucchini, mushroom caps, and cherry tomatoes. Brush with oil. Turn and brush frequently until done as desired.

MAUI LAULAU

• Weaving a slice of bacon between each piece of food, thread chunks of pineapple, squares of crisp red and green peppers, and jumbo ripe olives onto small skewers. Barbecue until bacon is crisp.

WIKIWIKI TIDBITS

• Stuff pitted prunes or dates with drained canned chunked pineapple and wrap in a strip of bacon. Secure with a wooden pick. Thread on small skewers and barbecue on grill, turning often until bacon is crisp. Serve warm.

Barbecued Bread

They'll do it every time: you go to a backyard barbecue and the burgers or franks or whatever-kabobs smell *delicious,* and you start getting that man-sized appetite that outdoor living stimulates. But when you get the meat, it comes with spongy store-bought buns. That's uncool.

Here are a couple of good solutions to the bread problem. Like instant garlic spread, these party buns bring bread out of the dark ages and into the 1950s. For frankfurters, try:

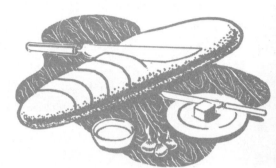

BEATNIK BUNS

1 can deviled ham spread	*Pepper*
2 tablespoons mayonnaise	*4 sprigs parsley, chopped*
1 teaspoon	*8 frankfurter rolls*
Worcestershire sauce	

• Mix ham spread, mayo, Worcestershire sauce, pepper, and parsley. Pull apart but do not tear frankfurter rolls. Spread mixture on each roll, close it up, then wrap each roll in heavy-duty foil and lay on grill for 10 minutes, turning once. (If desired, slices of cheese can be added to buns.)

For hamburgers try:

MOST HAPPY FELLA BREAD

8 tablespoons butter,	*3 tablespoons mustard*
softened	*8 large slices Italian bread*

• Mix butter and mustard (yellow preferred) and spread on both sides of bread slices. Grill until lightly browned, turning once.

Barbecued Dessert

There is no need to douse the fire when guests want their sweet tooth satisfied. End your cookout with one of these uncommon fruits from *Charkets Outdoor Chef.*

CAPE CANAVERAL BANANAS

• For each serving, peel 1 banana, brush with lemon juice, sprinkle generously with dark brown sugar, and dot with butter. Wrap securely in a double thickness of heavy-duty aluminum foil and lay on the grill for about 15 minutes, turning frequently. Unwrap and serve with shredded coconut.

GINGER-MINT PEARS

• For each serving, drain 2 canned pear halves and set on a double thickness of heavy-duty aluminum foil. Sprinkle with coarsely chopped crystallized ginger and a couple teaspoonfuls of apple-mint jelly. Wrap in foil, keeping cut side up so ginger and jelly stay in place. Barbecue about 12 minutes on grill. Unwrap and serve immediately.

HONEY-RUM GRAPEFRUIT

• Cut grapefruit in half, cut out core, and loosen each section with a grapefruit knife. In the center of each half, pour 1 tablespoon rum and top with ½ tablespoon honey and a sprinkle of ground mace. Wrap securely in a double thickness of heavy-duty aluminum foil. Grill cut side up about 20 minutes. Serve immediately.

If it's a hobo party, finish things off with round-the-fire folk songs and Camp Caramel Apples. "Everyone loves an apple on a stick," said *The Master Chef's Outdoor Grill Cookbook,* "especially when he creates his own golden work-of-art."

CAMP CARAMEL APPLES

• For each serving, spear 1 medium tart cooking apple through the stem end on a shish kebab skewer. Lay it on a lightly greased grill or hold over coals, turning occasionally, until skin breaks and may be easily pulled off.

Peel, then dip apple in a bowl of melted butter. Then immediately twirl apple in a deep bowl of brown sugar, covering it completely. Now hold apple over grill and slowly turn it until sugar turns into a rich caramel coating. Quickly dip top in finely chopped salted peanuts.

Let cool before eating. The caramel stays hot longer than you think!

Teen Food

Teenage culture flowered in the suburbs, and while the lazy kids dressed sloppily and ate too many french fries, good boys and girls studied how to become responsible, constructive adults.

One way to learn the art of being a grown-up was to mimic the rituals of grown-up social life—to entertain and cook just like Mom and Dad, but do it with youthful panache. "The sophisticated teen-ager," Kate Smith declared in the *Kate Smith Company's Coming Cookbook*, "will emulate mama by serving her party group Peachy Peach Sundaes, because she will be able to serve them *flambé*, just as mother does the Cherries Jubilee, and without a drop of brandy in sight."

Teen parties, according to *You're Entertaining—America's Junior Miss Party Guide*, were at the vanguard of a revolution in party-giving, the battle cry of which was informality. "Backyard, patio, porch, recreation room, even the magic half-circle around the television set have opened up attractive spots for new ideas in informal entertaining."

Informality means you can telephone your invitations instead of writing, you can set up a buffet instead of setting a formal table, and you can use Scott paper napkins instead of linen. (Did we mention that *You're Entertaining* was published by the Scott Paper Company?) However informal, you still must remember that, as a hostess, it is your job to set the tone of the evening by greeting guests at the front door with a "boot box" for muddy loafers, lined with superabsorbent ScotTowels.

For teen decor, all one need do is collect tubes left over from paper towels and bathroom tissue. For a mock candelabra, glue pink and yellow ScotTowels to the outside of towel tubes, cut a cardboard circle for their tops, and insert twisted wax paper as a wick. For a mock firecracker, cover a toilet tissue tube with red construction paper, then add a wick. You can make snowflakes from wax paper, Christmas tree favor holders with CutRite sandwich bags, and tiny parasols with pipe cleaners and small circles of double-thickness paper towels.

As for what to serve at a teen party, the basic assumption of teenage cookery, as set forth in 1950s cookbooks, is that teens will eat only hamburgers, hot dogs, and pizza, plus cookies and cake. Thus, teen food is a small cuisine, confined to permutations of shapes made from the limited repertoire of allowable ingredients.

ENGLISH MUFFIN PIZZAS

Everybody loves pizza, especially English muffin pizzas, because everybody can make their own. Set the ingredients out on the kitchen counter, and give each guest two muffin halves and five minutes. As to ingredients, only muffins, American cheese, and tomato ketchup are absolutely necessary, but the more variety you have, the merrier the pizza party. If your visiting chefs are budding gourmets, you might want to offer tomato sauce in lieu of ketchup, and sharp Cheddar or mozzarella cheese. And if you don't have any English muffins, no sweat—use miniature bagels, slices of cocktail rye, or plain white bread, formed into circles with a cookie cutter.

English muffins	*Topping*
(1 to 2 per person)	*(see suggestions below)*
Ketchup	*Garlic powder*
Sliced American cheese	

SUGGESTED PIZZA TOPPINGS

Bologna or salami	*Canned mushrooms*
Spam luncheon meat	*Tuna*
Chopped green or black olives	*Imitation bacon bits*
Chopped onions	*. . . even anchovies*

• Split English muffins, and flatten each half with a rolling pin. In a broiler, toast what was the outside surface of all muffin halves until just barely crisp. Remove and place on cookie sheet, untoasted side up.

On each half, spread a spoonful of ketchup and drape with cheese. Add whatever other toppings you desire, then sprinkle with garlic powder.

Return muffins to broiler and toast until cheese melts and just barely browns. Serve immediately.

MERRY PIZZA ROUNDS

We found these happy rounds in the Oakland, Iowa, Centennial Cookbook, among "Supper on a Bread Slice" and "Hamburger Maid Rites"—all quick to-fix food for teens. Rounds require a bit more culinary skill than basic English muffin pizzas, but they are more a whole meal than a snack.

2 8-ounce cans tomato sauce

2 tablespoons instant
   minced onion

½ teaspoon oregano

½ teaspoon garlic salt

½ teaspoon basil

1 pound mozzarella cheese

10 frankfurters

5 English muffins, split

• Simmer sauce with onion, oregano, salt, and basil for 10 minutes.

Cut 10 thin (1-ounce) slices from mozzarella cheese; grate remainder.

Score 10 franks at ½-inch intervals about three-quarters through, and shape into circles. Broil franks 2 to 3 minutes or until lightly browned.

Lightly toast bottoms of English muffins. Place 1 slice cheese on each muffin half. Broil 2 minutes or until melted. Place 1 cut frank on each split muffin and top with 2 tablespoons sauce. Fill center of frank circle with grated cheese. Sprinkle with oregano. Broil 2 minutes more.

Serves 5.

SLOPPY JOES

"Being a mother who knows what to serve while the Beatles are bleating will mark you as 'cool' forever," advised *The New Hamburger Cookbook* in 1965. Sloppy Joes, a "teen-agers' delight," come in many variations, but we think this minestrone soup recipe offers the ultimate in sloppiness.

2 pounds ground beef
1 large onion, diced
1 cup ketchup
1 cup water
1 7-ounce can mushroom stems
*   and pieces, drained*

½ teaspoon salt
¼ teaspoon pepper
1 10½-ounce can
*   minestrone soup*
8 hamburger buns

• Brown hamburger in large skillet and break apart until fine. Add onion and cook until translucent. Add ketchup, water, mushrooms, salt, pepper, and soup.

Cook over low heat 25 minutes, stirring occasionally. Heap onto burger buns.

Serves 8 adults or 4 teens.

DOWNBEAT DOGS ON A STICK

Similar in appearance to the corn dogs sold at Stuckey's drive-ins throughout the Midwest, these pups are an imaginative way to dress up wieners for teen parties. No utensils or plates needed!

10 wieners
10 6-inch wooden sticks
3 cups Bisquick baking mix
3 eggs

1 cup milk
Oil for frying
Mustard

• Stick each wiener firmly on a stick, and pat with a cloth to make sure it is dry.

Mix Bisquick, eggs, and milk to form thick batter. Dip each wiener in batter, thoroughly coating it.

Heat oil to 375°.

Slowly immerse wieners, 2 or 3 at a time, into hot oil. Cook 3 to 4 minutes, or until golden brown. Drain on paper towels.

Serve with a bowl of mustard, for dunking.

Serves 4 to 6 teens.

IMPOSSIBLE CHEESEBURGER PIE

The prototypical hamburger pizza; an essential Bisquick concoction. Ever since the "Impossible Bisquick" theme was introduced by General Mills, there have been innumerable Impossible Pie variations, both sweet and savory, but to the hungry teenager, this pile of burger meat, dough, and cheese is Impossibility at its finest. From the Bisquick box.

1 pound ground beef
1½ cups chopped onion
½ teaspoon salt
¼ teaspoon pepper
1½ cups milk

3 eggs
¾ cup Bisquick baking mix
2 tomatoes, sliced
1 cup shredded Cheddar cheese

• Preheat oven to 400°.

Cook ground beef and onion until beef is brown. Drain. Stir in salt and pepper. Spread mixture in greased 10-inch pie plate. Beat milk, eggs, and Bisquick until smooth. Pour into plate.

Bake 35 minutes. Top with tomatoes, then top tomatoes with cheese. Bake 8 to 10 minutes longer, or until knife inserted in center comes out clean.

Cool 5 to 8 minutes before serving.

Serves 6.

PEACHY PEACH SUNDAE

"Let's have a party!" Kate Smith says. "A sundae *flambé*, a rock-'n'-roll treat." For sophisticated teens only.

Vanilla ice cream   *Sugar cubes*

Canned sliced peaches   *Lemon extract*

• Place balls of vanilla ice cream in serving dishes. Top each with canned sliced peaches. Dip sugar cubes in lemon extract, and put 1 cube atop each sundae. At table, light sugar cubes.

FAMOUS CHOCOLATE WAFER ROLL

When Sis wants to impress her teenage football hero, here's just the ticket—the classic convenient dessert log. It seems so elegant, yet any idiot can make it. Not for teens only!

1 cup heavy cream   *½ teaspoon vanilla extract*

⅓ cup confectioners' sugar   *20 chocolate wafer cookies*

• Whip cream with sugar and vanilla. Reserve 1 cup, and spread each wafer with remaining cream, stacking them up in fives on wax paper. Chill 15 to 20 minutes.

Lay stacks on side, end to end, forming a long roll. Spread reserved cup of whipped cream over outside of roll. Cover arid chill at least 4 hours. Cut *diagonally*.

Serves 4 to 6.

VARIATIONS

Substitute peppermint extract for vanilla, and garnish log with crushed peppermint candies.

Substitute 1 tablespoon strong coffee for vanilla, and garnish log with shaved bittersweet chocolate curls.

Substitute 1 tablespoon almond extract for vanilla, and garnish log with crushed almonds.

COOKIES À LA KOOKIE

Other than his long hair and ever-present comb, the one thing Edd "Kookie" Byrnes was known for around the *77 Sunset Strip* set was the cookies his mom used to send him from home. According to *Cooking with the Stars— Hollywood's Favorite Recipes*, Kookie enjoyed these heavyweight confections while sipping espresso at a Sunset Strip coffeehouse.

*8 tablespoons butter, melted and
  cooled*
1 egg, beaten
*1 box white cake mix
  (18.25 ounces)*

*10 Brach's toffees, diced
  (about ⅔ cup)*

• Preheat oven to 350°.

Combine all ingredients. Drop in 1-inch balls on buttered cookie sheet. Bake 10 to 15 minutes or until light brown.

Remove from oven, let cool on cookie sheet a few minutes, then carefully remove with spatula to cookie rack.

Makes about 20.

Corn Flake Cookery

If there is a single generalization to be made about the cuisine of suburbia it is that it consists of things made from other things: soups turned into dips and casseroles; steaks cubed to form kabobs; graham crackers transformed into S'mores; Pepsi-Cola Cake and Ritz Pecan Pie. (Here we will merely draw—but not elaborate—the connecting line between this pronounced aspect of suburban gastronomy and suburban taste in general, which also consists of things made to look like other things: lawn fauna and garden gnomes made of concrete, Con-Tact paper "wood" on station wagons, spare rolls of toilet tissue hidden in the crocheted skirts of antebellum dolls.)

Nowhere is the celebration of unlikely material so accomplished as in the suburban cook's imaginative use of breakfast cereals, an approach that places the textures, colors, shapes, and tastes of everyday food in new and startling contexts. As a culinary movement, it is a style that foreshadowed what pop artists would be doing on canvas in the early 1960s. A complete retrospective of cereal cookery would include the likes of Product 19 Pancakes, Bran Bud Snacking Cake, Frozen Cheerio Dessert, Shredded Wheat Stroganoff, and Grape-Nut Chili.

But our interest is in the enduring formulations rather than esoteric anomalies, and so we have selected from the plethora of recipes only the germinal dishes of suburban cereal cookery.

OVEN-FRIED CORN FLAKE CHICKEN

Convenient, and surprisingly delicious. Moms like this recipe because it is neater than deep-frying, it's wholesome (anything with cereal in it *must* be healthy, right?), plus it's *fun*. And fun—the mischievous pleasure of turning breakfast food into dinner, and of baking something easy that seems difficult—is at the heart of the cereal cookery ethos.

1 3-pound frying chicken, cut up   *2 teaspoons salt*

2 eggs, slightly beaten   *½ teaspoon pepper*

4 tablespoons milk   *5 tablespoons butter, melted*

2½ cups corn flake crumbs

   (crushed but not pulverized)

• Preheat oven to 350°.

Wash chicken and pat dry. Mix together eggs and milk. Separately, mix corn flake crumbs, salt, and pepper. Dip chicken in milk-and-egg mixture, then in crumbs, evenly coating each piece. Set in well-greased baking pan. Drizzle with melted butter.

Bake, uncovered, 1 hour.

Serves 4 to 6.

BAKED CORN CHEX 'N' CHEESE CUSTARD

A Southern-style side dish to go with oven-fried chicken. It's like spoonbread, but with a Chex crunch. From *Cooking with Love 'n' Cereal*, a book we found while vacationing in a Holiday Inn in Ogallala, Nebraska.

¼ cup chopped green pepper   *⅛ teaspoon pepper*

⅓ cup finely chopped onion   *1 cup shredded*

2 tablespoons butter   *American cheese*

3 eggs   *1 pound canned corn, drained*

2 cups milk   *2 cups coarsely broken*

1 teaspoon salt   *Corn Chex*

½ teaspoon sugar

• Preheat oven to 325°.

Sauté green pepper and onion in butter until limp. Beat together eggs, milk, salt, sugar, and pepper. Stir in cheese, corn, sautéed peppers and onions, and 1½ cups cereal. Pour into buttered 2-quart casserole and top with remaining cereal.

Bake, uncovered, 45 to 50 minutes, or until set. Cool 10 minutes before serving.

Serves 6.

CHECKERBOARD SQUARE CLAM CRUNCH

Yankee cooking, suburban style—a winner of the Ralston Purina Create-a-Recipe Contest.

¼ cup flour	*1 6½-ounce can minced clams*
½ teaspoon baking powder	*with liquid*
¼ teaspoon salt	*1 egg, beaten*
⅛ teaspoon black pepper	*2 cups Rice Chex*
1 tablespoon chopped parsley	*Oil for frying*
Sour cream	

• Combine flour, baking powder, salt, pepper, and parsley. Slowly stir in liquid from canned clams until smooth. Add egg and clams. Mix well. Stir in Rice Chex to coat. Let stand 10 minutes.

Heat oil to ⅛-inch depth in skillet. Drop heaping tablespoons of clam mixture into hot oil, and pat with spoon to form 8 3-inch patties. Brown over medium heat. Turn. Brown.

Drain patties on absorbent paper. Serve topped with sour cream.

Serves 4.

CHOW MEIN CANDY CLUSTERS

No food is more stunning than a platter full of these Oriental-accented blobs, a "Space Age" candy from *Bayou Cuisine*. A powerhouse fusion of sugar and salt, these clusters demand the accompaniment of large glasses of bubbling club soda.

12 ounces butterscotch morsels   *2 cups cocktail peanuts*
1 3-ounce can chow mein noodles

• Melt butterscotch bits in top of double boiler. Remove from heat and immediately stir in chow mein noodles until all are coated, then quickly stir in peanuts. Drop on wax paper with a tablespoon.

Let cool until firm.

Makes about 2 dozen.

CLUSTERS ROYALE

• Substitute 2 cups Rice Krispies cereal for chow mein noodles. A lighter and less bludgeoning snack.

RICE KRISPIE COOKIES

Cereal cookies are a genre unto themselves, with Rice Krispies by far the most popular ingredient. You will still find these classic "marshmallow treats" on the back of some cereal boxes.

4 tablespoons butter   *5 cups Rice Krispies cereal*
10 ounces marshmallows (or 4
cups miniature marshmallows)

• Melt butter in large saucepan over low heat. Add marshmallows and stir until melted. Cook 3 minutes, stirring constantly. Remove from heat, add Rice Krispies, and stir until all are coated. Using buttered spatula, press mixture evenly into buttered 13-by-9-by-2-inch pan.

Cool. Cut into 2-inch squares.

Makes about 2 dozen.

VARIATIONS

Use Cocoa Krispies instead of Rice Krispies.

Melt 2 squares unsweetened chocolate with marshmallows.

Add ¼ cup peanut butter to marshmallows.

Add 1 cup raisins with Rice Krispies.

Add 1 cup salted peanuts with Rice Krispies.

CHOCO-SCOTCH CLUSTERS

For sweet and dense clusters, use only 3 cups of Rice Krispies cereal. For modern, lighter clusters, use 4.

6 ounces semisweet
   chocolate chips
6 ounces butterscotch morsels

¼ cup peanut butter
3 to 4 cups Rice Krispies cereal

• Melt chocolate, butterscotch, and peanut butter in top of double boiler, stirring constantly until well blended. Remove from heat, add Rice Krispies, and stir until cereal is thoroughly coated. Drop by tablespoon onto wax paper.

Cool until firm. (Listen to them crackle and pop!)

Makes 3 to 4 dozen,

JOHN BERESFORD TIPTON BARS

Like the coming of Technicolor to the movies, the invention of Froot Loops offered new expressive opportunities to the suburban cook. When we originally worked with this recipe, it called for a pound of almond bark, which was delicious, but required a trip to Woolworth's candy counter to buy it— too exhausting a safari. One day we were shaken by a brainstorm. Why not use Hershey's Golden Almond Bars in place of bark? They're the best— and richest-tasting—candy bar on earth, and so we named this confection after one of the world's richest men—John Beresford Tipton, the unseen, anonymous benefactor on the 1950s TV show *The Millionaire*. Why not make a batch some day and give them to a stranger whose name you find in the phone book?

1 pound Hershey's Golden	*1 cup Rice Krispies cereal*
Almond Bars (5 bars)	*1 cup miniature marshmallows*
1 cup Froot Loops cereal	

• Melt candy bars in double boiler. Remove from heat, add cereals, mix until coated, then add marshmallows. Mix well. Pour into buttered pan about 7 by 10 inches.

Let cool until set. Cut into 20 to 30 small squares.

TEENAGE ROCKY ROAD

What could be simpler, or more fun, than these lovely, loopy globules—another startlingly easy recipe from the Oakland, Iowa, Centennial Cookbook.

2 pounds white almond bark	*2 cups colored*
3 cups Froot Loops cereal	*miniature marshmallows*
3 cups Cheerios cereal	

• Melt almond bark in double boiler. Mix cereals in large bowl, and pour melted almond bark over them. Mix thoroughly, add marshmallows, mix again, then drop by tablespoonfuls onto wax paper.

Cool until firm.

Makes about 3 dozen.

CHOCOLATE CHIP TORTE

We shift perspective slightly now from cereal to potato chips and present for your consideration one of the strangest—and most disturbing—transformations of one kind of food into another. In this case, the leap is from the simple chip, suitable for munching with a Coke and a burger, to an elegant meringue dessert, in which crumbled potato chips create a bizarre and absolutely mysterious presence within the meringue. From *Recipes That Pep Up Meals with Wise Potato Chips.*

3 egg whites
⅛ teaspoon salt
⅛ teaspoon cream of tartar
1⅓ cups sugar
1 teaspoon vanilla extract
1 cup crushed potato chips
1½ ounces
    unsweetened chocolate

1 cup milk
1 tablespoon flour
¼ teaspoon salt
3 egg yolks, slightly beaten
1 tablespoon butter
½ teaspoon vanilla extract
½ cup heavy cream, sweetened
    and whipped

• Preheat oven to 300°.

Beat egg whites with salt and cream of tartar until foamy. Add 1 cup sugar slowly, and beat until meringue stands in very stiff peaks (10 to 15 minutes). Add vanilla and mix thoroughly. Fold in potato chips. Cover cookie sheet with unglazed paper (such as a brown paper bag). Spread meringue on paper in 2 rounds 9 inches in diameter and about ¾ inch thick.

Bake 45 minutes. Cool.

Place chocolate and milk in saucepan. Cook and stir over medium heat until chocolate is melted. Beat with rotary beater until blended. Combine ⅓ cup sugar, flour, and salt. Add to chocolate mixture slowly, stirring well. Cook and stir until thick, 10 to 15 minutes. Add egg yolks slowly to chocolate mixture, blending well. Cook for 3 minutes longer, stirring constantly. Remove from heat. Stir in butter and vanilla. Cool to room temperature.

Spread cooled chocolate filling on one meringue, then place second meringue on top. Spread sides with whipped cream. Chill until ready to serve, but don't keep in refrigerator more than a few hours, lest meringues wilt.

Serve with more whipped cream or vanilla ice cream.

Serves 6 to 8.

Look What You Can Do with Dr. Pepper

If breakfast cereal can be transformed into cookies and oven-fried chicken, why can't the fizz and wallop of soda pop infuse cakes, roasts, and congealed salads? So asks the restless suburban chef, eager to mix 'n' match disparate ingredients. Coca-Cola, 7-Up, Dr. Pepper, Vernors ginger ale: these are raw materials crying out to become something greater than soft drinks. Thus the cuisine of suburbia bubbles over with specialties flavored and glazed by soda pop. (In fact, long before convenience foods revolutionized the suburban diet, Southern country cooks had discovered that the best thing in the world for basting hams is Coke.)

We recommend keeping the recipe a secret if you plan on serving any of these dishes to food snobs. As soon as you say "Pepsi Cake" or "Duckling L'Vernors," their unadventurous palates close down for the night. Serve the duck, and then, after they clean their plates, wondering how you achieved the mysterious gingery resonance in the glaze, reveal the secret. They will be shocked . . . as we were, when we discovered that soft drink cookery produces startlingly delicious food.

DUCKLING L'VERNORS

If you haven't been to Detroit, you may not be familiar with the Motor City's great contribution to American gastronomy—its ginger ale. Like velvet cream soda with a strong ginger kick, Vernors makes all other ginger ales seem watered down. The syrup is aged four years in oak barrels, developing a deep amber color and the bite of a Michigan wolverine. Whenever we travel to Detroit, we take cases of it home, to drink straight, or as the basis for out-of-this-world Boston coolers (Vernors with a scoop of vanilla ice cream).

On our last trip to the Midwest, we discovered that Michiganders were way ahead of us in inventing new ways to enjoy ginger ale. In a small pamphlet called *The Vernors Lovers' Recipe Book,* we found this sensational recipe for duck.

We used it until we ran out of Vernors, then tried it with ordinary ginger ale. By doubling the amount of fresh ginger, and adding a dash of vanilla with the orange juice, we came close to the real thing. But we implore you—if you have any way of getting authentic Vernors from Detroit, don't settle for second best.

1 4-pound duckling, quartered	*½ cup dark brown sugar*
Salt and pepper	*½ cup orange marmalade*
24 ounces Vernors ginger ale	*2 teaspoons Dijon mustard*
2¼-inch-thick slices	*1 tablespoon minced scallions*
fresh ginger	*¼ cup brandy*
1 cup orange juice	*Orange slices for garnish*

• Preheat oven to 350°.

Remove fat from cavity of duck; cut off extra neck skin. Wipe quartered pieces with damp cloth; sprinkle with salt and pepper. Place skin side down on roasting pan.

Bake 50 minutes.

As duck bakes, combine Vernors and ginger slices in saucepan. Simmer until reduced to 1 cup. Add orange juice, brown sugar, marmalade, mustard, scallions, and 2 tablespoons brandy. Bring to boil, reduce heat, and simmer until mixture is like thin syrup, 20 to 25 minutes. Remove ginger.

Turn duck skin side up, drain fat, and baste thoroughly with Vernors sauce. Return to oven; bake 45 minutes more, basting every 10 minutes.

Add remaining brandy to sauce and simmer until thickened. Remove duck to heated platter, and pour on sauce. Garnish with orange slices. This is very good with Dr. Pepper Baked Beans.

Serves 4.

DR. PEPPER BAKED BEANS

This was a Vernors recipe, too; but when we ran out of the precious ginger ale, we decided that rather than substitute an inferior brand we would change the recipe and give the beans the full-bodied zest of Dr. Pepper soda. The alteration worked. These are hearty eats, good companions for pork chops, ham loaf, or wieners.

1 28-ounce can pork and beans　　*½ cup dark brown sugar*
1 onion, chopped fine　　　　　　*⅓ cup Dr. Pepper*
1 green pepper, chopped fine　　　*⅛ teaspoon ground cloves*
1 tomato, chopped fine

• Preheat oven to 350°.

Drain liquid from pork and beans. Pour into baking dish. Gently mix in onion, pepper, and tomato. Combine sugar, Dr. Pepper, and cloves until sugar is dissolved. Pour evenly over bean mixture.

Bake, covered, 30 minutes.

Serves 4 to 6.

LEMONADE FRIED CHICKEN

One of the all-time great chicken recipes was invented by Josie McCarthy, who had a regular cooking show in the 1950s on WRCA-TV in New York. Josie suggests that this syrupy sweet dish seems so much more difficult than it really is, and therefore makes a perfect entrée if you want to impress your mother-in-law or the boss.

1 6-ounce can frozen lemonade
   concentrate
1 cup water
1 2- to 2½-pound chicken, cut up
¼ cup all-purpose flour

1 teaspoon salt
¼ teaspoon ground
   black pepper
1 cup oil
2 tablespoons butter, melted

• Preheat oven to 350°.

Mix lemonade concentrate and water in small bowl. Pour over chicken in larger bowl. Refrigerate 2 hours or longer. Drain chicken and retain liquid.

Mix together flour, salt, and pepper in a small paper bag. Add well-drained chicken, one piece at a time. Grasp bag closed and shake to flour chicken evenly.

Heat oil in large skillet over moderate heat. Add floured chicken; cook until evenly browned, turning pieces over carefully.

Remove chicken and arrange in a single layer in a shallow baking pan. Brush chicken with melted butter. Add reserved lemonade.

Bake, uncovered, about 1 hour, basting chicken with lemonade from pan every fifteen minutes. About 15 minutes before chicken is done, drain off excess juice from pan.

Serves 4 or 5.

CHERRY COKE SALAD

Who said teens don't like salad? They will if it is this favorite flavor combination, served alongside burgers and French fries. A powerful dark Jell-O, for serious Coke drinkers, from the "Space Age" chapter of *Bayou Cuisine.*

1 16½-ounce can dark pitted
   cherries in heavy syrup
1 3-ounce package cherry Jell-O
   gelatin
1 8-ounce can crushed pineapple

1 cup Coca-Cola

• Heat cherries and their juice to boiling. Remove from heat and add Jell-O. Stir. Add pineapple, juice and all. Pour in Coke. Pour into oiled 6-cup mold.

Refrigerate at least 2 hours, or until set.

Serves 4 to 6.

PEPSI-COLA CAKE WITH BROILED PEANUT BUTTER FROSTING

A dreamy cake buoyed by Pepsi bubbles and moistened by miniature marshmallows which disappear into the chocolate, leaving no mallow blobs to embarrass you in front of gourmet guests. This fabulous cake comes from the Oakland, Iowa, Centennial Cookbook, but in place of the Iowans' Pepsi-chocolate frosting, we have substituted a peanut butter frosting we found in Swift's 1959 *Patio Picnic Cookbook.*

PEPSI-COLA CAKE

2 cups flour	*½ cup buttermilk*
2 cups sugar	*2 eggs, beaten*
½ pound butter	*1 teaspoon baking soda*
2 tablespoons	*1 teaspoon vanilla extract*
* unsweetened cocoa*	*1½ cups miniature*
1 cup Pepsi	* marshmallows*

• Preheat oven to 350°. Grease and flour a 9-by-13-by-2-inch pan.

Combine flour and sugar in large bowl. Melt butter, add cocoa and Pepsi. Pour over flour and sugar mixture, and stir until well blended. Add buttermilk, beaten eggs, soda, and vanilla. Mix well. Stir in marshmallows. Pour into prepared pan.

Bake 40 minutes. Remove cake from oven and frost while still warm.

BROILED PEANUT BUTTER FROSTING

6 tablespoons butter	*⅔ cup peanut butter*
1 cup packed tight dark brown	*¼ cup milk*
sugar	*⅔ cup chopped peanuts*

• Cream butter, sugar, and peanut butter. Add milk and stir well. Add nuts. Spread over warm cake.

Place frosted cake under broiler about 4 inches from heat source. Broil just a few seconds, or until topping starts to bubble. Do not scorch!

Let cool at least 30 minutes before serving.

FRESCA CAKE WITH MARASCHINO FROSTING

Like *The Defiant Ones,* in which Tony Curtis and Sidney Poitier were shackled together, Fresca Cake would seem to be a study in discord. Not true! In fact, the citrus diet soda and cherries mate perfectly, creating a lusciously moist, rather tropical sensation.

FRESCA CAKE

- 3 cups sugar
- ½ pound butter
- ½ cup vegetable shortening
- 6 eggs
- 3 cups sifted cake flour
- 7 ounces Fresca soda
- 1 teaspoon baking powder
- 1 teaspoon vanilla extract
- 1 tablespoon grated lemon rind
- 1 tablespoon grated lime rind

• Preheat oven to 350°.

Cream together sugar, butter, and shortening. Add eggs, one at a time, beating after each addition. Add flour and Fresca alternately. Add baking powder, and when mixture is fully creamed, add vanilla and fruit rinds. Pour into greased and floured 9-by-13-by-2-inch cake pan.

Bake 1 hour, or until cake tester comes out clean.

MARASCHINO FROSTING

- 2 egg whites
- 1 cup sugar
- 1 tablespoon water
- 2 tablespoons Maraschino cherry juice
- 1 tablespoon light corn syrup
- ¼ teaspoon cream of tartar
- 10 Maraschino cherries, chopped, or gumdrops

• Mix all ingredients except cherries and beat constantly while heating in top of double boiler. When thoroughly mixed, thick, and spreadable, frost cake. Decorate top of cake with chopped Maraschino cherries or gumdrops.

MR. PIBB PRALINES

Conjure up lazy Alabama Sundays with these gooey candies, made from a favorite Southern soft drink, Mr. Pibb. If no Mr. Pibb is available where you live. You can come close using Dr. Pepper soda, but it's not the same.

- 1 cup granulated sugar
- 1 cup dark brown sugar
- 1 cup Mr. Pibb
- 1 cup miniature marshmallows
- 2 to 3 cups pecan halves

• Cook sugars and Mr. Pibb in a saucepan over low heat, stirring constantly, then gradually bring to soft-ball stage (240°).

Remove mixture from heat; stir in marshmallows and pecans. Mix vigorously until marshmallows dissolve. Quickly drop by tablespoon onto wax paper to cool.

Makes 2 dozen pralines.

SPUTNIK TEA

A fabulous have-on-hand beverage called "Russian Tea" in *Bayou Cuisine*, where we found the recipe. In the winter, serve it hot in mugs; in the summer, pour over ice and garnish with lemon.

Tang, you will recall, is what astronauts drink in outer space.

1 18-ounce jar Tang mix	*1½ cups sugar*
¾ cup Lipton instant tea	*2 teaspoons ground cloves*
with lemon	*2 teaspoons cinnamon*

• Mix all ingredients and keep in tightly sealed jar. Use 2 teaspoons mix per cup of boiling water.

Dessert Ex Machina

To the creative pastry chef, prepackaged Hostess Twinkies are hardly adequate dessert. As one might expect, the cuisine of suburbia, driven as it is to create new dishes from off-the-shelf products, has generated fabulous original desserts out of mundane ingredients.

In the same genre as cookies made from breakfast cereal and cakes made from soda pop are cakes and pies made from crackers and candy bars. The classic expression of this aesthetic is mock apple pie made from Ritz crackers, the recipe for which is still printed on the box. But to the chef striving to be modern, mere mock apple pie is old hat (it dates back to the 1930s). What is needed is a new twist to the old recipe. We found Ritz Pecan Pie in the Oakland, Iowa, Centennial Cookbook.

RITZ PECAN PIE

A true space-age pie—a single unit with no articulation of crust and filling. As it bakes, the center will rise, then collapse; but when it is sliced, lo!—it has become the familiar translucent interior of a traditional pecan pie, but thinner.

20 Ritz crackers,
  crushed to crumbs
1 teaspoon baking powder
3 egg whites
1 cup sugar

1 teaspoon vanilla extract
½ cup halved pecans
3 ounces milk chocolate,
  finely shredded

• Preheat oven to 325°.

Mix crackers and baking powder. Beat egg whites stiff, then very gradually add sugar, continuing to beat. Add vanilla. Fold egg whites and crackers together. Put in a buttered 9-inch pie pan. Arrange pecans across top.

Bake 30 minutes.

Remove from oven, sprinkle with shredded chocolate, then put under broiler for a few seconds, watching vigilantly that chocolate melts but does not scorch.

Serve with ice cream or whipped cream.

MILKY WAY CAKE

The nougat texture of Milky Ways makes this cake, a Deep South favorite from *Bayou Cuisine,* perfect as a heavy, moist foundation for scoops of ice cream.

4 2.1-ounce Milky Way candy bars	*1 cup buttermilk*
½ pound butter	*2½ cups flour, sifted*
2 cups sugar	*¼ teaspoon baking soda*
4 eggs	*2 teaspoons vanilla extract*
	1 cup coarsely chopped pecans

• Melt Milky Ways and 8 tablespoons butter in double boiler. Let cool. Preheat oven to 350°.

Cream remaining butter with sugar. Add eggs one at a time. Add buttermilk alternately with flour and soda. Add vanilla and Milky Way mixture and mix until smooth. Fold in pecans. Pour into greased and floured bundt pan.

Bake 1 hour, or until cake tester comes out clean.

Cool 15 minutes in pan, then turn out on wire cake rack.

HYDROX COOKIE DESSERT

Hydrox and Oreo cookies are as essential to the pastry chef as miniature marshmallows. For grasshopper pie crusts, choco-peppermint ice cream bombes, or Swiss chocolate amandine torte, the chocolate cookies with the white gunk inside are irreplaceable. This is one of the plainest and best of the cookie desserts, from the Oakland, Iowa, Centennial Cookbook.

½ cup milk

2 egg yolks

24 full-size marshmallows

2 egg whites, beaten until stiff

1 cup heavy cream, whipped

36 Hydrox chocolate cookies

8 tablespoons butter, melted

• Mix milk, egg yolks, and marshmallows. Heat to custard consistency; cool. Add beaten egg whites and whipped cream.

Mash cookies thoroughly and add melted butter to crumbs. Place all but a few crumbs on the bottom of a 9-by-13-inch pan. Spread mixture neatly over crumbs, Sprinkle remaining crumbs on top.

Chill until firm.

Serves 8.

S'MORES

S'mores are the great-grandmother of the technique of making dessert from preexisting candy. Known as Princess Pats, Perfection Crisps, Slapsticks, and, rather formally, in Nika Hazleton's esteemed *American Home Cooking,* as "Somemores," they have been a Girl Scout favorite for years. S'mores are, of course, campfire food; but you can just as easily toast the marshmallows at an indoor fireplace, over a gas stove, or atop a can of Sterno.

Ever since Hershey stopped segmenting their small chocolate bars, the S'more chef's task has been more difficult, as it is necessary now to eyeball your measurements when cutting the bar into two or three equal pieces.

You will have to decide for yourself about cooking the marshmallow: either roast it slowly to a golden turn, or set it on fire, let the outside char, then blow out the flame. The latter method adds an extra flame-kissed taste to the sandwich.

2 graham cracker squares

⅓ plain small Hershey bar

1 large marshmallow

• Toast marshmallow. Put marshmallow on graham cracker. Put chocolate on marshmallow and cover with second graham cracker. (Heat from marshmallow will melt chocolate.)

Makes 1

TWINKIE PIE

Invented in 1930 by James A. Dewar of Continental Baking Company, Twinkies have only recently fallen into disrepute, as defense attorneys have begun to use their clients' Twinkie diets to explain insane criminal acts and diminished mental capacity. We always suspected as much. In the 1950s, when we were in high school, Twinkie-stuffing contests (how many can you put in your mouth at one time?) were all the rage among our—what shall we call them?—underachieving classmates. Nonetheless, eaten in moderation, as in this pie recipe from *Bayou Cuisine,* the spongy shortcakes are harmless; and quite a surprise for unsuspecting dinner guests!

Butter	*½ teaspoon vanilla extract*
9 Twinkies	*1 6-ounce package semisweet*
3 eggs, separated	*chocolate chips*
Dash cream of tartar	*1 cup chopped pecans*
½ cup sugar	*1 cup heavy cream, whipped*

• Grease Pyrex square or rectangular casserole with butter. Cut 8 Twinkies in thirds, *lengthwise,* and put one layer in bottom of pan.

Beat egg whites with cream of tartar and sugar, adding vanilla. Melt chocolate chips in top of double boiler. Add egg yolks to chocolate slowly, continuing to stir over boiling water. Fold chocolate into egg whites. Spread over Twinkies, then sprinkle with about one-third of the nuts. Layer on more Twinkies, more chocolate, more nuts. Continue layering. Top with whipped cream and a single whole Twinkie.

Chill and serve.

Serves 8.

Jell-O—
the Chef's Magic Powder

Jell-O and the suburban chef were made for each other. Jell-O is fast and convenient, pretty, and it mixes so well with other media. Preeminently modern, there is also something fabulously primitive about the process of Jell-O making—the rather bizarre ritual by which boiling water and cold water, mixed with powder made from hooves of cattle, turns into shimmering, jiggling molded shapes to be ornamented with miniature marshmallows, mandarin oranges, fruits, nuts, and berries. Jello-O is a registered trade mark of General Foods for its gelatin dessert.

In early 1983, our favorite morning talk show, Cleveland's *Morning Exchange,* did a segment called "Jell-O with Joel," in which the host asked for viewers' favorite recipes. It was a light, humorous few moments. But the repercussions were stunning. Joel was deluged with Jell-O recipes from all over Ohio, proving that even though you will not find it in the chichi pages of trendy food magazines, Jell-O cookery is thriving in the heartland. We're all for it. Give us a nice gelatin salad enriched with cream or cream cheese, or spiked with rum, and all is well with the world.

What Mrs. Dewey did *with the* NEW JELL-O !

JOEL'S BEST JELL-O

One of Joel's letters was an angry one, from Joyce Ferring of Stow, Ohio, who was furious with him for having his Jell-O contest while she was on vacation.

She submitted this simplest (and best) of all recipes in anticipation of "Jell-O with Joel II."

> 1 3-ounce package Jell-O,
>   any flavor
> 1 cup boiling water
> 8 ounces cold cola
> 1 8-ounce package cream cheese,
>   cut into ½-inch cubes

> 1 cup drained, pitted
>   dark cherries
> ½ cup chopped nuts, of choice,
>   if desired

• Dissolve Jell-O in boiling water. When cooled to room temperature, add cola, cream cheese, cherries, and nuts. Pour into oiled 6-cup mold.

Chill until set. Unmold to serve.

Serves 6 to 8.

SOUR CREAM JELL-O D'AKRON

Joel got this one from Gloria Jean Minnick of Akron. In the South it's called "congealed salad"—packed with health in the form of fruits and nuts. Sour cream turns the gelatin opaque green, a bit like the complexion of Frankenstein's monster, but as soon as you hit a Maraschino cherry, it's Christmas!

> 2 3-ounce packages lime Jell-O
> 1 cup boiling water
> 1 20-ounce can crushed
>   pineapple, with juice
> 1 pint sour cream

> ½ cup pecans, cut coarse
> 1 8-ounce jar
>   stemless Maraschino
>   cherries, drained
> Whipped cream

• Dissolve Jell-O in boiling water. Mix pineapple, sour cream, nuts, and cherries. Add to Jell-O. Pour into 8-inch-square oiled pan.

Refrigerate 2 hours or until set. Cut into squares and serve topped with whipped cream.

Serves 6.

SANDUSKY STRAWBERRY DAIQUIRI BAVARIAN

Mrs. Virginia Delp of Sandusky sent Joel the recipe for this cool pink beauty. It's a spiked version of the basic Bavarian concept of Jell-O and cream—what our *General Foods Kitchens Cookbook* calls "the aristocrat of the Jell-O family." Mrs. Delp told Joel, "You are going to love this one!" He did. So did we. So will you.

1 3-ounce package
strawberry Jell-O
1 cup boiling water
2 ounces light rum

1 pint heavy cream
1 teaspoon vanilla extract
1 10-ounce package frozen
strawberries, drained of syrup

• Dissolve Jell-O in boiling water. Set aside to cool.

Add rum to strawberries. Stir strawberries (which should still be cold) into Jell-O mixture. In a separate bowl, whip cream, adding vanilla. With the beater at low speed, combine cream and Jell-O mixture until thoroughly mixed, about 1 minute. Pour into oiled 6-cup mold.

Refrigerate 2 hours. Unmold onto plate.

Serves 6 to 8.

BARBECUE CUBES

Jell-O needn't be sweet and gloppy. To prove that point, *The Joy of Jell-O*, the gelatin-lover's bible, suggests salad blocks with a tang, suitable for serving on top of salad greens. Sandy Lutz of North Canton, Ohio, penned these words to express the goodness of just such a "barbecue salad":

Jell-O's quick and Jell-O's easy
But mostly it just makes me queasy.
Much too sweet—all that junk,
Marshmallows, Cool Whip, cream cheese chunks.

But this one's different with a subtle zing;
A simple aspic; why not give it a fling!
This too is Jell-O—easy and quick.
However it's tasty and good to the last lick!

1 3-ounce package lemon Jell-O	*½ teaspoon salt*
¾ cup boiling water	*Dash pepper*
1 8-ounce can tomato sauce	*1 tablespoon horseradish*
1½ teaspoons vinegar	

• Dissolve Jell-O in boiling water. Mix all other ingredients, and when Jell-O is at room temperature, add and mix. Pour into oiled 8-inch-square pan.

Chill until firm. Cut into cubes and serve atop salad.

Makes enough to garnish 6 small salads.

RED HOT SALAD

A simple, tongue-shocking recipe from the Oakland, Iowa, Centennial Cookbook. Red Hot Salad is excellent for teen parties, or to accompany Mexican food.

2 3-ounce packages	3 cups boiling water
cherry Jell-O	1 20-ounce can crushed
4 ounces Red Hots candy (also	pineapple, including liquid
known as Cinnamon	2 cups applesauce
Imperials)	

• Dissolve Jell-O and Red Hots in boiling water. When cooled to room temperature, add pineapple and applesauce. Pour into oiled 8-cup mold.

Chill before serving.

Serves 6.

POKE CAKE WITH JELL-O ICING

The classic goofy-textured cake. The secret of a good poke is to choose a cake mix and Jell-O that complement each other: white cake and raspberry Jell-O, banana cake and orange Jell-O, or, for a really mysterious creation in which the blobby sacs of pudding that ooze into the cake are nearly indistinguishable at first glance, devil's food cake and black cherry Jell-O.

POKE CAKE

1 18-ounce package pudding—	1 cup boiling water
included cake mix	½ cup cold water
1 3-ounce package Jell-O,	
any flavor	

• Preheat oven to 350°.

Prepare cake batter as directed on package. Pour into well-greased and floured 13-by-9-by-2-inch pan.

Bake 30 to 35 minutes, or until cake tester inserted in center comes out clean. Cool cake in pan 15 minutes, then prick with fork at ½-inch intervals.

Meanwhile, dissolve gelatin in boiling water. Add cold water and allow to cool to room temperature. Carefully pour Jell-O over cake.

Chill 3 to 4 hours. Garnish with Jell-O Icing.

JELL-O ICING

½ pound butter
2 cups confectioners' sugar
1 3-ounce package Jell-O, color to
complement cake

½ cup boiling water

• Cream butter and sugar. Dissolve Jell-O in boiling water; cool to room temperature. Slowly mix cooled Jell-O into butter-sugar mixture, until desired color is obtained.

Spread on Poke Cake.

CUT GLASS DESSERT

Talk about mixed media! This psychedelic tour de force is a stunner from the ladies of Oakland, Iowa. Each slice resembles a large helping of stained-glass window, edged with cream instead of lead.

CRUST

1⅔ cups vanilla wafer crumbs
¼ cup sugar

1 cup finely chopped pecans
8 tablespoons butter

• Preheat oven to 375°.

Combine vanilla wafer crumbs, sugar, and pecans. Cut in butter. Press into 9-by-13-by-2-inch pan.

Bake 8 to 10 minutes.

FILLING

3 3-ounce packages Jell-O in
complementary colors
1 3-ounce package lemon Jell-O
1 cup hot Pineapple juice

½ cup cold water
1 cup heavy cream
1 cup crushed pineapple, drained

• In separate greased 8-inch-square pans, set 3 flavors of Jell-O, mixing each according to directions on the package. When set, cut into ½-inch cubes.

Dissolve lemon Jell-O in hot pineapple juice, then add ½ cup cold water.

Place in refrigerator until it starts to set.

Whip cream. Fold crushed pineapple into whipped cream, then add semi-set lemon Jell-O. Fold in Jell-O cubes and pour into crust.

Chill about 1 hour before serving.

Serves 10 to 12.

UNDESCENDED TWINKIES

We cannot blame anyone other than ourselves for this, the *beau idéal* of suburban desserts, although inspirational credit is owed to our treasured Walnut, Iowa, Centennial Cookbook. After weeks of testing Pepsi cakes, we were infused with the spirit of suburbia, and when we came across the Walnut ladies' recipe for Twinkie Dessert (Lay the Twinks flat in the pan and cover with Jell-O), we were shaken with a vision. Why bury the Twinkies? Why not partially chill the Jell-O and lay them across the top, exploding the planar arrangement into three dimensions? Thus art is made, and a new Jell-O dessert is born.

2 3-ounce packages	*1 quart vanilla ice*
orange Jell-O	*cream, softened*
1 cup boiling water	*7 ounces 7-UP*
½ cup pineapple juice	*8 Twinkies*

• Dissolve Jell-O in boiling water. Add pineapple juice, ice cream, and 7-UP. Mix thoroughly (in a blender if necessary to dissolve ice cream), and pour into a deep pan, approximately 9 inches square. Chill until mixture begins to set.

Lay Twinkies flat side down in two rows of four across top of chilled gelatin.

If the gelatin is properly chilled, it will resist the Twinkies. You will push them in; they will slowly rise. It is a tense moment, like the scene in *Psycho* when Tony Perkins tries to sink Janet Leigh's car. But remember—you *don't want* them buried. Just semidescended in the lush, peach-colored ooze.

Chill until fully set.

Serves 4 to 6.

Index

blue Hawaii, 285
blue plate liver and onions, 76
blushing beetskis, 47
Boder's on the River (Mequon, Wis.), 21
boot camp spud soup, 213
Bosco, 112, 193
Boston, brown bread, 229
The Boston Cooking-School Cook Book
    (Farmer), 40, 197
Boston cooler, 101
Boston cream pie, 78–9
Brach's toffees, 305
braunschweiger en gelée, 263–4
bread, 9–10
    anadama, 134–5
    banana walnut, 12–13
    barbecued: beatnik buns, 296; most
        happy fella, 296–7
    biscuits; orange, 13–14; parsley, 209;
        pecan drop, 39–40
    blueberry gems, Frances Virginia, 10
    Boston brown, 229
    and butter pudding, 185–6
    chocolate, 171–2; pudding, 186–7
    cinnamon buns, Philadelphia, 11
    corn bread, salute to soya, 228–9
    corn gems, 14
    croutons, 271–2
    gingerbread, after school, 172
    for hamburgers (or other meat), 81,
        82–3, 296–7
    molasses johnnycake, 223
    molasses puffs, 52
    onion, pre-fab, 271
    popovers, Patricia Murphy's, 27–8
    queen of muffins, 45–6
    raisin bread pudding, cinnamon swirl,
        186
    rolls: carrot, sharpshooter, 228; clover-
        leaf, 142–3; tea, quick, 12
    scones, cream, 38
    souper dooper, 271–2
    spoonbread, best cook in town, 127–8
    for tea sandwiches, 33
    teatime London buns à la Bette Davis,
        43
    tomato juice, 227
    white (for toasting): to buy, 161–2; to

make, 162–3, 164–5
    in World War II, 226
    see also sandwiches; toast
bread crumbs
    butter crumb dumplings, 275
    crust coffee, 198
    as meat loaf extender, 68, 69
bridal showers, 51–7
Bridesmaid luncheon, 57–60
brown cow (soda), 101
brown sugar
    caramel coconut (toast topping), 168
    toast, 167
buns
    beatnik, 296
    for hamburgers (or other meat), 81,
        82–3
    Philadelphia cinnamon, 11
    teatime London, à la Bette Davis, 43
"burn one all the way" (double chocolate
    malt), 96
Butter
    crumb dumplings, 275
    frosting, 37–8
    spread, butterless, 224
    vanilla, 172
butterscotch
    banana pie, 178
    choco-scotch clusters, 310
    chow mein candy clusters, 308–9
    pudding, 179
    sauce, 23, 110
Byrnes, Edd "Kookie," 305

cabbage
    apple and pickle salad, 209–10
    celery seed cole slaw, 122
    evaporated milk dressing, 210
    head weenies, flaming, with pu-pu
        sauce, 288
    perfection salad, 140–1
cakes
    ambrosia layer, 21–2
    Boston cream pie, 78–9
    chocolate: angel food, with butterscotch
        sauce, 23; eggless, 235
    currant tea cakes, 39